WESTERN POLITICAL THOUGHT

WESTERN POLITICAL THOUGHT

Dr. Archna Chaturvedi

Commonwealth

Western Political Thought

Edition 2020

ISBN 81-7169-976-6

Published by :

COMMONWEALTH PUBLISHERS
4831/24, Prahlad Street,
Ansari Road, Darya Ganj,
New Delhi - 110002
Ph. : 23275511, 23257835
e-mail : commonwealthbooks@gmail.com

Typesetting by :

Rishu Computers
Delhi - 110051

Printed at :
Roshan Offset Printers
Delhi

PREFACE

Growth and development of modern political thought has been attributed to the wars and revolutions of our times. Conflicts between and within nations are over, power and advantage; but they also express profound cleavages of ideas and creeds rooted in conflicting ways of life. Hence for survival there developed a process for a deeper knowledge and keener appreciation of basic values, in the western civilization. This is how the process of western political thought began which is also termed as modern political thought.

We take this opportunity to record our indebtness and acknowledgements to the authorities on the subject.

In the process of preparing this work, we sought help from the librarians and their staff members. We thank them all.

My publisher and his staff worked hard. They deserve love and co-operation of my readers.

Dr. Archna Chaturvedi

Contents

1

The Basis of Political Philosophy

It has been well said that the message of Political Philosophy is a plea for freedom. Indeed that one concept–of freedom–when properly understood, can supply the most rational and legitimate foundation of our philosophy. If by freedom is meant absolute absence of restraint, the theory of *Human Government* is deprived of its moral basis, because such an interpretation of freedom must necessarily lead to some type of anarchism according to which any government is morally unsupportable and an unnecessary evil. It would, however, be obvious to any thoughtful individual that, in the context of a social life, absolute licence is not freedom; and that the idea of freedom includes certain types of restraints under the guiding influence of which we are able to realize our better or best selves. *To be free is to live according to the law of our being.*

But must we realize our better or best selves? Or, must we live according to the law of our being? The answer to that question can be but an emphatic "yes", because the law of our being, being what it is (*i.e.* the law of our BE-ING) is a *categorical imperative.* This imperative law inexorably demands that we should restlessly aspire to be better and attain the good. Co-eval with the emergence of man is the longing for the good and that is why man, in essence, is a *metaphysical being.* The craving in man for betterment, improvement and reforms assumes the possibility of betterment, the attainability of virtues and values and these again indicate the existence of a Goodness and a plan and a process. *To be free is to live according to this Master Plan or Evolution.*

How to make the Good available to society, is the task of the social philosopher. This obviously can be done by fitting our social, economic and political schemes of reform to the universal scheme of evolution, which is guided by the same law of or urge towards goodness as the law of our being. We have, in other words, to re-discover or Maker's Plan in the context of our social life. This voyage of re-discovering Goodness or justice or Freedom or *Dharma* is the life-long adventure of the political philosopher. He is the *Rishi* of *dharma*, the prophet of freedom and justice. Hence there is an inherent evangelism in the teaching of Political Philosophy.

It is obvious that no philosophy (or ideology for betterment of man) is possible without assuming the ultimate *goodness of our inner being*. The basis of nay philosophy must therefore be the respect for personality. Personality, however, cannot grow in the wildness of isolation: it can only grow in a freedom-pervading social ethos. The growth of human personality is not inimical to man's sociality; indeed as member of multiform voluntary association, discharging duties and enjoying rights, does an individual get the chance of developing into *a socially integrated personality*. Freedom in unit; liberty in association alone can result in dharma or social harmony. But association or sociality among less-than-the-perfectly-integrated individuals often results in differences and conflicts hence human government becomes a necessity.

The philosophical (and moral) obligation to obey the government cannot be based on force not only because force is immoral (i.e. based on an insult to personality) but also because such a coercive basis of governmental authority militates against the ultimate purpose of such an authority which lies not merely in securing obedience but in securing harmony *i.e. freedom in unity or liberty in association*. Political authority has moral validity to the extent it tries to secure justice or harmony. But justice itself becomes unjust if it is not meant for all on equal terms. Equality therefore is a *pre-condition* of liberty, for, political authority must make *justice available to all on equal terms*. Social privilege unconnected with social function (i.e. inequality) is the deadliest enemy of freedom or justice.

The conception of justice may differ from individual, to individual, from society to society (e.g. the recognition of slavery in Greece, caste in India and the House of Lords in Britain) but no system of Political Philosophy can be constructed without accepting the principle of justice or freedom or harmony as its primary theoretical basis. Further, since coercion without consent of the individual coerced is a negation of justice and freedom, political authority cannot be itself and still act without the consent of those on whom and on whose behalf it acts. Political authority or government may no doubt demand obedience to laws or respect for restrictions (created by it) but since political authority *is not any authority* which can coerce, but only that authority which is brought into being by the community for securing justice or freedom or harmony or for leading life according to the law of our being which is (being the law of being good to others or loving others) also the *law of love*, such an authority (to be legitimate and valid) must be based on the law of love or the law of goodness towards others or on self-imposed restrictions. In other words, restrictions placed on individuals by political authority, must be based on the *consent of the governed*.

This consentient basis of political authority was readily recognised by the ancients (in India and Greece). According to the Hindu *Nitishastras* if the coercive power (*danda*) is not exercised by the sovereign according to the dictates of dharma (i.e. justice or morality) then the *danda* will operate even against the sovereign and the ruler will fall; because the wieldier of the political authority or the *dandadhara* is a servant or agent of society and as such is answerable to the governed (or the people). In Christian Europe, owing probably to the interference of the Church in politics, the liberal or rather libertarian basis of Political Philosophy experienced an eclipse for some time under the influence of the Divine Right theory. With the progress of social evolution and of the social sciences a moral justification for political obligation began to be sought for in some sort of a Social Contract with indifferent results. Hobbes attempted to demolish democracy democratically; the teachings of Locke and Montesquieu failed to come to the prominence which they deserved, whereas Rousseau's "popular sovereignty" foundered in the abyss of his *General Will*. So that, in spite of occasional indications to the contrary, the net effect of "Classical Politics" was its anti-libertarian and authoritarian emphasis which however reached its high watermark in the idealist philosophy of Hegel.

Hegel's socio-political philosophy might have rescued "Classical Politics" from its over-emphasis of form (*at the cost of substance*) had it not, in its eagerness to help Germany's national unification and anxiety to support the Prussian despotism, missed the significance of the "community" (re-discovered by Rousseau) and erroneously identified it with the State. The result was that Hegel transferred the sanctity and sovereignty of the society (within which alone personality can grow and justice can emerge) to the State which is a mere instrument and creature of the communal will, which wills the weal of all. This communal will may be said to carry in its trail the glow of infallible divinity (i.e. if we prefer to talk in religious phraseology) and therefore against this will the individual may not claim any right. But the Hegelian deification of the State (as *die Wirklichkeit der sittlichen Idee*) was unwarrantable in logic, degrading as a philosophy and mischievous even as a social myth. The *Gang Gottes in der Welt* only paved the way for the godless dictators.

No wonder, freedom-loving people revolted against political Hegelianism; but, as is often the case in such circumstances, the first attack on Hegel's *embodiment of morality* or the State went too far and wide of the mark and included among its victims not merely the State but also the real store-house of morality, i.e. the society with its accumulated tradition and culture without which no morality could thrive. The result was an over-emphasised *individualism* (dissociated from the social context) based on the economic doctrine of *laissez-faire* and the biological doctrine of the survival of the fittest. Bentham and Spencer were the seducers of this age, capitalism and imperialism its fruits, Marxism and Freudism its reactions. Un-co-ordinated individualism can result only in the destruction of integrated unity (in man as well as in society) which means insanity or psychosis. Unimitigated self-lust—that natural product of ultra-individualism—has produced the psychosis of the nations which is being manifested in the general unrest and world-wars.

Nature, however, abhors monotony and works in alternate spasms and so before the reign of stark individualism could lead humanity to an irrevocable doom community-minded philosophers began to appear on the scene. But they were of two different types; their common element being their opposition to stark individualism. One of these may be described as the *Socialists* and the other the social-minded individualists (I prefer to call them the Neo-liberals). The socialists—Proudhon, Blanc, Marx, Engels, Lenin, Stalin, Trotsky—for our purposes (i.e., for the purposes of the search for the Basis of Political Philosophy) were not much helpful as they did not seriously address themselves to the task of evolving *a philosophy* of Government but they rather concentrated their efforts in exposing the weaknesses (moral and material) of the individualist-capitalist social order and to a great extent they succeeded in doing this very well.

It was indeed not at all difficult to expose the weakness of that social order, first because this social order came into being not on the ground of a morally justifiable social theory but as an accident of European history (i.e., the rise of Protestantism and the transition from the feudal to the capitalist stage) and secondly because such *ex post facto* philosophical bases as it pretended to have acquired were founded on very emphemeral and questionable theories like those of *pleasure-pain calculus* or *the survival of the fittest*. In the result "utilitarianism", "laissez-faire", "survival of the fittest" came to be looked down upon by the vast majority of the people in society (who are poor and unsuccessful in life's battle) as heartless, cynical and inhuman doctrines masquerading in the garb of high-brow philosophies for the sole purpose of safeguarding the vested interests of the rich and the successful who found life so comfortable under the existing dispensation that they tried to maintain the *status quo* at any cost and consequently *accumulated wealth* and *right of property* became the corner-stone of social security and "to safeguard the interests of the victors in life's battle," became the sole function of the State.

The utter hollowness of all this has become too obvious today. The incalculable pleasure-pain calculus of utilitarianism provides no safe guide to human behaviour (at least not on the highest human planes) nor the fact of survival any proof of moral or desirable fitness. As to economic *laissez-faire*, which is supposed to be based on the principle of freedom, it means, in the absence of economic security, freedom to be sick, to be ignorant, incapable, hungry; to vegetate or live without opportunities and to die like wretches. No freedom can be enjoyed in *absence of the freedom from want*, which, for the vast majority, must be secured (at least up to certain minimum level of requirements) by the society. If the Hegelian State harmed the individual interfering with him too much, the utilitarian State almost ruined him by following a policy of "splendid isolation" (or non-interference). No wonder that to the vast majority of the people in society the laissez-faire-State appeared to be a callous engine of calculated selfishness, a heartless stabilizer of social inequities.

Taking advantage of all this Marx and Marxians "diabolized" the State as a necessary evil, as an instrument of class-oppression. It was viewed as the executive committee of the ruling class (and in the capitalist social context), of the capitalist class and the only solution lay therefore in destroying the engine of class-oppression (i.e., the State) by a proletarian revolution (sine constitutionally it was incapable of being destroyed). By definition, political authority lacked and must always lack any moral justification, or a philosophical basis. In the whirlpool of confused problems raised by the State-philosophies of Hegel, Bentham and Marx, Political Philosophy lost the vestige of a theoretical or logical basis. It was left with the dogmatic beliefs of the different schools (represented by the above-named thinkers) according to which whatever their respective doctrines taught was alone conducive to the promotion of justice or freedom even when their interpretation of these concepts resulted in such absurd notions as the total eclipse of individual will and judgement (as suggested by Hegelian and Marxian views) or the freedom to starve and beg as suggested by the laissez-faire individualists.

Yet men must be governed and men (with even a moderate degree of enlightenment) cannot rest satisfied without being assured that that governance *has* a moral justification, which involves the reconciliation of authority and liberty. This is obviously a difficult task, made even more difficult, on the one hand, by the new self-respect that the common man had come to prize (as a result of the disappearance of feudalism and serfdom, urbanisation and organisation of labour in trade unions, parliamentary reforms and extension of franchise), and on the other, by the power and prestige won by the (sovereign) State through the circumstances of history (as directed in this period by Europe) and the teachings of philosophers from Bodin to Austin (via Hobbes, Hegel and others). It will be seen that two errors (generated probably by the necessity of evolving the nation-State or capitalist-democracy on the ruins of the feudal order in Europe) were responsible for the difficulty: (1) The over-dramatized antagonism between the "individual" and the "society" and (2) the identification between the "state" and the "society".

As to the individual-society antagonism, it is obvious that an assemblage of repellent individuals (without any sense of sociality, mutuality and honourable compromise) can never form into a society. The reconciliation of individual minds for the social or common good is necessary for the formation of a society, though the submersion of "minds" in a higher "social mind" is not needed. In other words the society, as Perry has said, is not a static substance but a composition and interaction. Both the extreme views according to which society is either an amorphous mass of repellent atoms (individuals) or an entirely new amalgam of humanity in which the component individual minds are completely lost, are faulty according to the findings of latest researches in Sociology and Psychology. The uniformity of social conduct (so necessary for social stability and life) is not due to any Bosanquetian "Real will" or "State-mind" in which the individual wills are drowned but it emerges through the reconciliation of individual minds and continues to survive on "the strength of continued reconciliation of minds". Without this reconciliation the moral society or community will not be evolved and without the community there can be no question of individual liberties, which are ultimately a system of moral values, assessed valuable by a community which is advanced enough to evolve a value-system or an ethical norm. In this perspective along it is possible to justify the dictum of the Greek political philosophy that the *polis is prior to the individual* which is sometimes mistranslated to mean that the State is prior to the individual and this brings us to the second confusion (i.e., the false identity between the State and the society).

There might have been a justification for identifying the Greek *polis* with the society, because though that term (*polis*) is often translated as city-state, the polis essentially was, what modern sociologists will call, a community (i.e., spontaneous in origin and universal in the scope of interests it pursues). On the same analogy, it is however a mistake to identify the society with the *modern State* which is essentially an association (i.e., artificial in origin and limited in the scope of interests which it pursues). The demand for the centralised sovereign nation State in Europe (at certain stage of her history) bloated up the prestige of the State till in political literature and popular mind it came to be regarded as synonymous with the community or *even superior to it*. While Sociology was still in the embryological state political philosophers of different schools however went on constructing political theories on its false foundations with tragic results. The idealists found in the State the bearer of the moral and real will of the society, the individualist-jurists (though reduced its function to the minimum of maintaining law and order) made it (within those limits) the omnipotent sovereign of unchangeable authority whose callousness to citizens' economic well-being virtually reduced it to an amoral machine and that too in the name of the highest moral principle, freedom. The Marxians, taking advantage of the implied moral bankruptcy of the juristic and idealistic views of the State, made it by definition an immoral instrument of class-oppression whose annihilation even by the (immoral) use of force (or revolution) could not be seriously questioned by philosophies which had reduced the individual to slave of the executive authority (as under *idealism*) or a victim of fate (as under individualism).

When this confused state of affairs was foreboding the very eclipse of a moral and rational basis of Political Philosophy, there appeared on the scene the newly developed science of Sociology (now shorn of much of its earlier shackles and superstitions) the inspirations and influences of which enriched the political philosophy of social minded individualists (like Green, Bourgeois, Durkheim, Hobhouse, Duguit, Ehrlich, Oppenheimer, Laski, Merriam and others).

Incidentally it might be noted that the insistence on the sociological (rather than the juristic and individual) approach in Politics had been the key-note of the Hindu *Dharmashastras* and some of us believe that the world can be cured of its social and international maladies by following the principles of the Hindu social philosophy (with necessary modifications to suit the needs of the modern age) and further that the ignorance of (most) western political philosophers of Sanskrit works (or their contempt for them) has been responsible for the delay (of some four centuries) in correcting the fallacies of Classical Politics and its concomitant evil, the individualist-socialist feud-though in the process of their inquiries the Westerners have brought out much analytical material which is bound to prove helpful in indicating what is to be taken as well as what is to be rejected in the reconstruction of society in the future.

Reverting our attention to the growth of our philosophy in the hands of the social-minded individualists of the West (or the neo-liberals) we find that the new sociological knowledge at their disposal obliged and enabled them to modify Classical Political Theory on various important points-law, sovereignty and the position of the State in the life of the community. It was found impossible for the purposes of Political Philosophy (though it might have been possible for the purposes of political organization irrespective of philosophy) to accept that the legal sovereign was an authority which could command absolute obedience because morally speaking the communal will alone was supreme. Neither was it possible to accept the view that law was the command of the determinate superior (except in a very formal sense) because in essence nothing (in a moral community) *would become the command of the sovereign* unless it reflected the "the sense of right of the right-minded majority." In the light of all this the position of the State in the community required re-examination, re-statement and re-assessment.

II

It is perhaps most convenient to start a discussion on the neo-individualist modifications of the classico-idealist political theory by referring first to the attack on the personality and will of the State. From the results of the progress made by the beginning of the present century in the fields of Sociology, Biology and Psychology it became more and more evident that the State was an organic unity but *not an organism* and that the personality of the State was but a poetic metaphor. This is however not deny the unity of social behaviour or purpose. The State, like the human individual, was a product of *integration* and yet, unlike the individual, was not a physical personality, because the nature of the integration which results in a human *personality* is different from that of the one which produced a corporation. In other words only a *special type of integration results in a personality.*

The type of integration which results in a personality has been described by Perry as *intraorganic* (as distinguished from the integration which results in associations like the State and which he calls inter-organic) the former type of integration takes place within the same physical organism which is connected by a single continuous and *concentric nervous system* and in which purposive activities or interests are so subordinated to each other as to generate a hierarchy of purposes (through intermediation of interests). Integration in which this *intermediation of interests* takes place alone given rise to personalities. Such an integrated personality alone possesses the *prerogatives of personality such as, will, rationality, judgement* and *responsibility* and they are peculiar to organic individuals of the human species i.e. organisms endowed with a highly developed nervous system.

The inter-organic variety of integration obtains among organisms which are neurally discontinuous and eccentric. Here, as in the intra-organic integration, there is community and mutuality of interests but unlike in the personal type of integration, the community and *mutuality of interests* are not combined with the principle of *intermediation of interests.* This type of integration gives rise to associations (like the State) but not to personality. An association is *an inter-action of persons,* not a personality, i.e. persons do not by association compose a super person. Associations exhibit personality in the parts (i.e. in individual members) but not in the whole.

But though State-personality is but a metaphor, social sense or sociality in the individual personality is a fact in any society. Under the influence of this sociality we sacrifice our own desires for the sake of the larger good of the society, which means no *the negation but the reconciliation of individual wills.* That is why the unity of social order or social stability is not permanently there but has to be re-created on the basis of continued reconciliation of will of individual citizens, wherein lies the real test of their freedom.

The second modification needed in the classico-idealist political theory is that tough the State has some formal or legal preeminence, it is but one among many associations in the society.

This preeminence (1) is not absolute because the State has been brought into being for serving certain specific social purposes (i.e. regulating the "universal and external conditions of social life") and whenever it acts beyond its commission it acts without authority. This preeminence (2) again is not substantial or factual because beneath the *legal superstructure* represented by the State, the existence and superior claims of the *social and political structure* have got to be recognised as a matter of stark reality of social life. This socio-political structure includes among it component parts the State and Non-state groups (like the family, the church, the guild etc.) whose seniority (to the State) is a historical fact, whose utility to society can be challenged by an arrogant State at the risk of its own experience.

The over-emphasis on the importance of the State in social life due to a great extent, to the lack of historical perspective among juristic and idealistic thinkers who were responsible for the development of the theory of monistic sovereignty (which was perhaps convenient for political organization in a Particular Philosophy). According to most of these thinkers political evolution took palace by means of a sudden jump-from men in the state of nature to a fully developed civil state (via a Social contract)- and therefore private associations existed in society to the extent they were servile to and tolerated by the State. The history of hitherto known societies, however, teaches us that the State is a product of gradual evolution the stages of which are, family, clan gens, village and city communities, voluntary associations in and across the communities with traditional culture and family, the State.

As a result of (associational) living together, culture and tradition, the sense of right and wrong grow in a community, which, by way of insurance against the risk of loss of the value system thus evolved by it, brings into being a public authority (the State) for the definite object of defending these values and maintaining peace and justice. The State must, therefore, neither go against the social will which brings it into being, nor function in excess of the duties for which it is created, nor capriciously enslave or destroy groups and associations (like the family) which are of much greater antiquity than the State. The modern State is a new-comer among the social associations and its arrogance betrays only it youthful immaturity. The jurisdiction within which the State must function is strictly limited *in fact* and *philosophy*.

This brings us to the third modification needed in the classico-idealist political theory, viz, that the State *does not represent the totality of the political authority* and as such is not the dispenser of total or all round justice. The State may be "a people organised for law" but, as has been well said, there is much law outside the State just as there is much charity outside the Church. The trade unions. The trade unions, the press, the political parties are political institutions of at least as much importance and influence as the State. If they do not shape the dressing up of law, they certainly weave the texture and the patterns of justice which the laws are going to realize.

In other words, as Merriam has shown there are formal as well as informal agencies of human government; the former being represented by the State, the latter by non-State political agencies (like political parties and the like) which latter also influence government, define political values and make justice available. The formal and informal agencies of government taken together therefore constitute the totality of political authority and these alone can dispense all-round social justice. Left to its own restricted resources, the State can dispense only formal justice, that is can remedy breaches of rules which have specifically secured the formal status of law, i.e. criminal and civil offences for punishing which specific provisions have been made through civil and criminal courts. But for all sorts of exploitations short of breach contract, intimidations and extortions short of crime there is no State-remedy. In such cases private associations (like the family, the school, the church, the trade union) are the dispensers of justice, which therefore are political institutions of highest import and which the State can ignore at its own peril.

If these three modifications are admitted the classico-idealist State loses much of its absoluteness which was based on the three false assumptions of its personality, superiority (over other associations), and monopoly of political power. Now we find it has no personality (but it represents the sense of social unity which is a mark of some sort of integration though not of the personal type), that it enjoys no *ab initio* superior authority over other associations (but can interfere with them only when they disturb the social harmony) and that it has no monopoly of political authority (though it has the *monopoly of legal authority* i.e., it is the sole authority to endow any rules with the formal sanction of law though the decision as to which rules should receive the legal sanctity is made mostly and ultimately by non-State political agencies i.e., *public opinion*). As a result of these modifications emerges a truncated but modest and chastened State—a State which (unlike the classico-idealist type) does not cut off the root of Political Physiology by trying to appear either as a sub-human *Leviathan* or a superhuman *Deity*. Such a State places Political Philosophy on the soundest foundation of *freedom* both in its *spiritual* and *institutional* aspects.

By the spiritual aspect of freedom. I mean the freedom of the human spirit which is possible to promote only within a particular *social ethos*. This implies the evolution of a social climate which will help citizens to be trained to *resist the encroachments of authority* on their liberties. In such a perspective law, viewed as an instrument of coercion, in an invasion of personality. To be able to claim any rational and moral validity loyalty to law must be voluntary and the contents of law must satisfy the conscience of the individuals who are required to obey it. Liberty certainly is not a permanent display of the disobedient mood and social life no doubt will be made well-high impossible without our willingness to acquiesce to higher orders, but as Laski has said, "the decision to acquiesce is a decision which should be my own", for, 'to do otherwise is to betray freedom' i.e. to discard the law of our being which we can do only at the peril of our better selves. Such a view helps the growth of an enlightened citizenship by encouraging freedom of speech, association and though and thus enriches the experiences which the citizen may bring to bear upon public questions. As a voluntary member of multiform free associations he develops into a socially integrated personality and a society in which a large number of such personalities live and work is certainly a society "where the mind is without fear and the head is held high." Such a social atmosphere will itself be a great safeguard against the emergence of tyranny and eclipse of freedom.

But important as the social ethos is for defending our liberty and personality against invasions of authority, that (ethos) alone cannot prove to be an adequate safeguard against power which left unguarded in variably tends to be abused. Safeguards against abuse of authority therefore should be reflected and embodied in the *patterns of our institutions* which, to act even with moderate adequacy, must guarantee the basic rights of citizens including the right to choose their rulers at intervals, separation of the judiciary from the executive, right of the individual to sue the State in tort, decentralization of authority as far as possible without weakening the central authority unduly, widest consultation of those affected by legislation and increasing voice of workers in the constitution of the economic institutions of society. It will be readily seen that these changes can be effected in the body politic only if the position of the State is modified in accordance with the suggestions made above.

To sum up: it is possible to talk and think of a subject like Political Philosophy, because it is possible to find a morally valid basis for human government. Whether or not the governments of the world are being run in accordance with this moral basis or standard is a problem of the practical art of government not of its *philosophy*. *The philosophy of government* is concerned, primarily, with the *moral justification* of the phenomenon of government in society. We have seen that such a justification is *possible* but only when government or authority is based upon the recognition of the *principle of freedom*, that is, the principle of being true to oneself or being true to the law of our being, which is the law of enlarging and elevating ourselves, which again is possible by being good to others or by recognising the *principle of love*. So that the law of our being is the law of freedom and that again ultimately means the law of love. *Life in freedom*, in other words, means *life in love*. This principle of freedom or love is the only valid basis of Political Philosophy or the Philosophy of Government.

But government, in the ultimate analysis involves acquiescence to authority and how can it be possible to govern or exert authority and at the same time respect the principle of freedom? Further, how can it be possible to enjoy freedom and at the same time love others which tends to curtail one's own freedom? Taking the second question first, we find that freedom is based on the assumption of goodness of our being finds its expression in being serviceable to or in loving others. True freedom and love of others are therefore not contradictory but almost identical conceptions.

Taking up now the first question, we find that authority based on the love of (the personality of) others will not destroy but rather fulfil the cause of freedom. But can authority be based on love? Is not authority by nature, coercive and therefore indifferent to the susceptibilities of the personalities of those over whom it is exercises? Yes, sometimes (though not always) authority may take a coercive form of manifesting itself but this coercive manifestation (of authority) alone will not make it morally invalid if the sanction behind the authority so exercised had been (not merely superior brute force but) the support and sympathy of the social sense of unity and fair play. This social sense of unity, however, is not a super will (in which the individual wills have been submerged) but a sense of solidarity and mutuality secured by the voluntary reconciliation of individual will for the Common Purpose, for which (Common Purpose) the individuals in society have the greatest concern because the growth of individual personality (though a matter primarily of intra-organic integration) takes place and can take place within a social *milieu* so that intra-organic integration or growth of personality is affected by inter-organic integration or growth of sociality and vice versa.

Obviously, this reconciliation of personal (individual) wills cannot be effected once for all (*a la* Hobbes), because at every critical turn (i.e., decision making moment) these individual wills will have to be *consulted and reconciled afresh* in order that the lamp of liberty may be kept eternally burning. That is why, eternal vigilance is said to be the price of liberty. In fine, in face of a given social situation it is the *individuals* (though undoubtedly influenced by the social ethos and cultural climate) who *must decide*, and to that extent Political Philosophy must remain *libertarian and individualistic*. The task of Political Philosophy is to rediscover the meaning of freedom for every age; it lies in other words in re-interpreting liberty in the context of contemporary social history.

Such a view necessarily rejects the personality, political superiority and monopoly of authority on the part of the State, because on the basis of that rejection alone freedom or justice, as we have understood it to be, may become available to all on, as far as possible, equal terms. It pleads therefor neither for State-despotism nor State-socialism nor Stateless pluralism nor anarchism but for a modes and truncated State, a welfare association, working within the limits of its legitimate functions, enforcing as well as respecting law. Such a State alone can promote welfare without sacrificing freedom, which we maintain is the basis of Political Philosophy.

The main task of the philosopher is theoretically over when he has discovered a moral basis or validity for this philosophy; the philosophy however, loses much of its social worth if it is so theoretical as not at all to be applicable to the problems of real life. Such however, I believe, is not the case with our Philosophy. Realizing the difficulty of attaining the ideal of freedom—difficulties which are inherent in the realization of any great ideal—we reject, however, any suggestion to the effect that Political Philosophy (or the Philosophy of Freedom) is a mere theoretically desirable utopia. The ideal of liberty, like any other ideal, is only progressively realizable in the practices of the governments of countries which have any sense of *human values of civilization*. In other words, the aims of Political Philosophy are a realizable ideal, but realizable only under suitable social and spiritual conditions and in gradual stages. The institutional and functional patterns of the State, in the context of the present age, go a long way to make or mar those conditions. An additional lecture on that topic therefore may not be out of place in a series of lectures specifically meant to be delivered on the Basis of Political Philosophy.

III

We shall now address ourselves to the task of exploring the main patterns of the institutional and functional order within which the State (with its auxiliaries) can help the realization of the ideals of freedom. From our previous observations it would be evident that Political Philosophy (or the Philosophy of Freedom) must necessarily advocate some sort of libertarianism or respect for the individual. But such a philosophy can never mean a creed of selfish individualism (*a la laissez-faire* theory) because what it inculcates is the promotion or growth of personality as the highest aim of social organization and not *mere governmental non-interference* in private and business life. It is clear that (governmental) interferences which help the growth of personality—like factory law, poor law, compul:ory education—are liberal (or libertarian) methods because they help to extend our freedom and heighten our personalities. Growth of personality involves the realization by individuals of certain social values and virtues such as, love, compassion, charity, toleration etc. which include therefore the development also of the highest type of sociality.

At the present moment sociality, however, is being tried to be developed through two processes,—*voluntary* and *compulsory*. The philosophy of freedom (or libertarianism) teaches voluntary *sociality*. It emphasizes not *selfishness* but the bringing into operation of the *voluntary principle* in the practice of *unselfishness*, through which alone the self can be enriched. On the other hand sociality practised under compulsion (as under revolutionary socialism) not only insults personality but makes even the sociality it engenders precarious, short-lived and lacking in ethical quality. It is very important to realize fully that today the choice before us is not between sociality and selfishness but between voluntary and forced sociality (or socialism). The latter has no theoretical foundation, except the inadequacy of the *programme* of the former which has however a sound theoretical basis. The defects of liberalism (or libertarianism) is no the inadequacy or absence of philosophy but the insufficiency and inefficiency of its practical programme.

The task of Political Philosophy, I have said, is *primarily* to re-interpret liberty in the context of current social life but *secondarily* its task is also to show the applicability of the philosophy of liberty in that life through suitable institutions. This, it will be seen, is possible at the present juncture, if we reject the purely legal (*State-al*) view of Politics and accept a sociological (Societal) view of it. Political Philosophy, being the philosophy of all-round freedom or justice, is concerned with the totality of political authority which includes the entire range of (social) transactions and negotiations which in any shape or form deal with the patterns of (social) justice and not merely the patterns of *formal* justice maintained by the State, for, the State is the controller of the *legal order* but not of the entire *political order*. Our first task therefore, is to re-define the position of the State *vis-à-vis* the other organized social groups which may be spontaneous *communities* or artificial *associations*. Here we encounter among others the family, the church, the trade union and the political party—i.e., groups and organizations engaged ultimately in the same task in which the State is also engaged, viz, realization of freedom or making justice available to all.

It is straightway desirable to give up the State's claim to *personality* (not only because such a claim, as shown earlier, is morally and logically untenable but also) because if that is insisted upon, then the other social groups, by the same token, would claim personality on their behalf and social life only of the confused or the slavish sort would be possible. Even so what about its monopoly of authority and superiority among social groups? Authority can retain its moral validity and at the same time be the monopoly of a body if and only if that body has the power and jurisdiction to safeguard liberty or justice (because in the *context of liberty alone is authority justifiable*) and since the State cannot ensure total liberty, cannot dispense all round justice (but only formal or legal justice) the State cannot claim total authority i.e. monopoly of authority. Permit me to repeat that formal or legal justice does not exhaust the entire contents of justice or harmony in society and that total justice is dispensed by the totality of political agencies, viz. the State and the non-State agencies (i.e., private bodies like the family, the school the church, the press etc.). Breaches of contracts (or civil offences) and breaches of peace (crimes) are social inequities against which alone there are remedies available form the State (in the civil and criminal courts). But against innumerable cases of exploitations short of breach of contract, intimidations and suppressions short of crime committed at the instance of the economic, educational and religious orders or by individuals stationed in places of authority (like the father, the teacher, the employer) there is practically no remedy in any court unless it be the non-State tribunal of public opinion organised at private levels as free associations. The *State is co-extensive with the legal order, not with the political order* and hence the State's superiority is legal (and formal) not political or factual.

It will therefore be obvious that in order to make freedom prevail and make justice available to all in a given society, the community must be regarded as an integrated mosaic of many organized groups which are as much important for the realisation of the supreme aim of society (i.e. freedom) as the State. The composition of such a society, in other words, must be federal (without however emphasizing too much the constitutional significance of the term "federal"). Society is federal in the sense that organized groups and associations have rights of existence and development which must be respected by the State unless the objects they pursue are against public opinion and taste. It also means that of this *federation of groups* (i.e., the society) the State is *not the dictator* but a *fellow-member* each one of whom, like the State, performs valuable (though not always spectacular) service to the society. The distinguishing feature of the State lies not so much in its superiority as the *spectacularity* of the function which it performs—a spectacularity akin to that manifested by the *referee* on the foot-ball ground, the *secretary* in the club or the manager in the business concern. It will be an obvious mistake to think of the referee as the dictator of the game and the directions of his whistle are effective only to the extent the parties have greed to play the game (according to the rules) and have placed their confidence in the referee's decisions which therefore, have authority to the extent they can command the respect of those concerned. Even so the State-authority: its apparent and formal omnipotence has meaning only in the context of the *loyalty* which is decisions can command and the *cooperation* that its behaviour can evoke from the society, which, *in effect*, is the same as the *organised groups* and associations in society.

Evidently genuine loyalty to and cooperation with the State on the part of other groups in society are dependant upon the *respect* and *confidence* which these others can expect from the authority which seeks their loyalty and cooperation. In these circumstances it is not difficult to see that the modern State (with a political ideal i.e., the ideal of freedom or justice) must discard the superior arrogance and conceit of the classico-idealist State and accept the obligation of *consulting* and *respecting* the wishes of other associations as far as that is consistent with the State's ultimate obligation of maintaining social harmony and peace. It is in this sense and only in this sense that the society is federal.

This, however, in my opinion, does not necessarily lead to an extreme form of pluralism, if by that term is meant the co-ordinate (legal) jurisdiction of all associations in society (including the State). The State is no doubt one among many associations in society, but a peculiar one, being the only one of its kind (in a given society), the only one that is to say which enforces law and coordinates the centrifugal social forces into an integrated system. This peculiar and characteristic obligation it must discharge because the social whole, for the very sake of its existence, will it so. The State thus is the Supervisor-General of the society: its right to supervise, however is based not on any inherent superiority on its part. The source of this right or obligation of the State (to supervise the affairs of the society) is the will of the society and the exercise of this supervision has to take place within the definite scope indicated by the social will. The authority of the State, therefore, is *neither original* (in source) no *omnicompetent* (in scope) and *yet peculiar* in its characteristics, viz., it is (a) *supervisory*, (b) *extensive* and (c) *spectacular*. These characteristics lend to it the appearance of absolute irresponsibility, which is a myth, though like all myths it is believed by the crowd but like all myths without any foundation in fact or philosophy. The personality, political superiority and monopoly of authority of the State therefore must be rejected as unsupportable by facts and untenable in theory.

In the light of these observations, it will seen that the realization of liberty in a society does not really depend upon minimum interference by the State, nor is such an interference necessarily anti-liberal; because, whether or not this is so depends upon (i) whether or not any particular interference is backed by the ratification of the society and (ii) whether or not such an interference results in the enlargement of freedom and elevation of personality. State non-interference as a *sine qua non* of liberty was one of the specious presumptions of the doctrine of economic laissez-faire which was perhaps the greatest single influence to bring into disrepute the entire liberal philosophy of government. The demolition of that doctrine cannot be regretted by any genuine lover of liberty. Interferences which promote general welfare and growth of personality—like compulsory education prevention of child labour or child marriage—are not only not anti-liberal but instrumentalities of "positive freedom" without which, as Green has shown, negative freedom (or non-interference) is a questionable benefit.

The failure of the *laissez-faire* doctrine, however, is not the failure of the *philosophy* of freedom, which believes not in spiritual isolationism or dictatorial socialism (which philosophically speaking is a contradiction in terms) but in viewing sociality and individuality a complementary conceptions. The growth of individuality is possible (as I have shown earlier) only in society; society is conceivable only among unit-minded individuals. *Freedom unrelated to unity is chaos* (which is very different form the state of happiness experienced by an integrated personality); *unity unrelated to freedom is undiluted slavery* (which is very different from the state of joy arising out of the communion of free spirits). *Freedom in unity* alone is productive of *personality* and progress.

It is certainly easier to talk of *freedom in unity* than to make such a compounded conception operative in our social behaviour and institutions; and it must be frankly admitted that it is an extremely difficult task to decide at any particular moment the *comparative claims of freedom* and unity or to decide how much of freedom should be sacrificed for how much of unity or *vice versa*. All that can be stated in general terms is that the ideal of freedom will not be degraded if whenever such an issue presents itself, it is decided on the *widest basis of social consultation*. *Dictation* by the State is not a necessary consequence of State interference: *totalitarianism* is not a necessary sequel to positive *State activities*, provided public opinion is wide awake.

The social consultation referred before, in the context of the modern life, however, very often tends to be evaded due to the expanding scope of the activities of the State (or State-functions). The modern State, it might be observed, is not merely a *negative welfare agency* (i.e. a co-ordinating and supervisory body to which reference has been made earlier) but also a *positive welfare agency*. This, however, is so not because any authoritarian right (on the part of the state) to meddle in social affairs at random but because the accumulated social experience of mankind has taught us that certain services are best or adequately performed only by the State. As a result, the police-State has given place to the *welfare-State*. What those services are that are best performed by voluntary associations and individuals and what others are best performed by the State must, as I have said, be decided by public opinion (if liberty in society is not to be eclipsed). We can only indicate here the broad principles on which the division of functions between State and non-State agencies should be effected by a society which is aspiring to realise the maximum freedom and welfare of its members.

A probe into the intricacies of human nature cannot fail to show that man, an associational animal, encounters in the course of his life-process not merely the *"struggle for existence"* but as Dr. Bhagawandas has said, also the spirit of *"alliance for existence"*. Human life originates in physical alliance but thrives, prospers, improves and elevates in more rational and altruistic alliances. To emphasise merely the struggle-aspect or rivalry in life is to neglect the fundamental opposite principle in life i.e., unity, alliance, cooperation, sociality, call it what you will but the most generic name is love, i.e. the enlargement or extension of the self in others or *altruism*.

It may, however, be asked that if love or altruism is so very natural to man, why do we encounter so much rivalry and hatred in society? The only thoughtful answer to that is that man, like all things created, is a product of the principle of *dwandam* or duality, the matter-spirit, the evil-good, the higher-lower, the attraction-repulsion, the light-darkness. But so far as we know, it has been given to man alone to be self-conscious, that is the ability to see through the play of duality and to vote for the higher the better, the nobler of the two aspects of the twin-principle in life. The higher and the lower (i.e., *altruism and egoism*) however are inextricably mixed up with each other and we can prepare schemes of social reconstruction by ignoring any one of them only at our own peril. The lower (or egoistic) part of our nature has therefore also to be recognised in any social scheme but institutional provisions should be made so as not to allow the lower to preponderate over the higher principle. The mundane, the material aspect of life (which is concerned with food, clothing, housing, population, migration, trade and commerce) should not therefore be ignored; rather it should be properly developed but should be made subservient to the spiritual, emotional and aesthetic aspect of life. However interdependent the two aspects of life may be, *by nature*, the *glory of civilization* will lie in the degree it is able to subordinate the material to the spiritual and aesthetic values.

In the context of man's dual (spirito-material) nature a society of spiritual (or libertarian) values would mean a society in which no one is deprived of that modicum of creature comforts or rather one in which every one is assured of those comforts and knowledge without which no one can live like a human being. In addition persons trying to realise the higher values should receive the maximum help from the society and enjoy the maximum freedom to do so. It is necessary to accept this stratification in man and society because no thoughtful man (however egalitarian) can be blind to the fact that there are two inextricably entwined aspects of life, the *creative* and *corporate* (the *spiritual* and the *institutional*).

The common experience of mankind, I believe, has also shown that for the common good it is best to entrust the ministry of mundane side of our life (that is matters relating to food, health, clothing, transport, migration etc.) to the State. This I call the *corporate side* of life and is the field suitable for *regimentation* provided of course the social will is adequately consulted. The other aspect of life, which I call the higher, consists of of the spritual, emotional and aesthetic man. This is the creative aspect of man and in this field he should enjoy the maximum freedom form governmental control or interference.

Such a scheme of society will necessarily include many socialistic items, and yet being based on the recognition of individual liberty and personality, will not result in totalitarianism. Indeed the ideal of society should be to produce individuals, who as members of multiform associations would develop into socially integrated personalities. Within the ambit of a social life it is not possible to talk of an *absolute individualist* nor, with due respect to man's personality, is it possible to talk of an *absolute socialist*. The absolute socialist is to be found in a *slave colony*; the absolute individualist in the wilderness. The over dramatization of *individuality* and *sociality* is the most dangerous defect of modern political ideologies and movements.

2

Plato: The Republic

The imperial ambitions of Athens perished with her defeat in the Peloponnesian War, but though her role was changed, her influence upon Greece, and ultimately upon the whole of the ancient world, was by no means diminished. After the loss of her empire she became more and more the educational center of the Mediterranean world, a position which she retained even after her political independence had vanished and indeed far down into the Christian Era. Her schools of philosophy and science and rhetoric were the first great institutions in Europe devoted to higher education and to the research which necessarily accompanies advanced instruction, and to them came students from Rome and all parts of the ancient world. Plato's Academy was the first of the philosophical schools, though Isocrates, who taught especially rhetoric and oratory, probably opened his school a few years earlier. Aristotle's school at the Lyceum was opened some fifty years later, and the two other great schools, the Epicurean and the Stoic, began some thirty years after Aristotle.

Those who have mastered the fine spontaneity, both of life and of art, in the Periclean Age can hardly avoid looking upon this academic specialization of Athenian genius as a decline. Probably it is true that the Greeks would not have turned to philosophy, at least in the manner they did, had the life of Athens remained as happy and as prosperous as it seemed to be when Pericles's Funeral Oration struck its dominant note. And yet no one can doubt that the teaching of the Athenian Schools played as large a part in European civilization as the art of the fifth century. For these Schools mark the beginning of European philosophy, especially in its relations with politics and the other social studies. In this field the writing of Plato and Aristotle were the first great pioneering operations of the European intellect. At the start they have only rudimentary beginnings and nothing that can properly be called a body of sciences, distinguished and classified in the way that now seems obvious. The subjects and their interrelations were in process of creation. But by the time the corpus of Aristotelian writings was completed in 323, the general outline of knowledge—into philosophy, natural science, the sciences of human conduct, and the criticism of art—was fixed in a form that is recognizable for any later age of European thought. Certainly no scholar can afford to belittle the advancing specialization, and the higher standard of professional accuracy which came with the Schools, even though it brought something academic and remote from civic activity.

The Need for political Science

Plato was born about 427 B.C. of an eminent Athenian family. Many commentators have attributed his critical attitude toward democracy to his aristocratic birth, and it is a fact that one of his relatives was prominently connected with oligarchic revolt of 404. But the fact can be perfectly well explained otherwise; his distrust of democracy was no greater than Aristotle's, who was not noble by birth nor even Athenian. The outstanding fact of Plato's intellectual development was his association as a young man with Socrates, and from Socrates he derived what was always the controlling thought of his political philosophy—the idea that virtue is knowledge. Otherwise stated, this meant the belief that there is objectively a good life, both for individuals and for states, which may be made the object of study, which may be defined by methodical intellectual processes, and which may therefore be intelligently pursued. This in itself explains why Plato must in some sense be an aristocrat, since the standard of scholarly attainment can never be left to numbers or popular opinion. Coming to manhood at the conclusion of Peloponnesian War, he could hardly be expected to share Pericles's enthusiasm for the "happy versatility" of democratic life. His earliest thought on politics, that recorded in the Republic, fell just at the time when an Athenian was most likely to be impressed by the discipline of Sparta and before the hollowness of that discipline was made evident by the disastrous history of the Spartan Empire.

In the autobiography attached to the Seventh Letter[1] Plato tells how, as a young man, he had hoed for a political career and had even expected that the aristocratic revolt of the Thirty (404 B.C.) would bring substantial reforms in which he might bear a part. But experience with oligarchy soon made the democracy seem like a golden age, though forthwith the restored democracy proved its unfitness by the execution of Socrates.

> *The result was that I, who had at first been full of eagerness for a public career, as I gazed upon the whirlpool of public life and saw the incessant movement of shifting currents, at last felt dizzy . . . and finally saw clearly in regard to all states now existing that without exception their system of government is bad. Their constitutions are almost beyond redemption except through some miraculous plan accompanied by good luck. Hence I was forced to say in praise of the correct philosophy that it affords a vantage-point from which we can discern in all cases what is just for communities and for individuals; and that accordingly the human race will not see better days until either the stock of those who rightly and genuinely follow philosophy acquire political authority, or else the class who have political control be led by some dispensation of providence to become real philosophers.*[2]

It is exceedingly tempting to see in this passage an important reason for the founding Plato's School, though rather curiously the School is not mentioned in the letter. The date must have been within a few years after the conclusion of his rather extensive travels and his return to Athens in 388. Doubtless the Academy was not founded exclusively for any single purpose and therefore it would be an exaggeration to say that Plato intended to build an institution for the scientific study of politics and the training of statesman. Specialization had not yet reached this point, and Plato hardly thought of the need for the philosopher in politics as a need for men trained *ad hoc* in the professions of administration and legislation. He though of it rather as a need for men in whom an adequate intellectual training had sharpened the perception of the good life and who were therefore prepared to discriminate between true and false goods and between adequate and inadequate means of attaining the true good. The problem was an out-growth of the distinction between nature and convention which had been before the minds of reflective

Greeks during the second half of the fifth century. It was, therefore, in Plato's conception, an important part of the general problem of discriminating true knowledge from appearance, opinion and downright illusion. To it no branch of advanced study, such for example as logic or mathematics, was irrelevant. At the same time it would be hard to believe that Plato, convinced as he was that such knowledge and its acquisition by rulers was the only salvation for states, did not hope and expect that the Academy would disseminate true knowledge and philosophy, not spurious arts such as rhetoric. Certainly he believed later that statesmanship is the supreme or "kingly" science.

In 367 and 361 Plato made his famous journeys to Syracuse to aid his friend Dion in the education and guidance of the young king Dionysius in whose accession he saw what he hoped was the auspicious occasion for radical political reform—a youthful ruler with unlimited power and a willingness to profit by the combined advice of a scholar and of an experienced statesman. The story is told with great vividness in the Seventh Letter. Plato soon found that he had been wholly misled by the report of Dionysius's willingness to take advice and to apply himself either to study or to business. The project was a complete failure, and yet it does not appear that there was anything essentially visionary about Plato's purposes. The advice contained in his letters to Dion's followers is sound and moderate, and it seems clear that Dion's plans were wrecked by his own failure to meet the Syrcusans with a conciliatory policy. Some parts of Plato's Seventh Letter imply that he perceived the great importance for the whole Greek world of a strong Greek power in Sicily to offset the Carthaginians,[3] which was certainly a statesman-like project, and if he believed that an adequate power was impossible without monarchy, this was a conclusion which the Hellenization of the East by Alexander did much to justify. So far as the Sicilian adventure concerned Plato personally, he manifestly felt that no serious scholar who, for a generation, had been preaching the doctrine that politics required philosophy could refuse the support which Dion asked.

> I feared to see myself at last altogether nothing but words, so to speak—a man who would never willingly lay hand to any concrete task.

Matters more or less connected with political philosophy are discussed in many of Plato's Dialogues, but there are three which deal mainly with the subject and from these his theories must be mainly gathered. These are the Republic, the Statesman, and the Laws. The Republic was written in Plato's mature but comparatively early manhood, probably within a decade of the opening of his School. Though it was certainly intended to be a unit and has so impressed its best critics, its composition may well have extended over several years, and there is good stylistic evidence that the discussion of justice in Book I is relatively early. The Laws, on the other hand, was the work of Plato's old age and according to the tradition he was still at work on it when he died in 347. Thirty years (or possibly even more) elapsed, therefore, between the writing of the Republic and the writing of the laws. It is plausible to see in the former work the enthusiasm of Plato's first maturity, of the time which saw the founding of the School, and in the latter the disillusionment which came with age, perhaps accentuated by the failure of his venture in Syracuse. The Statesman was written between the other two dialogues, but probably nearer the Laws than the Republic.

Virtue is knowledge

The Republic is a book which defies classification. It fits into none of the categories either of modern social studies or of modern science. In it practically every side of Plato's philosophy is touched upon or developed, and its range of subject-matter is such that it may be said to deal with the whole of human life. It has to do with the good man and the good life, which for Plato connoted life in a good state, and with the means for knowing what these are and for attaining them. And to a problem so general no side of individual or social activity is alien. Hence the Republic is not a treatise of any sort, nor does it belong to politics, or ethics, or economics or psychology, though it includes all these and more, for art and education and philosophy are not excluded. For this breadth of subject-matter, which is a little disconcerting to an academically trained reader, several facts account. The mere literary mechanics of the dialogue-form which Plato used permitted an inclusiveness and a freedom of arrangement which a treatise could not tolerate. Moreover, when Plato wrote, the various "sciences" mentioned above did not yet have the distinctness that was later somewhat artificially assigned to them. But more important than either literary or scientific technique is the fact to which reference has already been made, that in the city-state life itself was not classified and subdivided so much as it now is. Since all of a man's activities were pretty intimately connected with his citizenship, since his religion was the religion of the state, and his art very largely a civic art, there could be no very sharp separation of these questions. The good man must be a good citizen; a good man could hardly exist except in a good state; and it would be idle to discuss what was good for the man without considering also what was good for the city. For this reason an interweaving of psychological and social questions, of ethical and political considerations, was intrinsic to what Plato was trying to do.

The richness and variety of the problem and subject-matter that figure in the Republic did not prevent the political theory contained in the work from being highly unified and rather simple in its logical structure. The main positions developed, and those most characteristic of Plato, may be reduced to a few propositions, and all these propositions were not only dominated by a single point of view but were deduced pretty rigorously by a process of abstract reasoning which was not, indeed, divorced from the observation of actual institutions but did not profess to depend upon it. To this statement the classification of forms of government in Books VIII and IX in some degree an exception, but the discussion of actual states was introduced to point the contrast with the ideal state and may therefore be neglected in considering the central argument of the Republic. Aside from this the theory of the state is developed is a closely concatenated line of thought which is both unified and simple. Indeed, it is necessary to insist that this theory is far too much dominated by a single idea and far too simple to do justice to Plato's subject, the political life of the city-state. This explains why he felt obliged to formulate a second theory—without however admitting the unsoundness of the first—and also why the greatest of his students, Aristotle, while accepting some of the most general conclusions of the Republic, stood much closer on the whole to the form of political philosophy developed in the Statesman and the Laws than to the ideal state of the Republic. The over-simplification of the political theory contained in the earlier work made it, except in respect of very general principles, an episode in the development of the subject.

The fundamental idea of the Republic came to Plato in the form of his master's doctrine that virtue is knowledge. His own unhappy political experience reinforced the idea and crystallized it in the founding of the Academy to inculcate the spirit of true knowledge as the foundation for a philosophic statecraft. But the proposition that virtue is knowledge implies that there is an objective good to be known and that it can in fact be known by rational or logical investigation rather than by intuition, guesswork, luck. The good is objectively real, whatever anybody thinks about it, and it ought to be realized not because men want it but because it is good. In other words, will comes into the matter only secondarily; what men want depends upon how much they see of the good but nothing is good merely because they want it. From this if follows that the man who knows—the philosopher or scholar or scientist —ought to have decisive power in government and that it is his knowledge alone which entitles him to this. This is the belief which underlies everything else in *Republic* and causes Plato to sacrifice every aspect of the state that cannot be brought under the principle of enlightened despotism.

Upon examination, however, this principle is more broadly based than might at first be supposed. For it appears upon analysis that the association of man with man in society depends upon reciprocal needs and the resulting exchange of goods and services. Consequently the philosopher's claim to power is only a very important case of what is found wherever men live together, namely, that any co-operative enterprise depends upon everyone attending to his own part of the work. In order to see what this involves for the state, it is necessary to know what sorts of work are essential, an investigation which leads to the three classes of which the philosopher-ruler will obviously be the most important. But this dividing of tasks and securing the most perfect performance of each—the specialization of function which is the root of society—depends upon two factors, natural aptitude and training. The first is innate and the second is a matter of experience and education. As a practical enterprise the state depends on controlling and inter-relating these two factors; in other words, upon getting the best human capacity and developing it by the best education. The whole analysis reinforces the initial conception: there is no hope for states unless power lies in the hands of those who know—who know, first what tasks the good state requires, and, second, what heredity and education will supply the citizens fitted to perform them.

Plato's theory is therefore divisible into two main parts or theses first, that government ought to be an art depending on exact knowledge and, second, that society is a mutual satisfaction of needs by persons whose capacities supplement each other. Logically the second proposition is a premise for the first. But since Plato presumably derived the first almost ready-formed from Socrates, it is reasonable to suppose that temporally the second was generalization or extension of the first. The Socratic principle that virtue is knowledge proved to have a large applicability than appeared on its face.

The Incompetence of Opinion

The thesis that the good is a matter of exact knowledge descends to Plato directly from the already ancient distinction of nature and convention and the quarrel between Socrates and the Sophists. Unless something is good, really and objectively, and unless reasonable men can agree about it, there is no standard for an art of statesmanship such as Plato hoped to found. The question in its various ramifications is spread at large over Plato's earlier dialogues, in the continually recurring analogy between the statesman and the physician or the skilled artisan, in the counter comparison in the Gorgias of oratory to the pampering of appetite by cookery, in the lack of method and the pretentiousness attributed to the teaching of the Sophists in the Protagoras, and on a more speculative level in the frequently recurring question about the relative positions of reason and inspiration, or of methodical knowledge and intuition. In the same category belong the long discussions of art in the Republic and the not very flattering estimate of artists as men who get an effect without knowing how or why. This parallels precisely the charge that statesmen, even the greatest of them have governed by a kind of "divine madness." Obviously no one can seriously hope to teach divine madness.

The difficulties of the city-state, however, are not in Plato's opinion the result of defective education alone and still less of moral deficiencies in its statesmen or its teachers. They arise rather from a sickness of the whole body-public and of human nature itself. The public itself, he said, is the great sophist. A constantly recurring note in his ethics is the conviction that human nature is at war with itself, that there is a lower man from whom the higher man must at all costs save himself. It was this which made Plato seem to the Fathers of the Church "almost a Christian." Quite gone is the faith in "happy versatility" so magnificently praised in the Funeral Oration. The happy confidence of a generation that had created both spontaneously and successfully has given place to the doubt and uncertainty of a more critical age, in Plato the hope still persisted that it may be possible to recapture the happier frame of mind, but only through methodical self-examination and rigid self-discipline. In origin, therefore, the Republic was critical study of the city-state as it actually was, with all the concrete defects that Plato saw in it, though for special reasons he chose to cast his theory in the form of an ideal city. This ideal was to reveal those eternal principles of nature which existing cities tried to defy.

Chief among the abuses that Plato attacked was the ignorance and incompetence of politicians, which is the special curse of democracies. Artisans have to know their trades, but politicians know nothing at all, unless it be the ignoble art of pandering to the "great beast." After the disastrous outcome of the Peloponnesian War, the generation in which the Republic was written was peculiarly a time in which Athenians would be likely to admire the thoroughness and discipline of Sparta Xenophon went farther than Plato in this direction, and indeed Plato never could have admired whole-heartedly a one-sided military education like that at Sparta, however much he might ad:nire the devotion to duty that it produced. But it is noticeable that he was more sharply critical of Sparta at the end of his life, when he wrote the *Laws*, than he was in *Republic*. Moreover, the idea of expert skill professionally trained was one which, in Plato's day, was just dawning upon Greece. Not many years before the Academy was opened a professional soldier, Iphicrates, had astonished the world by showing what a body of light-armed, professionally trained troops could do even against the heavy infantry of Sparta. Professional oratory may be said to have started about the same time with the school of Isocrates. Thus Plato was merely making explicit an idea that was already growing up. What he rightly perceived was that the whole question is much larger than the training of soldiers or orators, or even than training itself. Behind training lies the need of knowing what to teach and what to train men to do. It cannot be assumed that somebody already has the knowledge which shall be taught; what is most urgently needed is more knowledge. The really distinctive thing in Plato is the coupling of training with investigation, or of professional standards of skill with scientific standards of knowledge. Herein lies the originality of his theory of higher education in the Republic and something of this sort, it is tempting to believe, he must have tried to realize in the founding of the Academy.

Incompetence is a special fault of democratic states but there is another defect which Plato saw in all existing forms of government equally. This is the extreme violence and selfishness of party-struggles, which might at any time cause a faction to prefer its own advantage above that of the state itself. The harmony of political life—that adjustment of public and private interests which Pericles boasted had been achieved in Athens—was indeed, as Plato perceived, for the most part an ideal. Loyalty to the city was at best a precariously founded virtue, while the political virtue of ordinary custom was likely to be loyalty to some type of class-government. The aristocrat was loyal to an oligarchical form of constitution, the man of common birth to a democratic constitution, and both alike were only too likely to make common cause with their own kind in another state. Practices which by standards of modern political ethics would be counted treasonable were in Greek politics rather common. The best-known example, but by no means the worst, is Alcibiades, who did not hesitate to intrigue against Athens both with Sparta and Persia, in order to re-establish his own political influence and that of his party. Sparta, which was oligarchic in its form of government, was regularly looked to for support by the oligarchic party of all the cities within her sphere of influence, and in the same way Athens made common cause with the popular factions.

This fierce spirit of factionalism and party-selfishness was manifestly a chief cause of the relative instability of government in the city state. Plato attributed it largely to the discrepancy of economic interests between those who have property and those who have none. The oligarch is interested in the protection of his property and the collection of his debts whatever hardship this works upon the poor. The democrat is prone to schemes for supporting idle and indigent citizens at public expense, that is, with money taken from the well-to-do. Thus is even the smallest city there are, Plato said, two cities, a city of the rich and a city of the poor, eternally at war with each other. So serious is this condition that Plato can see no cure for factionalism in Greek politics unless there is a profound change in the institution of private property. As a root-and-branch remedy he would abolish it outright, but at the very least he believes it necessary to do away with the great extremes of poverty and wealth. And the education of citizens to prefer civic welfare before everything else is hardly less important than the education of rulers. Incompetence and factionalism are two fundamental political evils that any plan for perfecting the city-state must meet.

The State as a Type

The theoretical or scientific implications of Plato's principle are not less important for him than the critical. There is a good both for men and for states and to grasp this good, to see what it is and by what means it may be enjoyed, is a matter of knowledge. Men have, indeed, all sorts of opinions about it and all sorts of impressionistic notions about how to reach it, but of opinions there is no end and among them there is little to choosé. Knowledge about the good, if it could be attained, would be quite a different sort of thing. There would, in the first place, be some rational guarantee for it, it would justify itself to some faculty other than that by which men hold opinions. And in the second place, it would be one and unchanging, not one thing at Athens and another at Sparta, but the same always and everywhere. In short, it would belong to nature and not to the shifting winds of custom and convention. In man as in other parts of the world there is something permanent, a "nature" as distinct from an appearance, and to grasp nature is just what discriminates knowledge from opinion. When Plato says that it is the philosopher who knows the good, this is no boast of omniscience, it is merely the assertion that three is an objective standard and that knowledge is better than guess-work. The analogy of professional or scientific knowledge is never far from Plato's mind. The statesman ought to know the good of a state as the physician knows health, and similarly he should understand the operation of disturbing or preserving causes. It is knowledge alone which distinguishes the true statesman form the false, as it is knowledge that distinguishes the physician from the quack.

To Plato when he wrote the Republic this determination to be scientific implied that his theory must sketch an ideal state and not merely describe and existing state. Though it may seem paradoxical, it is literally true that the Republic pictures a utopia not because it is a "romance", as Dunning imagines,[5] but because Plato intended it to be the start of a scientific attack upon the "idea of the good." The statesman was really to know what the good is and consequently what is required to make a good state. He must know also what the state is, not in its accidental variations but as it is intrinsically or essentially. Incidentally, the philosopher's right to rule could only be vindicated if this were shown to be implied by the nature of the state. Plato's state must be a "state as such," a type or model of all states. No merely descriptive account of existing states would serve his purpose, and no merely utilitarian argument would vindicate the philosopher's right. The general nature of the state as a kind or type is the subject of the book, and it is a secondary question whether actual states live up to the model or not. This procedure accounts for the rather cavalier way in which Plato treats questions of practicability, which are likely to bother the modern reader. It is easy to exaggerate his remoteness from actual conditions, but as he understood the problem, the question whether his ideal state could be produced really was irrelevant. He was trying to show what in principle a state must be; if the facts are not like the principle, so much the worse for the facts. Or to put it a little differently, he was assuming that the good is what it objectively is; whether men like it or can be persuaded to want it is another matter. To be sure, if virtue is knowledge, it may be presumed that men will want the good when they find out what it is, but the good will be none the better for that.

Plato's way of proceeding here will be much more intelligible if it is realized that his conception of what would make a satisfactory science of politics is, in a way harking back to the ancient Egyptians, built upon the procedure of geometry. The relation of his philosophy to Greek mathematics was exceedingly close, both because of the influence upon him of the Pythagoreans and because of the inclusion in his own school of at least two of the most important mathematicians and astronomers of the day. There is a tradition, indeed, that he refused to admit students who had not studied geometry. Moreover, Plato himself propounded to his student the problem of reducing the apparently erratic motions of the planets to simple geometric figures and the problem was solved by Eudoxus of Cnidos.[6] This feat produced a scientific theory of the planetary system and also an approximation to a mathematical explanation of nay natural phenomenon. In short, the method and the ideal of exact scientific explanation, which appeared in Greek geometry and astronomy and which reappeared in the astronomy and mathematical physics of the seventeenth century, is one strand in the great Platonic tradition. It has its beginning precisely in the generation which saw the founding of the Academy and the writing of the Republic.

It is no way surprising, therefore, that Plato should have imagined that progress in the rational understanding of the good life lay along a similar line. It was obvious to him that the precision of exact science depended upon a grasp of types; there is no geometry unless one is content to deal with idealized figures, neglecting the divergences and complications that occur in every representation of the type. All that empirical fact can claim, for example in astronomy, is that the types used shall "save the appearances"; in short, that the astronomer's deductions shall yield a result in agreement with what apparently is happening in the heavens. Manifestly the astronomer's types—his true circles and triangles—tell what is "really" happening.[7] In the same manner the Republic aims not to describe states but to find what is essential or typical in them—the general sociological principles upon which any society of human beings depends, in so far as it aims at a good life. The line of thought is substantially similar to that which caused Herbert Spencer to argue for a deductive "Absolute Ethics," applying to the perfectly adapted man in the completely evolved society, as an ideal standard of reference for descriptive social studies.[8] The utility or even the possibility of such a project, as conceived either by Plato or Spencer, may doubted, but is a gross error to think that Plato intended to loose his imagination for flight into the regions of fancy.

Reciprocal Needs and Division of Labour

The proposition that the statesman should be a scientist who knows the idea of the good supplied Plato with a point of view from which he could criticise the city-state and also with a method that led to the ideal state. From this point he was led directly to his analysis of the typical state, and here again he found that he could follow the rule of specialization. The frequent analogies between the statesman and other kinds of skilled workers, artisans, or professional men, are in truth more than analogies. This is true because societies arise in the first place out of the needs of men, which can be satisfied only as they supplement each other. Men have many wants and no man is self-sufficient. Accordingly they take helpers and exchange with one another. The simplest example is, of course, the production and exchange of food and the other means of physical maintenance, but the argument can be extended far beyond the economic needs of a society. For Plato it afforded a general analysis for all association of men in social groups. Wherever there is society there is some sort of satisfaction of needs and some exchange of services for this purpose.

This analysis, introduced so simply and unobtrusively by Plato into his construction of the ideal state, was one of the profoundest discoveries which his social philosophy contains. It brought to light an aspect of society which is admittedly of the greatest importance for any social theory and it stated once for all a point of view which the social theory of the city-state never abandoned. Briefly stated it amounts to this: society is to be conceived as a system of services in which every member both gives and receives. What the state takes cognizance of is this mutual exchange and what it tries to arrange is the most adequate satisfaction of needs and the most harmonious interchange of services. Men figure in such a system as the performers of a needed task and their social importance depends upon the value of the work they do. What the individual possesses, therefore, is first and foremost a status in which he is privileged to act, and the freedom which the state secures him is not so much for the exercise of his free will as for the practice of his calling.

Such a theory differs from one which pictures social relations in terms of contract or agreement and which therefore conceives the state as primarily concerned with maintaining liberty of choice. A theory of the latter sort occurs, as was pointed out in the last chapter, both in the fragment of Antiphon the Sophist and in the remarks on justice by Glaucon early in the second book of the *Republic*.[9] But Plato rejected it because agreement, resting solely upon the will, can never show that justice is intrinsically a virtue. Social arrangements can be shown to rest on nature rather than convention only if it can be shown that what a man does has meaning beyond the mere fact that he wants to do it. How convincing the argument was found is shown by the fact that Aristotle, who was not greatly influenced by most of Plato's argument for his ideal state, was quite at one with him in this. The analysis of the community in the opening pages of the Politics was merely a new version of Plato's argument that a society depends upon mutual needs.

But exchange of services implies another principle of almost equal importance, the division of labour and the specializing of tasks. For if needs are satisfied by exchange, each must have more than he needs of the commodity which he offers, just as he must have less than he needs of that which he receives. It is clearly necessary, therefore, that there should be some specialization. The farmer produces more food than he needs while the shoemaker produces more shoes than he can wear. Hence it is advantageous to both that each should produce for the other, since both will be better fed and clothed by working together than by each dividing his work to make all the various things he needs. This rests, according to Plato, upon two fundamental facts of human psychology, first that different men have different aptitudes and so do some kinds of work better than others and, second, that skill is gained only where men apply themselves steadily to the work for which they are naturally fitted.

> We must infer that all things are produced more plentifully and easily and of a better quality when one man does one thing which is natural to him and does it at the right time, and leaves other things.[10]

Upon this brief but exceedingly penetrating analysis of society and of human nature Plato's further construction of the state depends.

It turns out, therefore, that the philosopher-ruler is not peculiar but that his claim to power is justified by the same principle which is at work throughout all society. Banish specialization entirely and all social interchange is banished with it. Imagine men with no difference of natural aptitude and the basis for specialization is gone. Take away all training by which natural aptitude is perfected into developed skill and specialization becomes meaningless. These, then, are the forces in human nature upon which society and with it the state have to rely. The question, then, is not whether they shall be used but only whether they shall be used well. Shall men be divided according to their real aptitudes? Shall these aptitudes be wisely and adequately trained to bring them to their most perfect form? Shall the needs which men seek to satisfy cooperatively be their highest and most genuine needs, or merely the wants of their lower and more luxurious natures? These questions can be answered only in the light of what Plato calls inclusively a knowledge of the good. To know the good is to know how to answer them. And this is the special function of the philosopher. His knowledge is at once his right and his duty to rule.

Classes and Souls

It will be clear upon reflection that this argument makes an important assumption which is not explicitly stated by Plato. Individual capacities are assumed to be of such a sort that, when developed by a properly devised and controlled education, they will result in a harmonious social group. The difficulty with existing states has been that education has been wrong; or at all events, if better breeding is needed—and Plato believes that it is—an improvement of existing strains will accomplish the purpose. In other words, he takes for granted that there is nothing radically unsocial or antisocial in well-bred human beings which might result in disharmony precisely because of a complete and perfect development of individual powers. This assumption is not obviously and true and many thinkers since Plato have questioned it; some have even gone to the length of supposing the opposite, namely, that socialized training must be more or less repressive of individual self-expression. But this possibility does not enter into Plato's calculations. While the assumption just mentioned is not explicitly stated, it does enter into the argument of the Republic at one point which is likely, without explanation, to be a little puzzling. This is the point at which the state is assumed to be merely the individual "writ large"[11] and at which, accordingly, the question about justice is transformed from the search for an individual virtue into the search for a property of the state. The difficulty of the transition, which seems to a modern reader a little artificial, is masked for Plato by the presumption that there is an inherent fitness of human nature for society and of society for human nature, and this fitness he interprets as parallelism. Both man and the state have single underlying structure which prevents the good for one from being essentially different form the good for the other.

It must be admitted that this assumption is responsible for much that is most attractive in the ethical ideal of the city-state and in Plato's representation of it. It explains why, in Plato's ethics, there is no ultimate cleft between inclination and duty or between the interests of individuals and those of the society to which they belong. Where such conflicts arise—and the Republic was written because they do arise—the problem is one of development and adjustment, not of repression and force. What the unsocial individual needs is a better understanding of his own nature and a fuller development of his powers in accordance with that knowledge. His internal conflict is not an unappeasable strife between what he wants to do and what he ought to do, because in the last resort the full expression of his natural powers is both what he really wants and what he is entitled to have. On the other hand, what the inharmonious society needs is to provide just those possibilities of complete development for its citizens which their needs demand. The problem of the good state and of the good man are two sides of the same question, and the answer to one must at the same time give the answer to the other. Morality ought to be at once private and public and if it is not so, the solution lies in correcting the state and improving the individual until they reach their possible harmony. It may very well be doubted whether, in general terms, any better moral ideal than this has ever been stated.

At the same time Plato's attempt to make one analysis do duty for both the state and the individual yields him a theory much too simple to solve his problem. The analysis of the state shows that there are three necessary functions to be performed.

The underlying physical needs must be supplied and the state must be protected and governed. The principle of specialization demands that essential services should be distinguished, and it follows that there are three classes: the workers who produce and the "guardians", who in turn are divided, though not so sharply, into the soldiers and the rulers, or the philosopher-king if he be a single ruler. But since division of functions rests on difference of aptitude, the three classes depend upon the fact that there are three kinds of men, those who are fitted by nature to work but not to rule, those who are fit to rule but only under the control and direction of other, and finally those who are fit for the highest duties of statesmanship such as the final choice of means and ends. These three aptitudes imply on the psychological side three vital powers or "souls," that which includes the appetitive or nutritive faculties and which Plato supposes to reside below the diaphragm, that which is executive or "spirited" and which resides in the chest, and that which knows or thinks, the rational soul which is situated in the head. It would seem natural that each soul should have its own special excellence or virtue, and Plato does in fact carry out this plan in part. Wisdom is the excellence of the rational soul and courage of the active, but he hesitates to say that temperance can be confined to the nutritive soul. Justice is the proper interrelation of the three functions, whether of the classes in the state or of the faculties in an individual.

It would probably be a mistake to put too much stress upon this theory of the "three souls." Plato seems never to have tried seriously to develop it, and often in psychological discussion he does not use it. Moreover, it is certainly not true that in the Republic the three classes are so sharply separated as his schematic statement of the theory would lead one to expect. The classes are certainly not castes, for membership in them is not hereditary. On the contrary his ideal seems to be a society in which every child born is given the highest training that his natural powers permit him to profit by, and in which every individual is advanced to the highest position in the state that his achievements (his capacity plus his education and experience) enable him to fill adequately. Plato in the Republic showed himself remarkable free from temperamental class-prejudice, much freer than Aristotle, for example, and freer than he seems to be in the outline of the second-best state in the laws. But when all these allowances are made, the fact remains that the parallelism assumed between mental capacities and social classes is a restricting influence which prevented him from doing justice in the Republic to the complexity of the political problems under discussion. The theory obliged him to assume that all the intelligence in the state was concentrated in the rulers, though his repeated references to the skill of the artisans in their own kind of work shows that he did not literally believe this. On the other hand, in their political capacity the workers have nothing to do but obey, which is nearly the same thing as to say that they have no properly political capacity at all. The position to which they are assigned cannot be corrected even by education, because they seem not to need education for civic activity or for participation in the self-governing activities of the community. In this part of the state's life they are onlookers.

This result has often been attributed, as for example by Edward Zeller,[12] to a contempt for artisans and the handicrafts as compared with intellectual labour, but in truth Plato showed a more genuine admiration for manual skill than Aristotle. The explanation is to be found rather in the assumption that good government is nothing but a matter of knowledge and that knowledge is always the possession of a class of experts, like the practice of medicine. According to Plato most men are permanently in the relation to their rulers of a patient to his physician. Aristotle asked a pertinent question on this point when he inquired whether there are not cases where experience is a better guide than the knowledge of an expert.[13] A man who has to live in a house need not rely on a builder to tell him whether it is commodious or not. But Plato's ideas about sound knowledge when he wrote the Republic allowed little importance to experience. The result was that he failed to grasp one of the most significant political aspects of the city-state whose civil life he desired to perfect. His distrust of "happy versatility" was so great that he swung to the opposite extreme and allowed to artisans no capacity for public service except their trades. The old free give and take of the town-meeting and the council is utterly gone, and this side of human personality, which the Athenian democrat valued above everything, must be quite eradicated from the masses. So far as the higher activities of life are concerned, they live in a state of tutelage to wiser men.

Justice

The theory of the state in the Republic culminates in the conception of justice. Justice is the bond which holds a society together, a harmonious union of individuals each of whom has found his life-work in accordance with his natural fitness and his training. It is both a public and a private virtue because the highest good both of the state and of its members is thereby conserved. There is nothing better for a man than to have his work and to be fitted to do it; there is nothing better for other men and for the whole society than that each should thus be filling the station to which he is entitled.

> Social justice thus may be defined as the principle of a society, consisting of different types of men . . . who have combined under the impulse of their need for one another, and by their combination in one society, and their concentration on their separate functions, have made a whole which is perfect because it is the product and the image of the whole of the human mind.[14]

This is Plato's elaboration of the *prima facie* definition of justice as "giving to every man has due." For what is due to him is that he should be treated as what he is, in the light of his capacity and his training, while what his due from him is the honest performance of those tasks which the place accorded him requires.

To a modern reader such a definition of justice is at least as striking for what it omits as for what it includes. In no sense is it a juristic definition. For it lacks notion, connoted by the Latin word ius and the English word right, of powers of voluntary action in the exercise of which a man will be protected by law and supported by the authority of the state. Lacking this conception Plato does not mean by justice, except remotely, the maintenance of public peace and order; at least, external order is but a small part of the harmony which makes the state. What the state provides its citizens is not so much freedom and protection as a life—all the opportunities for social interchange which make up the necessaries and the amenities of a civilised existence. It is true that in such a social life there are rights, just as there are duties, but they can hardly be said to belong in any peculiar sense to individuals. They are inherent rather in the services or functions that individuals perform. Resting as it does upon the principle that the state is created by mutual needs, the analysis runs necessarily in terms of services and not of powers. Even the ruler is no exception, for he has merely the special function to which his wisdom entitles him. The notion of authority or sovereign power, such as the Roman attached to his magistracies, has practically no part in Plato's political theory, nor indeed in that of any Greek philosopher.

This completes the general outline of Plato's theory of the state. Starting form the conception that the good must be known by methodical study, the theory constructs society around this idea by showing that the principle is implicit in all society. The division of labour and the specialization of tasks are the conditions of social co-operation, and the problem of the philosopher-king is to arrange these matters in the most advantageous way. Because human nature is innately and inherently social, the maximum advantage to the state means also the maximum advantage to citizens. The goal is therefore a perfect adjustment of human beings to the possibilities of significant employment which the state affords. The remainder of Plato's argument might almost be described as a corollary. The only remaining question concerns the means by which the statesman can bring about the adjustment required. Broadly speaking there are only two ways to take hold of this problem. Either the special hindrances to good citizenship may be removed or the positive conditions of good citizenship may be developed. The first results in the theory of communism and the second in the theory of education.

Property and the family

Plato's communism takes two main forms which meet in the abolition of the family. The first is the prohibition of private property, whether houses or land or money, to the rulers and the provision that they shall live in barracks and have their meals at common table. The second is the abolition of a permanent monogamous sexual relation and the substitution of regulated breeding at the behest of the rulers for the purpose of securing the best possible offspring. This bracketing of the two social functions of procreating children and of producing and owning goods was more obvious in a society that lived mainly under a household economy than it is now. A radical innovation in respect to the one coalesced readily with an innovation in respect to the other. Communism in the Republic, however, applies only to the guardian class, that is, to the soldiers and rulers, while the artisans are to be left in possession of their private families, both property and wives, how this is to be made consistent with promotion form the lower rank to the higher is not explained. But the truth is that Plato does not take the trouble to work out his plan in much detail. Still more striking is the fact that, in connection property, he does not have anything to say about slaves. It is a fact that Palto's state seemingly might exist without slavery, since no work especially to be done by slaves is mentioned, a respect in which the state of the laws is strikingly different. This has led Constantin Ritter to argue that in the Republic slavery is "in principle abolished."[15] But it is almost incredible that Plato intended to abolish a universal institution without mentioning it. It is more probable that the merely regarded slavery as unimportant.

Plato was in no way unique in believing that an economic cleavage between the citizens of a state is a most dangerous political condition. In general, the Greeks were quite frank in admitting that economic motives are very influential in determining political action and political affiliation. Long before the Republic was written Euripides had divided citizens into three classes, the useless rich who are always greedy for more, the poor who have nothing and are devoured by envy, and the middle class, the sturdy yeomanry, who "save states."[16] The oligarchical state to a Greek meant a state governed by, and in the interest of, the well-born among whom the possession of property is hereditary, while a democratic state was one governed by and for the "many," who have neither birth nor property. The economic difference was the key to the political distinction, as is quite clear from Plato's account of oligarchy.[17] The importance of economic causes in politics was therefore no new idea, and in believing that great diversity of wealth was inconsistent with good government Plato was following a common conviction which represented Greek experience through many generations. The causes of civic unrest in Athens had been mainly of this sort from at least the days of Solon.

So firmly was Plato convinced of the pernicious effects of wealth upon government that he saw no way to abolish the evil except by abolishing wealth itself, so far as soldiers and rulers are concerned. To cure the agreed of rulers there is no way short of denying them the right to call anything their own. Devotion to their civic calling admits no private rival. The example of Sparta, where citizens were denied the use of money and the privilege of engaging in trade, doubtless weighed with Plato in reaching this conclusion. His reasons, however, should be carefully noted. He was not in the least concerned to do away with inequalities of wealth because they are unjust to the individuals concerned. His purpose was to produce the greatest degree of unity in the state, and private property is incompatible with this. The emphasis is characteristic of Greek thought, for when Aristotle criticises communism, he does so not on the ground that it is unfair but on the ground that it would not in fact produce the unity desired. Plato's communism has, therefore, a strictly political purpose. The order of ideas is exactly the reverse of that which has mainly animated modern socialist utopias; he does not mean to use government to equalize wealth, but he equalizes wealth in order to remove a disturbing influence in government.

The same is true also of Plato's purpose in abolishing marriage, since he regards family affection, directed toward particular persons, as another potent rival to the state in competing for the loyalty of rulers. Anxiety for one's children is a form of self-seeking more insidious than the desire for property, and the training of children in private homes he regards as a poor preparation for the whole-souled devotion which the state has right to demand. But in the case of marriage Plato had other purposes as well. He was appalled at the casualness of human mating, which, as he says, would not be tolerated in the breeding of any domestic animal. The improvement of the race demands a more controlled and a more selective type of union. Finally, the abolition of marriage was probably an implied criticism of the position of women in Athens, where her activities were summed upon in keeping the house and rearing her children. To Plato his seems to deny to the state the services of half its potential guardians. Moreover, the he was unable to see that there is anything in the natural capacity of women that corresponds to the Athenian practice, since many women are as well qualified as men to take part in political or even military duties. The women of the guardian class will consequently share all the work of the men, which makes it necessary both that they shall receive the same education and be free form strictly domestic duties.

To a modern taste there is something a little starting about the coolly unsentimental way in which Plato argues from the breeding of domestic animals to the sexual relations of men and women. It is not that he regards sex casually, for the reverse is emphatically true; in fact, he demands a degree of control and of self-control that has never been realized among any large population. The point is rather that he carries out a line of thought relentlessly and with little regard for difficulties that are manifest to feeling even when they are not explicitly stated. The unity of the state is to be secured; property and family stand in the way; therefore property and marriage must go. There can be no doubt that here Plato spoke the authentic language of doctrinaire radicalism, which is prepared to follow the argument where it may lead. On the score of common sense. Aristotle's answer left nothing to be said. It is possible, he pointed out, to unify a state to the point where it ceases to be a state. A family is one thing and a state is something different, and it is better that one should not try to ape the other.

Education

However much importance Plato attached to communism as a means for removing hindrances form the path of the statesman, it was not upon communism but upon education that he placed his main reliance. For education is the positive means by which the ruler can shape human nature in the right direction to produce a harmonious state. A modern reader cannot fail to be astonished at the amount of space devoted to education, at the meticulous care with which the effect of different studies is discussed, or at the way in which Plato frankly assumes that the state is first and foremost an educational institution. He himself called it "the one great think"; if the citizens are well educated they will readily see through the difficulties that beset them and meet emergencies as they arise. So striking is the part played in Plato's ideal state by education that some have considered this to be the chief topic of the Republic. Rousseau said that the book was hardly a political work at all, but was the greatest work on education ever written.[18] Obviously this was no accident but a logical result of the point of view form which the work was written. If virtue is knowledge, it can be taught, and the educational system to teach it is the one indispensable part of a good state. From Plato's point of view, with a good system of education almost any improvement is possible; if education is neglected, it matters little what else the state does.

This degree of importance being conceded, it follows as matter of course that the state cannot leave education to private demand and a commercialized source of supply but must itself provide the needed means, must see that citizens actually get the training they require, and must be sure that the education supplied is consonant with the harmony and well-being of the state. Plato's plan is therefore for a state-controlled system of compulsory education. His educational scheme falls naturally into two parts, the elementary education, which includes the training of young persons up to about the age of twenty and culminates in the beginning of military service,[19] and the higher education, intended for those selected persons of both sexes who are to be members of the two ruling classes and extending from the age of twenty to thirty-five. It is necessary to consider these two branches of education separately, as Plato himself does.

The plan for a compulsory, state-directed scheme of education was probably the most important innovation upon Athenian practice which Plato had to suggest, and his insistence upon it in the Republic maybe interpreted as a running criticism upon the democratic custom of leaving every man to purchase for his children such education as he fancies or as the market affords. In the Protagoras he broadly implied that often they give less thought to training their children than to breaking a good colt. The Athenian exclusion of women from education falls under the same criticism. Since Plato believed that there was no difference in kind between the native capacities of boys and girls, he logically concluded that both should receive the same kind of instruction and that women should be eligible to the same offices as men. This, of course, is in no sense an argument for women's rights but merely a plan for making the whole supply of natural capacity available to the state. In view of the importance which education has in the state, it is extraordinary that Plato never discusses the training of the artisans and does not even make clear how, if at all, they are to be included in the plan of elementary instruction.

This fact illustrates again the surprising looseness and generality of his conclusions, since his unquestionable intention to promote promising children born of artisan parents seems to be wholly unworkable unless a competitive educational system made selection possible. On the other hand, he did not exclude the artisans and it is an open question whether those commentators, especially, Zeller, are right who regard the omission as evidence of Plato's aristocratic contempt for the workers. It is at least true that he set no great store by general education, much as he relied on selective education for the more gifted youth.

The plan of elementary education sketched in the Republic was rather a reform of existing practice than the invention of a wholly new system. The reform may be said roughly to consist in combining the training usually given to the son of an Athenian gentleman with the state-controlled training given to a youthful Spartan and in revising pretty drastically the content of both. The curriculum was therefore divided into two parts, gymnastics for training the body the and "music" for training the mind. By music Plato meant especially the study and interpretation of the masterpieces of poetry, as well as singing and playing the lyre. It is easy to exaggerate the influence of Sparta upon Plato's theory of education. Its most genuinely Spartan feature was the dedication of education exclusively to civic training. Its content was typically Athenian, and its purpose was dominated by the end of moral and intellectual cultivation. This is true even of gymnastics, which aims only secondarily at giving physical prowess. Gymnastics might be called a training of the mind through the body, as distinguished from direct training of the mind by music. It is meant to teach such soldierly qualities as self-control and courage, a physical keenness tempered by gentleness, as Plato himself defines it. Plato's plan of training represents therefore an Athenian, not a Spartan, conception of what constitutes an educated man. Any other conclusion would have been unthinkable for a philosopher who believed that the only salvation for states lay in the exercise of trained intelligence.

But while the content of elementary education was mainly poetry and the higher forms of literature, it cannot be said that Plato desired particularly an esthetic appreciation of these works. He regarded them rather as a means of moral and religious education, somewhat in the way that Christians have regarded the Bible.[20] For this reason he proposed not only to expurgate drastically the poets of the past, but to submit the poets of the future to censorship by the rulers of the state, in order that nothing of bad moral influence might fall into the hands of the young. For a man who was a consummate artist himself Plato had a singularly philistine conception of art. Or perhaps it would be truer to say that when he wrote about the moral purpose of art a certain puritanical, almost an ascetic, strain is apparent which seems in general out of character for a fourth-century Greek, though it is a strain which appears elsewhere in Plato. In rejecting the poetic form for the dialogue from Plato is perhaps suggesting that poetry stresses the emotional side of human behaviour while the more prose-like dialogue highlights the rational, Philosophically this is connected with the very sharp contrast of mind and body, most evident in the Phaedo, which passed from Plato to Christianity. The poverty which Plato exacts of his rulers perhaps shows the same tendency, as do also the preference which he expressed for a very primitive (non-luxurious) sort of state at the beginning of his construction of the ideal state, and the suggestion accompanying the Myth of the Den that the philosopher may have to be forced to descend from a life of contemplation to take part in the affairs of man. Obviously the rule of philosophers might easily become the rule of saints. Probably the closest analogue that has ever existed to Plato's ideal is state is a monastic order.

Undoubtedly the most original as well as the most characteristic proposal in the Republic is the system of higher education, by which selected students are to be prepared, between the ages of twenty and thirty-five, for the highest positions in the guardian class. The relation of such a conception of higher education to the founding of the Academy and to the whole plan for a science and art of statesmanship has been sufficiently stressed. Unless it be the Academy, there was nothing in Greek education upon which Plato could have built; the idea was entirely and characteristically his own. The higher education of the guardians was in purpose professional and for his curriculum Plato chose the only scientific studies known to him—mathematics, astronomy and logic. Beyond doubt he believed that these most exact studies are the only adequate introduction to the study of philosophy, and there is little reason to doubt that he expected the philosopher's special object of study—the idea of the good—to yield results of comparable precision and exactness. For this reason the outline of the ideal state properly culminates in the plan for an education in which such studies would be fostered, in which new investigations would be undertaken and new knowledge placed at the disposal of rulers. In order to appreciate the greatness of such a conception it is not necessary to believe that Plato was right in hoping for a science of politics as exact as mathematics. It is hardly fair to demand more of him than that he should have tried to follow the lead which, in his own hands and those of his students, was creating in mathematics perhaps the truest monument to human intelligence.

The Omission of Law

Few books that claim to be treatises on politics are so closely reasoned or so well co-ordinated as the Republic. None perhaps contains a line of thought so bold, so original, or so provocative. It is this quality which has made it a book for all time, from which later ages have drawn the most varied inspiration. For the same reason its greatest importance is general and diffused, rather than the result of specific imitation. The Republic was, in the eyes of some, the greatest of utopias and the whole tribe of utopian philosophers followed it, but this phase of the book interested Plato so little that he was almost careless in carrying through the details of the plan. The true romance of the Republic is the romance of free intelligence, unbound by custom, untrammeled by human stupidity and self-will able to direct the forces even of custom and stupidity themselves along the road to a rational life. The Republic is eternally the voice of the scholar, the profession of faith of the intellectual, who sees in knowledge and enlightenment the force upon which social progress must rely. And indeed, who can say what are the limits of knowledge as a political force, and what society has yet brought to bear upon its problems the full power of trained scientific intelligence?

Yet it is impossible to avoid the conclusion that in the Republic Plato, like most intellectuals, simplified his problem beyond what the province of human relations will bear. And enlightened despotism—and Plato is right when he concludes that government by intelligence must be government by the few—cannot be merely assumed to be the last word in politics. The presumption that government is purely a matter of scientific knowledge, which the mass of men can resign into the hands of a few highly trained experts, leaves out of account the profound conviction that there are some decisions which a man must make for himself. This is no argument certainly for "muddling through" in cases where muddling means only the bungling choice of means for recognized ends. But Plato's argument assumes that the choice of ends is exactly comparable with the choice of means for an end already agreed upon, and this appears to be simply not true. His comparison of government to medicine, carried through to its farthest extreme, reduces politics to something that is not politics. For an adult, responsible human being, even though he be something less than a philosopher, is certainly not a sick man who requires nothing but expert care. Among other things he requires the privilege of taking care of himself and of acting responsibly with other like responsible human beings. A principle which reduces political subordination to one type, the relation of those who know to those who do not know, is simpler than the facts.

Not the least significant aspect of the Republic is what it omits, namely, law and the influence of public opinion. The omission is perfectly logical, for Plato's argument is unanswerable if his premise is granted. If rulers are qualified merely by their superior knowledge, either the judgement of public opinion upon their acts is irrelevant or else the pretense of consulting it is mere piece of political jesuitry by which the "discontent of the masses" is held in check. Similarly, it is as foolish to bind the hands of the philosopher-king with rules of law as to force an expert physician to copy his prescription from the recipes in a medical textbook. But in reality the argument begs the question. For it assumes that public opinion is nothing but a muddled representation of what the ruler already knows more clearly, and that law has no meaning other than to give the least bungling rule that will fit an average case. And this not a description but a caricature. As Aristotle said, the knowledge of a thing in use and by direct experience is different in kind from a scientist's knowledge about it, and presumably it is just this immediate experience of the pressures and burdens of government, of their bearing upon human interests and ends, that public opinion expresses. Presumably also the law contains not merely an average rule but also an accumulation of the results of applying intelligence to concrete cases and also an ideal of equitable treatment of like cases.

At all events the ideal state of Republic was imply a denial of the political faith of the city-state, with its deal of free citizenship and its hope that every man, within the limits of his powers, might be made a sharer in the duties and privileges of government. For this ideal was founded on the conviction that there is an ineradicable moral distinction between subjection to the law and subjection to the will of another human being, even though, that other be a wise and benevolent despot. The difference is that the first is compatible with a sense of freedom and dignity while the second is not. The sense of his own freedom under the law was precisely the element in the city-state upon which the Greek set the highest moral valuation and which made the difference, to his mind, between a Greek and a barbarian. And this conviction, it must be acknowledged, has passed from the Greeks into the moral ideals of most European governments. It was expressed in the principle that "governments derive their just powers from the consent of the governed," and vague as the meaning of consent is, it is hard to imagine that the ideal itself will disappear. For this reason Plato's omission of law from his ideal state cannot be interpreted otherwise than as a failure to perceive a striking moral aspect of the very society which he desired to perfect.

At the same time it is clear that Plato could not have included that law as an essential element of the state without reconstructing the whole philosophical framework of which the ideal state is a part. Its omission was not a matter of caprice but a logical consequences of the philosophy itself. For if scientific knowledge has always the superiority to popular opinion which Plato supposes, there is no ground for that respect for law which would make it the sovereign power in the state. Law belongs to the class of convention; it rises through use and wont; it is the product of experience growing slowly from precedent to precedent. A wisdom which arises by rational insight into nature cannot abdicate its claims before the claim of law unless law itself has access to a kind of wisdom different from that which scientific reason possesses. If, then, Plato is wrong in trying to make the state over into an educational institution, if this puts a load upon education which it is not able to bear, the philosophical principles—especially the sharp contrast of nature and convention and of reason and experience—need to be re-examined. It is the suspicion that this might be the case, at least the sense that the theory in the Republic had not got to the bottom of all the problems involved, that led Plato in his later years to canvass the place of law in the state and to formulate in the Laws another type of state in which law rather than knowledge should be the ruling force.

NOTES

1. The account of Plato's adventure in Sicily presumes the historical reliability, if not the actual authenticity, of Letters III, VII, and VIII. For this there is now ample authority.
2. Letter VII, 325d-326b; L.A. Post's trans. Plato was writing in 353 B.C The last sentence echoes the famous passage in the Republic (473d) about philosophers becoming kings.
3. 332e-333a.
4. Letter VII, 328c.
5. History of Political *Theories, Ancient and Mediaeval* (1905), p. 24.
6. Sir Thomas Heath, *Aristarchus of Samos* (1913), chs. xv, xvi.
7. Cf. The contrast of real astronomy and "star-gazing" (*Republic,* 529b-530c) and of science with computation throughout Plato's account of the higher education in mathematics (522c-527c).
8. *Data of Ethics,* ch. xv.
9. 358e ff.
10. *Republic,* 370c.
11. 368d.
12. Plato and the Older Academy. Trans. by S. F. Alleyne and Alfred Goodwin, 1888, p. 473.
13. *Politics,* 3, 11; 1282a 17 ff.
14. E. Barker, *Greek Political Theory, Plato and his Predecessors* (1925), pp. 176 f.
15. *Platon, seine Leben, seine Schriften, siene Lehre* (1923), Vol. II, p. 596.
16. *The suppliants,* II. 238-245.
17. *Republic,* 551d.
18. See also Eric A. Havelock, *Preface to Plato* (Cambridge: Harvard University Press, 1963).

19. The compulsory military service of Athenian boys between the ages of eighteen and twenty was probably not yet in force when Plato wrote, though it was adopted not many years after, as Wilamowitz suppose, because of the *Laws* (*Aristoteles and Athen*, 1893, Vol. I, pp. 191 ff.).

20. Poetry is the means a preliterate culture employs to retain and pass on useful information both of a moral and technical sort. Rhythm and rhyme are memory aids as is the story form. The Odyssey and the Illiad are, thus, not simply "works of art" in the modern sense, but early Greek encyclopedias containing what preliterate Greek elders passed on to their young—including information on everything form morality to ship building. Interestingly enough, in the twentieth century some illiterates in the Balkan mountains have been encountered who can recite the entire *illiad* and *Odyssey* from memory. See Havelock, op. cit. And Albert B. Lord, A. *Singer of Tales* (Cambridge: Harvard University Press, 1960).

3

Aristotle: Political Ideals

About the time when Plato was asked by Dion to undertake the venture in Syracuse for the education of the young Dionysius and the improvement of Syracusan government, the greatest of Plato's students joined the Academy. Aristotle was not an Athenian but a native of Stagira in Thrace, where he was born in 384. His father was a physician, which probably contributed to the prevailing interest in biological studies that Aristotle's work shows, and had been attached in that capacity to the Macedonian court. Aristotle was probably attracted to Plato's school in the first place because it was the best place in Greece to carry on advanced studies. Once there, he remained a member of the school as long as Plato lived – a period of twenty years –and his mind received indelibly the impression of Plato's teaching. Every page of his later philosophical writing bears witness to this connection. After Plato's death in 347 Aristotle left Athens and during the next twelve years was variously employed. To this period belongs the first of his independent writing. In 343 he became the instructor of the young prince Alexander of Macedon, but one looks in vain in his political writing for any effect of his Macedonian connection upon his ideas. He seems to have lacked the imagination necessary to see the revolutionary importance of Alexander's conquest of the East, with the consequent mingling of Greek and oriental civilization. The choice of such a policy was directly contrary to everything that he must have taught his royal pupil about politics. In 335 Aristotle opened his own School in Athens, the second of the four great philosophical Schools, and during the next twelve years most of his books were written, though they probably included work begun during the earlier period. Aristotle survived his great pupil by a year; he died in Euboea in 322, after leaving Athens to escape the anti- Macedonian disturbance that followed Alexander's death.

The New Scic ce of Politics

The Aristotelian writings present a problem very different from that of Plato's Dialogues. His extant works, neglecting fragments of early popular writings, were for the most part not books completed and prepared for publication. They were used in connection with his teaching, though important parts of them were probably written before the Lyceum was opened. In fact, they were not published in their present form until four centuries after his death but remained the property of the School and were doubtless used by later instructors. It seems probable that the twelve years of Aristotle's life as head of the Lyceum were largely occupied in directing a number of extensive projects of research, shared by the students, such as the famous investigation of the constitutional history of a hundred and fifty-eight Greek cities, of which the *Constitution of Athens* (discovered in 1891) is the only surviving example. These researches, of which the study of the constitutions was only one, were mainly historical rather than philosophical; they were genuinely empirical investigations and in the light of them Aristotle from time to time made additions to the body of writings which he already had by him when the School was opened.

The great political treatise which goes by the name of the *Politics* cannot therefore be regarded as a finished book such as Aristotle would have produced had he been writing for a general public. It has been doubted, in fact, whether Aristotle himself arranged it in its existing form or whether it may not have been put together by his editors from several bodies of manuscript.[1] The difficulties lie upon the surface and could hardly be missed by any attentive reader, but the solution of them is another matter. Later editors have shifted the books about in an attempt to improve the order, but no rearrangement of the text will make a unified and finished work of the *Politics*.[2] Thus Book VII, in which Aristotle takes up the construction of an ideal state, apparently goes on from the end of Book III, while Books IV, V, VI, dealing with actual and not ideal states, form a group by themselves. For this reasons Books VII and VIII are usually put after Book III, and Books IV to VI at the end; yet there is a connection between the discussion monarchy near the end of Book III and the discussion of oligarchy and democracy in Book IV. So far as the reading of the text goes, there are difficulties in any order, and probably Ross is right when he says that the reader might as well take it as it stands traditionally.

The best hypothesis which has so far been advanced to explain the Politics is that by Werner Jaeger[3] and while this is not demonstrated, it at least offers a reasonable way of envisaging the development of Aristotle's political Philosophy. According to Jaeger the Politics as it stands is Aristotle's work and not that of an editor. But the next belongs to two stages and therefore falls into two main strata. There is, in the first place, a work dealing with the ideal state, and with previous theories of it. This includes Book II, an historical study of earlier theories and chiefly notable for the criticism of Plato; Book III, a study of the nature of the state and of citizenship but intended to be introductory to a theory of the ideal state; and Books VII and VIII on the construction of the ideal state. These four books Jaeger assigns to a date not long after Aristotle's departure from Athens following the death of Plato. There is, in the second place, a study of actual states, mainly democracy and oligarchy, together with the causes of their decay and the best means of giving them stability, which makes up Books IV, V, and VI. This Jaeger assigns to a date after the opening of the Lyceum,[4] supposing that it represents a return to political philosophy after or during the investigation of the hundred and fifty-eight constitutions. Books IV, V, and VI were interested by Aristotle in the middle of the original draft, and result in enlarging the work on the ideal state into a general treatise on political science. Finally, Jaeger believes, Book I was written last of all as a general introduction to the enlarged treatise, though it was joined hastily and imperfectly to Book II. According to Jaeger's conception, therefore, the *Politics* was intended to form a treatise on a single science, but was never subjected to the rewriting that would have been necessary to bring the parts, written as they were over a period of perhaps fifteen years, into a well-unified form.

If this hypothesis be correct, the Politics represents two stages in Aristotle's thought which are distinguished by the distance that he has travelled in emancipating himself from the influence of Plato, or perhaps it would be better to say, in striking out a line of thought and investigation characteristically his own. In the first he still thinks of political philosophy as the construction of an ideal state upon lines already laid down especially in the *Statesman* and the *Laws*. Plato's prevailingly ethical interest in the subject still predominates; the good man and the good citizen are one and the same, or at all events they ought to be, and the end of the state is to produce the highest moral type of human being. It is not to be supposed that Aristotle consciously abandoned this point of view, since the treatise on the ideal state was left standing as an important part of *Politics*. At some data not far removed from the opening of the Lyceum, however, he conceived a science or art of politics on a much large scale. The new science was to be general; that is, it should deal with actual as well as ideal forms of government and it should teach the art of governing and organizing states of any sort in any desired manner. This new general science of politics, therefore, was not only empirical and descriptive, but even in some respects independent of any ethical purpose, since a statesman might need to be expert in governing even a bad state. The whole science of politics, according to the new idea, included the knowledge both of the political good, relative as well as absolute, and also of political mechanics employed perhaps for an inferior or even a bad end. This enlargement of the definition of political philosophy is Aristotle's most characteristic conception.

The description of Aristotle's political theory can therefore be advantageously divided into two parts. The source for the first is Books II, III, VII, and VIII. The questions to be considered here are the relations of his thought to Plato's in the first attempt at an independent philosophy and especially the suggestions, in so far as they can be discerned, the presage the final step which took him quite beyond Plato. The source for the second is Books IV, V, and VI, and the questions here are his final thoughts on the kinds of government, his conception of the social forces behind political organization and change, and his description of the means with which the statesman has to work. Finally, in the opening chapters of Book I he said his last word about the great philosophical problem upon which both he and Plato had been engaged, the distinction of nature from appearance or convention, and suggested and conception of nature to which his ripest political reflection led him.

The Kinds of Rule

True to a custom which he follows in works on other subjects, Aristotle begins his book on the ideal state with a survey of what other writers have written on the subject. The point of greatest interest here is his criticism of Plato, since one would expect to find the key to the differences of which he was conscious between himself and his master. The result is rather disappointing. So far as the *Republic* is concerned he is emphatic in his objections to the abolition of private property and the family. These objections to have already been referred to and nothing further need be said about them. His criticism of the *Laws*, on the other moreover it is sometimes astonishingly inaccurate. This is surprising in view of the fact that, in his construction of the ideal state, almost every subject discussed is suggested by the *Laws*, and there are many parallelism (even verbal) in small points.[5] Evidently when the passage was written he did not regard it as worth while to analyze the *Laws* and state his dissent from its principles. The tone of his criticism suggests what may be the reason. Apparently he felt about both Plato's political works, and perhaps about his philosophy in general, that they are brilliant and suggestive but too radical and speculative. They are, as he says, never commonplace and always original. But the query in his mind seems to be, Are they reliable? The general ground of his dissent is stated in a dryly humorous remark which sums up better than pages of comment the fundamental difference of temper between Aristotle and his master:

> *Let us remember that we should not disregard the experience of ages; in the multitude of years these things, if they were good, would certainly not have been unknown; for almost everything has been found out, although sometimes they are not put together; in other cases men do not use the knowledge which they have.*[6]

In short, Aristotle's is the soberer if less original genius. He feels that too great a departure from common experience probably has a fallacy in it somewhere, eve though it appears to be irreproachable logical.

One essential difference between Plato and Aristotle is apparent in all parts of the *Politics* that have to do with the ideal state: what Aristotle calls the ideal state is always Plato's second-best state. The rejection of communism just referred to shows that the ideal state of the *Republic* was never entertained by Aristotle, even as an ideal. His ideal was always constitutional and never despotic rule, even though it were the enlightened despotism of the philosopher-king. Consequently, Aristotle accepted from the start the point of view of the *laws*, that in any good state the law must be the ultimate sovereign and not any person whatsoever. He accepted this not as a concession to human frailty but as an intrinsic part of good government and therefore as a characteristics of an ideal state. The relation of the constitutional ruler to his subjects is different in kind from any other sort of subjection because it is consistent with both parties remaining free men, and for this reason it requires a degree of moral equality or likeness of kind between them, despite the undoubted differences which must exist.

This distinction between different kinds of rule is so important for Aristotle that he returns to it again and again, and it had evidently been an object of early interest with him.[7] The authority of a constitutional ruler over his subjects is quite different from that of a master over his salves, because the salve is presumed to be different in nature, a lower sort of being who is inferior from birth an incapable of ruling himself. Aristotle admits, to be sure, that this is often not true in fact, but at all events it is the theory upon which slavery is justified. For this reason the slave is the master's living too, to be kindly used, but still used for the master's good. Political authority differs also from that which a man exercises over his wife and children, though the latter is certainly for the good of the dependent as well as for that of the father. The failure to distinguish household from political authority Aristotle regarded as one of Plato's serious errors, since it led him in the *Statesman* to assert that the state is like the family only larger. The child is not an adult and even though he is ruled for his own good, he is still not in a position of equality. The case of the wife is not so clear but apparently Aristotle believed that women were too different in nature from men (though not necessarily inferior) to stand with them on the peculiar footing of equality which alone permits the political relationship. The ideal state, therefore, if not a democracy, at least includes a democratic element. It is "a community of equals, aiming at the best life possible"[8] and it ceases to be constitutional or genuinely political if the discrepancy between its members is so great that they cease to have the same "virtue."

The Rule of Law

Constitutional rule in the state is closely connected, also, with the question whether it is better to be ruled by the best man or the best laws, since a government which consults the good of its subjects is also government in accordance with law. Accordingly the supremacy of law is accepted by Aristotle as a mark of a good state and not merely as an unfortunate necessity. His argument of his position is that Plato is mistaken when, in the *Statesman*, he makes government by law and government by wise rulers alternatives. Even the wisest ruler cannot dispense with law because the law has an impersonal quality which no man, however good, can attain. The law is "reason unaffected by desire".[9] and the analogy which Plato was accustomed to draw between politics and medicine is wrong. The political relationship, if it is to permit of freedom, must be of such a kind that the subject does not wholly resign his judgement and his responsibility, and this is possible provided both the ruler and the ruled have a legal status. The "passionless" authority of law does not take the place of a magistrate, but it gives to the magistrate's authority a moral quality which it could not otherwise have. Constitutional rule is consistent with the dignity of the subject, whereas a personal or despotic rule is not. The constitutional ruler, as Aristotle sometimes says, rules over willing subjects; he rules by consent and is quite different from a dictator. The precise moral property which Aristotle means to point out is as elusive as the consent of the governed in modern theories, but no one can doubt its reality.

Constitutional rule as Aristotle understands the expression has three main elements: First, it is rule in the public or general interest as distinguished from a functional or tyrannous rule in the interest of a single class or individual. Second, it is lawful rule in the sense that the government is carried on by general regulations and not by arbitrary decrees, and also in the vaguer sense that the government does not flout standing customs and conventions of the constitution. Third, constitutional government means the government of willing subjects as distinguished from a despotism that is supported merely by force. Though these three properties of constitutional rule are clearly mentioned by Aristotle, he nowhere examines them systematically to find out either if the list is complete or what is the relationship between the three. He was aware that one of the properties might be absent from a government while the others were present; for example, a tyrant may act despotically and yet in the public interest, or a lawful government may be unjustly favourable to one class. But constitutional rule was never really defined by Aristotle.

The emphasis upon constitutional rule is the consequence of taking seriously the suggestion in the *Laws* that law may be regarded not as a makeshifts but as an indispensable condition of a moral and civilized life. An introductory passage in the *Politics* was evidently written with one of Plato's remarkable utterances in mind. "Man, when perfected, is the best of animals, but, when separated from law and justice, he is the worst of all."[10] But this view of law is impossible unless it be supposed that there is a gradual increase of wisdom through the accumulation of experience and that this growing stock of social intelligence is embedded in law and custom. The point is of fundamental philosophical importance because if wisdom and knowledge are the prerogatives of scholars, the experience of the ordinary man never brings him more than unreliable opinion, and Plato's reasoning unanswerable. To put the case the other way about, if Plato's philosophy is mistaken in neglecting the experience of the ages, than that experience must represent a genuine growth in knowledge, though this growth registers itself in custom rather than in science and is produced by common sense rather than by learning. Public opinion must be admitted to be not only an unavoidable force but also, up to a point, a justifiable standard in politics.

It is possible to argue, Aristotle says that in the making of law the collective wisdom of a people is superior to that of even the wisest law-giver. He develops the argument still farther in connection with his discussion of the political ability of popular assemblies. Men in the mass supplement each other in a singular fashion, so that by one understanding one part of a question and another part, they all together get around the whole subject. He illustrates this by the assertion (perhaps not quite obvious) that popular taste in the arts is reliable in the long run, while experts make notorious blunders at the moment. To somewhat the same effect is his marked preference for customary as compared with written law. He is even prepared to admit that possibly Plato's plan for abolishing law would be an advantage if only the written law were at stake. But he holds it clearly impossible that the knowledge of the wisest ruler can be better than the customary law. The rigid distinction between nature and convention, with the extreme intellectualism or rationalism to which this distinction had committed Socrates and Plato, was thus broken down by Aristotle. The reason of the statesman in a good state cannot be detached from the reason embodied in the law and custom of the community he rules.

At the same time, Aristotle's political ideal was quite at one with Plato's in setting up an ethical purpose as the chief end of the state. He never changed his opinion on this point, even after he had enlarged his definition of political philosophy to include a practical manual for statesmen who have to do with governments which are very far from ideal. The real purpose of a state ought to include the moral improvement of its citizens, because it ought to be an association of men living together to achieve the best possible life. This is the "idea" or meaning of a state; Aristotle's ultimate effort at a definition turns upon his conviction that the state alone is "self-sufficing," in the sense that it alone provides all the conditions within which the highest type of moral development can take place. Like Plato, also, Aristotle confined his ideal to the city –state, the small and intimate group in which the life of the state in the social life of its citizens, overlapping the interests of family, of religion, and of friendly personal intercourse. Even in his examination of actual states there is nothing to show that his connection with Philip and Alexander enabled him to perceive the political significance of the Macedonian conquest of the Greek world and of the East. The political failure of the city-state did not, in his eyes, take from it the character of an ideal.

Aristotle's theory of political ideals, therefore, stands upon ground which he had clearly occupied because of his association with Plato. It follows from an effort to adopt and take seriously the chief elements of the theory developed in the *Statesman* and the *Laws*, with such changes as were required to make that theory clear and self-consistent. This applies particularly to the distinctive feature of Plato's later theory, that law must be treated as an indispensable constituent of the state. This being true, it is necessary to take account of the conditions of human nature which make it true. Law must be admitted to include real wisdom, and the accumulation of such wisdom in social custom must be allowed for. And the moral requirements which make law necessary must be incorporated as part of the moral ideals of the state. True political rule must therefore include the factors of subordination to law and of freedom and consent on the part of its subjects. These become factors not of a second-best state but of the ideal state itself.

About Aristotle's ideal state itself not much need be said. In truth his avowed purpose to construct an ideal state never eventuated, and the reader feels that the task was really little to his taste. What he does is to write a book not on an ideal state but upon the ideals of the state.

The sketch of an ideal state, begun in Books VII and VIII, was apparently never finished , which is significant, specially if it be correct to suppose that these books belong to the earlier draft of the *Politics*. The good life requires conditions both physical and mental, and it is upon these that Aristotle expends his attention. The list of conditions is derived from the *Laws*. It includes specifications regarding the population needed, both its amount and character, the territory most suitable in size, nature and situation. It is not the case that Aristotle always agrees with Plato. He is distinctly more favourable to a situation on or near the sea, for example, but the differences are matters of details, and the list of relevant conditions is substantially that which Plato had proposed. Aside from physical conditions of the good life, the most important force in molding citizens, is for Aristotle as for Plato, a compulsory system of education. In his general theory of education Aristotle differs from Plato, as might be expected, in allowing greater weight to the formation of good habits. Thus he places habit between nature and reason among the three things which make men virtuous. Such a change was necessary in view of the importance which custom must have in a state subject to law. Aristotle's discussion is wholly devoted to liberal education and shows, far more than Plato's, an actual contempt for the useful.

A plan of higher education such as had formed so notable a part of the *Republic* is conspicuous by its absence – an omission which may of course be due to the fact that the book is unfinished. The government of the ideal state also suggests the *Laws*. Property is to be privately owned but used in common. The soil is to be tilled by slaves, and artisans are to be excluded from citizenship on the ground that virtue is impossible for men whose time is consumed in manual labour.

Conflict of the Ideal and the Actual

So far Aristotle's political ideals have been outlined without raising any questions about the discrepancies and difficulties that would be encountered if these ideals were brought into relation with the actual institutions and practices of cities. The ideal is in itself almost as deductive as Plato's and apparently it had been formed by a kind of dialectical analysis of the defects of the earlier theory. But it is obvious that discrepancies with practice and with ends actually pursued in government are much more serious for Aristotle than for Plato. The latter had never supposed that an ideal need be embodied in practice to be valid, and he had never allowed to custom any such claim to wisdom as Aristotle's theory required. If fact fail to square with deal truth, Plato could always say, like the mathematician or the mystic, so much the worse for facts. Aristotle, with a heavy obligation to common sense and the wisdom of the ages, is in no position to be so radical. He might be reformist but never revolutionary. The whole bent and bias of his thought must be toward the view that the ideal, while conceded to be an effective force, must still be a force within the actual current of affairs and not dead against it. The wisdom inherent in custom must, so to speak, be a guiding principle that takes advantage of such plasticity as actual conditions include to lift them gradually to a better confirmation. This is the view of nature which Aristotle finally evolved as a result of his reflection upon both social and biological problems.

That Aristotle was by no means at peace with this problem, even when he wrote the treatise on the ideal state, is written large in the complexities of Book III, in which the crucial questions of the whole work are discussed. The conclusion of the book shows that it was designed as an introduction to an ideal state. Book VII and VIII, however, show that Aristotle found the carrying out of this project so unsatisfactory that he never completed it, and when the first draft was enlarged, it was not by proceeding with the sketch of the ideal state but by the insertion of Books IV to VI. These are conspicuously realistic in their purpose and tone but carry forward lines of thought that are started in Book III. It is safe to conclude that the construction of an ideal state became less and less congenial to Aristotle's mode of thought as he grew older, and also that he finally found in Book III an introduction to a line of investigation which he had not originally intended to pursue. This conclusion is borne out by the reading of Book III itself. Its complexities are due, in part at least, to the fact that an introduction to the ideal state involves, to Aristotle's mind, a rather extended study of existing kinds of states. Often he is evidently more interested in the empirical study than in the purpose that he had set himself. In short, the reasons which led Aristotle to insert Books IV to VI after Book III were sound, though presumably they were not the reasons which led him to write Book III in the first place. The plan outgrew its original scope, but it grew from interests that were present at the start.

The general nature of the difficulty which Aristotle confronts is not difficult to see. The political ideal which came to him from Plato presumed that city and citizen are strictly correlative terms. This accounts for three questions which he places at the opening of Book III: What is a state? Who is a citizen? Is the virtue of a good man the same as the virtue of a good citizen? A state is an association of men for the sake of the best moral life. The type of life which a group of men will live in common depends upon what kind of men they are and what ends they design to realize, and reciprocally the end of the state will determine who can be members of it and what kind of life they can individually live. From this point of view a constitution is, as Aristotle says, an arrangement of citizens, or as he says elsewhere, a kind of life, and a form of government is the expression of the kind of life which the state is designed to foster. The ethical nature of the state not only dominates but, so to speak, completely overlaps its political and legal nature. Thus Aristotle concludes that a state lasts only so long as its form of government endures, since a change on form of government would signify a change in the constitution or the underlying "kind of life" that the citizens are trying to realize. Law, constitution, state, form of government all tend to coalesce, since from a moral point of view they are all equally relative to the purpose which causes the association to exist.

In so far as the object is to formulate an ideal state, this is not an insuperable objection. For such a state would be dominated by the highest possible kind of life, and Plato, at least, had supposed that an understanding of the ideas of the good would show what this is. But to arrive at the idea of the good first and then to use this as a standard for criticising and evaluating actual lives and actual states, was just what made Aristotle despair. If, on the other hand, one begins with the observation and description of actual states, distinctions evidently have to be made. The good man and the good citizen cannot be quite identical, as Aristotle points out, except in an ideal state. For unless the purposes of the state are the best possible, their realization will required a kind of life in the citizens which fall below the best possible. In actual states there must be different kinds of citizens with different kinds of "virtue". Similarly, when Aristotle defines the citizen as one who is eligible to take part in the assembly and to serve on juries- a definition based upon Athenian practice – he is obliged to point out at once that the definition will not fit any but a democratic state. Or again, when he concludes that the identity of the state changes with its form of government, he has to add a warning that the new state is not therefore justified in defaulting the debts and other obligations contracted by the previous state. Distinctions must in practice be made. A constitution is not only a way of life for the citizens but also an organization of officers to carry on public business, and therefore its political aspects cannot be forthwith identified with its ethical purpose. Merely to observe these complexities is to feel a difficulty about the construction of an ideal state to serve as a standard for them all.

A similar sense of the complexities of his problem is apparent when Aristotle passes on the discuss the classification of forms of government. Here he adopts the sixfold classification already used by Plato in the Statesman. Having distinguished constitutional from despotic rule by the principle that the former is for the good of all and the latter for the good of the ruling class only, he crosses this division upon the traditional threefold classification and thus gets a group of three true (or constitutional) states-monarchy, aristocracy, and moderate democracy (polity) - and three perverted (or despotic) states-tyranny, oligarchy and extreme democracy or mob-rule. The only difference between Plato's treatment and Aristotle's - and it appears to be unimportant - is that the former describes his true states as law-abiding while the latter describes them as governed for the general good. In view of his analysis of what constitutional government means, Aristotle must have thought that the two descriptions came to nearly the same thing. No sooner does he complete the sixfold classification, however, than he points out that there are serious difficulties about it. The first of these is that the popular classification by the number of rulers is superficial and does not say, except by accident, what those who use it mean. What everybody means by an oligarchy is a government by the rich, just as a democracy is a government by the poor. It is true that there are many poor and few rich, but this does not make the relative numbers descriptive of the two kinds of state. The essence of the matter is that there are two distinct claims to power, one based upon the rights of property and the other upon the welfare of the greater number of human beings.

Conflicting Claims to Power

This correction of the formal classification carries Aristotle a long way, for it raises the question, what are the justifiable claims to power in the state? And if there are more than one, how can they be adjusted to each other in such a way as to save them all? Similar questions, as has been said, had already presented themselves to Plato.[11] These questions, be it noted, do not really concern an ideal state—and Plato had not supposed that they did—but the relative merits of actual states and relative claims of various classes in the same state. Wisdom and virtue might be said to have an absolute claim to power; at least Plato had thought so and Aristotle did not deny it. But this point is academic. The dispute is not about a general moral principle but about the way to approximate it in practice. Everyone will admit, Aristotle says, that the state ought to realize the largest measure of justice possible and also that justice means some kind of equality. But does equality mean that everybody is to count for one and nobody for more than one, as the democrat supposes? Or does it mean that a man with large property-interests and perhaps a good social position and education ought to count for more than one, as the oligarch believes? Granted that government ought to be carried on by wise and virtuous rulers, where must you lodge power to get wisdom and virtue, or at least the best available approximation to them?

When the question is put in this way Aristotle immediately perceives that a relative question requires a relative answer. He shows easily enough that wealth has no absolute moral claim to power, for the state is not a trading company or a contract, as Lycophron the Sophist had said. It is easy to show also that counting everybody for one is at most a convenient fiction. But on the other hand, can it be said that property has no rights? Aristotle was convinced that Plato's venture in that direction had proved disastrous, and in any case, as he points out, a plundering democracy is no more honest than an exploiting oligarchy. Property has moral consequences and for this reason is too important to be left entirely out of the picture by anyone who is trying to be realistic. Good birth, good education, good associations, leisure – and these go in some degree with wealth – are not negligible as claims to political influence. The democrat also has something to say relatively for his claim. The number of persons affected surely is a moral consideration in estimating political consequences, and moreover a sober public opinion, Aristotle is convinced, often is right where professedly wise persons are wrong. The upshot of the discussion is that there are objections against every claim to power that can be advanced and also that all the usual claims have a certain amount of merit. It is hard to see just how this conclusion can advance the construction of an ideal state, but it is also obvious that Aristotle has treated a perennial dispute in political ethics with incomparable common sense. In fact, this examination of the conflicting claims of democracy and oligarchy led Aristotle later to lay aside the search for an ideal state and to take up the more modest problem of the best form of government attainable by most states.

The conclusion that no class has an absolute claim to power re-enforces the principle that the law must be supreme, since its impersonal authority is less subject to passion than men can claim to be. But Aristotle recognizes that even this, one of his most deeply-held convictions, cannot be asserted quite absolutely. For the law is relative to the constitution and consequently a bad state will be likely to have bad laws. Legality itself then is only a relative guarantee of goodness, better than force or personal power, but quite possibly bad. A good state must be ruled according to law but this is not the same as saying that a state ruled according to law is good.

Apparently Aristotle believed that monarchy and aristocracy alone have any claim to be regarded as ideal states. He has very little to say about aristocracy but he treats monarchy at some length. It is precisely this discussion of a supposedly ideal state that shows clearest how little he has to say on the subject and connects most clearly with the quite realistic rediscussion of democracy and oligarchy placed in book IV. The monarchy ought theoretically to be the best form of government if it be assumed that a wise and virtuous king can be found. Plato's philosopher-king would come nearest to having an absolute claim to his power. But then, he would be a God among men. To allow other man to make law for a moral God would be ridiculous and to ostracize him would not be quite just. The only alternative is to allow him to rule. And yet Aristotle is not perfectly certain that even such a man has an indefeasible right to rule. So much importance does he attach to the equality which ought to exist between citizens of the same state that he questions whether even perfect virtue would be an expectation. The problem of equality concerns every form of government, good as well as perverted. Still, Aristotle is willing to admit that monarchy would be suitable for a society in which one family was far superior to all others in virtue and political skill. The truth is that the ideal monarchy is for Aristotle perfectly academic. Except for the authority of Plato he probably would never have mentioned it. He remarks that monarchy according to law is law is not really a constitution at all, and if this be taken literally, the fact that good government must recognize the supremacy of law really puts the monarchy out of consideration as a true form of government. A monarchy of the ideal type would belong to domestic rather than political rule. Nothing but his acceptance of Plato's sixfold classification brings it into consideration.

When Aristotle turns to an examination of existing monarchies he drops the consideration of an ideal state entirely. Two legal forms of monarchy he knows, the Soartan kingship and the dictatorship, but neither of these is a constitution, and two kinds of monarchical constitution, the Oriental monarchy and the monarchy of the heroic age. The latter, of course, is conjectural and really outside Aristotle's experience. The Oriental monarchy is more truly a form of tyranny, though it is lawful after a barbarian fashion, since Asiaties are slaves by nature and do not object to despotic government. Substantially, therefore, actual monarchy, as Aristotle knows it, is equivalent to such government as that of Persia. However, the significance of this discussion is less in what he says about monarchy than in the fact that he distinguishes the different kinds. Evidently the sixfold classification of states had already lost its meaning for him as compared with an empirical study of the actual working of governments. It was precisely at this point that he took up again the examination of oligarchy and democracy-that is to say, Greek forms of government –in Book IV.

The reasons should now be clear why Aristotle's political ideals did not eventuate in the construction of an ideal state. The ideal state represented a conception of political philosophy which he inherited from Plato and which was in fact little congenial to his genius. The more he struck out an independent line of thought and investigation, the more he turned toward the analysis and description of actual constitutions. The great collection of one hundred and fifty-eight constitutional histories made by him and his students marks the turning point in his thought and suggested a border conception of political theory. This did not mean that Aristotle turned to description alone. The essence of the new conception was the uniting of empirical investigation with the more speculative consideration of political ideals. Moral ideals-the sovereignty of law, the freedom and equality of citizens, constitutional government, the perfecting of men in a civilized life –are always for Aristotle the ends for which the state ought to exist. What he discovered was that these ideals were infinitely complicated in the realization and required infinite adjustment to the conditions of actual government. Ideals must exist not like Plato's pattern in the Heavens but as forces working in and through agencies by no means ideal.

NOTES

1. Thus, for example, Ernest Barker (*Political thought of Plato and Aristotle, 1906*, p.259) believes that notes of three distinct sets of lectures are combined in the *Politics*, while W.D. Ross (Aristotle, 1924, p. 236) calls it a "conflation of five separate treatises."
2. References to the books by number mean the order of the manuscript; so many experiments have been tried that, beyond Books I to III, the numbers are very ambiguous. There is a table giving the order in the principal editions in Immisch's Teubner text, p. vii.
3. *Aristotees* (1923); Eng. Trans. By Richard Robinson, 1934, ch. 10.
4. For a criticism of Jaeger's hypothesis see Ernest Barker's translation of the *Politics* (1948), Introduction II, $4; pp. xii-xivi.
5. A considerable lists of parallels is given by E. Barker, *Greek Political Theory, Plato and his Predecessors* (1925), pp. 380 ff.
6. *Politics*, 2, 5; 1264 a 1 ff. (Jowett's trans).
7. *Cf. Politics* 3, 6; in 1278 b 31 he refers to his early popular dialogues, while only a few lines before, 1278 b 18, he refers to the discussion of household authority in Book I, though the subject is evidently the same.
8. 7,8; 1328 a 36.
9. 3, 16; 1287 a 32.
10. 1,2; 1253 a 31 ff. Cf. *Laws*, 874 e.
11. *Laws*, 690 a ff.

4

The Twilight of the City-State

The political philosophy of Plato and Aristotle was singularly devoid of immediate influence both of a practical and a theoretical kind. In fact, if it were judged by the part that it played in the two centuries following Aristotle's death, it could only be described as a magnificent failure. The reason for this is that the two philosophers between them had stated more completely and perfectly than any successor could hope to do the ideals and the principles of the type of political institution with which they dealt, the city-state. There was in truth no further progress to be made upon that line. This is not to say that what Plato and Aristotle had written had value only as applying to the city-state. The presumption upon which Plato worked –that human relation may be made the object of rational study and may be subjected to intelligent direction-is a *sine qua non* of any social science whatever. And the more general ethical principles of Aristotle's political theory- the conviction that a state ought to be a relation between free citizens morally equal, conducting itself according to law and resting upon discussion and consent rather than force- have never vanished from European political philosophy. These great qualities explain why later, thinkers, even down to the present, have repeatedly gone back to Plato and Aristotle. But though much that they wrote thus had permanent significance, it is a fact that Plato and Aristotle believed it to apply to the city-state and to that alone. They never conceived of these or of any political ideals as capable of being realized in any other form of civil society. There assumption was justified by the facts as they then were, for it is hard to imagine political philosophy taking its rise in any society that then existed except the Greek cities.

Plato and Aristotle were quite aware, of course, that no city in Greece had realized the ideals which they believed to be implicit in the city-state. Had the need for criticism and correction not been clearly present to their minds, they would never have tried to analyze the society in which they lived or to distinguish its perversions from its successes. But while they criticized-and often sharply-they still believed that the conditions of a good life did measurably exist in the city-state. And while they would gladly have changed many of its practices, they never doubted that the city-state was fundamentally sound and the only ethically sound foundation for the higher forms of civilization. Their criticism was, therefore, basically friendly. They spoke for the class of Greeks that found life in the city-state substantially satisfying, though by no means perfect. But it is ominous symptom that both men, certainly without intending to be spokesmen for a class, were driven to make citizenship more and more explicitly a privilege and therefore the prerogative of those who had the property and the leisure to enjoy the luxury of political position. The deeper Plato and Aristotle penetrate into the underlying ethical meaning of the city-state, the more they are forced to the conclusion that this meaning exists only for a few and not for the whole mass of artisans and farmers and wage-earners, as the democracy of the Periclean Age had imagined. This in itself suggests – what was the fact –that other less vocal or less favorably situated might see in the city-state a form of society that needed not to be improved but to be superseded; at least they might regard it as a thing to be neglected by men in search of a good life. Such a criticism, of protestor at least of indifference, did exist, somewhat obscurely, in the age of Plato and Aristotle. But the historical circumstances were such that the immediate future lay with it rather than with the more imposing theories of the greater men, and this explains the temporary eclipse of their political philosophy after Aristotle's death. When the city-state had been relegated to history and it was no longer possible to picture political values as realizable only in it, men could return to exploit the infinite fertility of the *Republic*, the *Laws*, and the *Politics*.

The common form taken by these diverse philosophies of protest or indifference – and their startling significance in the fourth and third centuries-can be grasped only by keeping clearly in mind the ethical presumption which lay behind all that Plato and Aristotle wrote about the state. This is the presumption that a good life implies participation in the life of the state. It was this which enabled Plato to start with the propositions that the state is at bottom a division of labour in which men of differing capacity satisfy their needs by mutual exchange. Plato's conception was made merely more complete in Aristotle's analysis of the community. The presumption caused both men to regard participation as a conception ethically more important than either duties or rights, and to see in citizenship a sharing of the common life. From his point of view citizenship stands at the summit of human goods, or at least this would be so if both the city and human nature were developed to the top of their bent. This presumption represents the very genius of the ethics and politics of the city-state. And for this reason the essence of protest is the denial of it. Assert that a man, in order to live a good life, must live outside the city-state, or being in it should at any rate not be of it, and you have set up a scale of values not only foreign to but essentially opposed to that assumed by Plato and Aristotle. Say that the wise man will have as little to do with politics as he can, that he will never willingly take the responsibilities or the honors of public office, but will shun both as a useless cause of anxiety, and you have said that Plato and Aristotle have set up a wholly erroneous notion of wisdom and goodness. For such a good is private, something which a man gains or loses in himself and by himself, and not something that requires a common life. Self-sufficiency, which Plato and Aristotle regarded as an attribute of the state, becomes an attribute of the individual human being. The good becomes something not strictly conceivable within the confines of the city-state-a good of privacy and withdrawal. It is the growth of this kind of ethical theory that marks the twilight of the city-state.

The attitude of Plato and Aristotle toward this ethics of with-drawl is significant. They know its existence but they cannot quite take it seriously. Thus there is perhaps a gibe at the Cynic scheme of life in the "pig-state" of the *Republic*,[1] where living is reduced to the barest and rudest necessaries. There is almost certainly a sneer behind Aristotle's remark that the man who can live without the state is either a beast or a God. The moralist who sets up the ideal of individual self-sufficiency claims the attributes of a god, but he is likely to live the life of a beast. Only in the introduction to his ideal state does Aristotle propose to argue the relative merits of the statesman's and the philosopher's life, and here he does not really argue. He merely asserts that "happiness is activity" and that "he who does nothing cannot do well."[2] He almost certainly is thinking of the Cynics, and it is not improbable, as Jaeger suggests, that some of Plato's students had enlarged upon the ideal of the contemplative life in the spirit of Plato's own remark that the philosopher might have to be compelled to return to the den. At all events the Academy certainly had moved in this direction a generation later. But for Aristotle the argument has really not got beyond the level of epigram. The whole structure of his political thought assumes that the citizen's activity is the chief good and he never takes any other view seriously.

The Failure of the City-State

Beside the theoretical assumption that only the city-state is morally self-sufficient there is also in the reformist political philosophy of Plato and Aristotle a practical assumption of great importance and one which had the misfortune to be not quite true under existing circumstances. The improvement of the city-state within limits set by that form of government took for granted that its rulers were free agents, able by the choice of wise policies to correct its internal defects. The complete acceptance of it as a moral institution by Plato and Aristotle meant in effect that their political horizon was bounded by it. In consequence neither of them was as keenly aware as he should have been of the part which foreign affairs played even in the internal economy of the city-state. It is true that Aristotle criticized Plato for this omission,[3] but it cannot be said that he did better himself. If Plato had been as closely associated with Macedonia as Aristotle, he would hardly have failed to perceive the epoch-making importance of the career of Alexander. It is interesting to conjecture what might have happened if it had occurred to Aristotle to consider the hypothesis that the city-state needed to be absorbed into some still more self-sufficing political unit, as it had itself absorbed the family and the village. But this was beyond his power of political imagination. In fact, however, the fate of the city-state depended not upon the wisdom with which it managed its internal affairs upon its interrelations with the rest of the Greek world and upon the relations of Greece to Asia on the east and to Carthage and Italy on the west. The supposition that the city-state could choose its mode of life regardless of limits fixed by these foreign relations was fundamentally false. Plato and Aristotle might deplore, like many other intelligent Greeks, the contentiousness and belligerency of the relations between the Greek cities, but as the event proved, these vices were ineradicable so long as the cities remained independent.

As Professor W.S. Ferguson has pointed out,[4] the Greek city-state from a date early in its history was confronted by a political dilemma which it never was able to cope with. It could not attain self-sufficiency, either in its economics or its politics, without adopting a policy of isolation, and it could not isolate itself without suffering stagnation in that very culture and civilization which Aristotle regarded as its crown of glory. On the other hand, if it chose not to isolate itself., it was driven by political necessity to seek alliances with other cities, and these alliances could not be successful without impairing the independence of their members. The dilemma ought to be comprehensible to a modern political observer, for it was substantially similar to that in which a more inclusive economy has placed the nation-state. The modern nation can neither isolate itself nor, as yet at least, curb its independence enough to form a more viable political unit. All the modern fictions about complete national sovereignty united with international regulation find their parallel in the Greek alliances of allegedly independent cities. By the middle of the fourth century these federations were the prevailing form of government in the Greek world, but they quite failed to make permanent and stable states. Even as late as the formation of the Panhellenic League by Philip, at Corinth in 338, the cities, had they been able to work together, might have gone far toward influencing and even controlling the policy of Macedonia, but the inherent particularism of the city-state was unable to rise to the opportunity. It is a matter of speculation whether, had the Greek cities been left to themselves, they could ever have succeeded in producing a really effective kind of federal government. It was of the essence of the situation that they could never hope to be left to themselves.

Greek particularism and its danger to Greek political life were an old story even in Plato's day. Especially the orators, from the beginning of the fourth century, had urged the cities to unite against the barbarians either of the east or of the west. Gorgias of Leontini had made it the subject of an oration at the Olympian Games, as had also Lysias a little later in 388. Isocrates had urged unity and lived to see in Philip of Macedon, as he believed, the man of destiny who might bring it about. Yet the treaty of Antalcidas (387-6) had established the suzerainty of Persia over the Greek world in matters of war and peace, and the Persian power persisted until it passed into the hands of Philip by the formation of the League at Corinth. Two centuries later the control of Greece was taken over by the expanding power of Rome. In foreign affairs, therefore, the city-state had failed permanently and more or less obviously from a date quite early in the fourth century. Even if the confederation had succeeded in stabilizing relations among the cities themselves, they would still have had to deal with the great political forces that surrounded the Greek world on the east, north, and west. And this they were doubly incapable of doing.

The failure of the cities to stabilize their relations with one another was not, however, a failure only in a special branch of administration. Foreign and domestic affairs were never really separable in the city-states, for the class interests which were oligarchic or democratic in internal politics were similar from city to city and continually made common cause. No important aspect of local government could avoid making its peace in some fashion or other with the political and economic ties which ran between cities. And this is as true of the Macedonian intervention as the relations between cities. The interests of property were in general on the side of Macedonia and this is one important reason why the more prosperous classes tended to look with complaisance upon the rise of Philip's power. For obvious reasons democratic interests had more local patriotism. The inextricable intertwining of foreign and domestic policy is admirably illustrated by the treaties between Alexander and the cities of the League of Corinth.

In addition to the control of foreign affairs, Macedonia and the League were given the reasonability of repressing, in the cities of the League, any movement for the abolition of debt, the redivision of land, the confiscation of property, or the liberation of salves. Later leagues included similar provisions.[5] The old issue between wealth and poverty, which Plato and Aristotle regarded as the essential difference between oligarchy and democracy, was in no way dimished as time went on. If anything it grew sharper;

foreign intervention might draw the lines anew but the lines were still here.

The truth is that the social and political problems of the Greek world were not soluble by the city-states. It would be false to imply that they were really solved by the confederations and the monarchies that followed the conquests of Alexander. What became ever clearer was that the politics of the city-state did not even-state the problems. The rise of Macedonia forced home the recognition of two facts that has existed but that Plato and Aristotle had for the most part over looked. The one fact was that the city-state was too small and too contentious to govern even the Greek world and that no perfecting of it would make it commensurable with the economy of the world in which it lived. The other fact was that the assumed political superiority of Greeks over barbarians was not viable in the eastern Mediterranean, in view of the economic and cultural relations which had long existed between the Greek cities and the Asiatic hinterland. When Alexander deliberately adopted the policy of merging his Greek and his oriental subjects-a policy which must have been flatly contradictory of all that Aristotle had thought him about politics-he was at once accepting a fact whose importance his master had missed and also taking a step which made his master's political presumptions definitely obsolete.

Withdrawal or Protest

It is clear, then, that there was nothing accidental about the existence and the spread of a political philosophy much more negative in its attitude toward the values native to the city-state than that of Plato and Aristotle. The city-state of course continued to exist, and most of them continued for a long time to control their local affairs by the old governing bodies. No general statement can be made that will cover all the degrees and kinds of control over them in the Hellenistic Period. But no intelligent observer who had a sense of humor could take them quite so seriously as to suppose that their offices formed the capstone of a very significant career. A negative attitude might arise merely from a perception of the fact that the government of the city was not so important as men had imagined, that the life of any city was not for the most part in its own power, and that the most gifted statesman could not hope to accomplish much in that arena.

The result would be a defeatist attitude, a mood of disillusionment, a disposition to withdraw and to create a private life in which public interests had a small or even a negative part; a public career would be indifferent or even an actual misfortune. This point of view was perhaps best illustrated by the Epicureans or the Skeptics. On the other hand, a much more fortright negation of the city-state and its value might arise in so far as the unfortunate and dispossessed succeeded in making themselves vocal. Here it might be expected that with drawl would be accompanied by a note of protest or a stress upon the seamy side of the existing social order. Such a protest might well be unable to state an adequate ideal of its own and might therefore run to fantastic or even indecent extremes. This tendency was illustrated best by the Cynic School.

It was characteristics of all these Schools, as has been said, that they did not follow the lines laid down by Plato and Aristotle. Their significance lies in the fact that they branched out in a new direction and began lines of thought to which the fortune was to give importance. For this reason they stand in some respects upon a much lower level of perfection than the work of the great theorists of the city-state. None of their authors possessed the transcendent genius of Plato and none had Aristotle's incomparable mastery of the history and government of the city-states. Their importance lies in the fact that they present a different point of view, that they raise questions about first principles, and that they make an opening for the restatement of these principles in a situation very different from that which Plato and Aristotle had envisaged. Considered sympathetically the failure of the city-state must be interpreted as a major moral disaster, at least for those classes that were mainly affected. It meant infinitely more than the closing of a political career can possibly mean in an age when in any case the whole scheme of values is largely private and personal. It forced upon men the creation for the first time of ideals of personal character and private happiness such as a Greek, trained in the ideals of the city-state, could scarcely see as other than a makeshift and a renunciation. This may be perceived in the growth of large numbers of private societies for religious or social purposes, such as the classical age had felt no need for, a tendency characteristic of the Hellenistic age.[6] These are manifestly an effort to compensate for the social interests left unsatisfied by the recession of the city from a place of first-rate importance. To Plato and Aristotle the values offered by citizenship still seemed fundamentally satisfying, or at least capable of being made so; to a few of their contemporaries and increasingly to their successors this appeared to be false. It was this profound difference of point of view that made it necessary for the time being to turn aside from the political philosophy which they had left.

All the schools that taught the ideal of individual self-sufficiency professed to arise directly from the teaching of Socrates. How much truth there may have been in any of these claims is impossible to say, and after the generation had passed that had known him in person, his professed followers probably knew little more about it than is known now. Socrates became and remained almost a myth, the ideal wise man and philosophic hero, whom every school set up as the professed example of its teaching. In one sense, however, the philosophical problem really did return to the posture in which it had stood before the work of Plato. It was a recanvassing of the old issue about the meaning of nature and its relation to customary and conventional rules of popular morals. This was of course true for the generation to which Plato belonged, since everyone really did begin where Socrates left off, but it was true at a later date also for those who found themselves unable to accept the elaborate solutions offered by Plato and Aristotle. The more it became doubtful whether the city-state actually did provide the only conditions upon which a civilized life can be lived, the more it was necessary to re-examine the previous question : what are the essential and permanent factors in human nature from which a theory of the good life can be derived? Theories that Plato considered and rejected get a new hearing.

There were, as has been said, two chief forms of political philosophy to be considered in this connection. The one was most fully developed in the Epicurean School, though the differences between Epicureans and Skeptics were not very important, so far as the negations of their political theories were concerned. The second was the very different political philosophy of the Cynic School. It will be convenient to consider the two forms of theory in this order.

The Epicureans

The purpose of Epicureanism[7] was, in general terms, the same as that of all the ethical philosophy of the period after Aristotle, namely, to produce in its students a state of individual self-sufficiency. To this end it taught that a good life consists in the enjoyment of pleasure, but it interpreted this negatively. Happiness consists actually in the avoidance of all pain, worry, and anxiety. The pleasures of congenial friendship, which Epicurus sought to realize within the circle of his pupils, were those which formed the positive content of his doctrine of happiness, and this involved a withdrawal from the useless cares of public life. The wise man, therefore, will have nothing to do with politics unless circumstances compel him to do so. The philosophical basis of this teaching is a system of thoroughgoing materialism adopted from earlier philosophies, and apparently chosen less because it was certainly true than because of the consolations which it was believed to hold out. The secret of its power of consolation lay in the fact that Epicurus counted the anxieties of religion, of divine retribution, and the incomprehensible whims of Gods and spirits, as among the most serious to which men are heir. The Gods, we may be sure, care nothing about men and do not interfere either for good or ill in the course of their lives. This was in fact the most virile part of the Epicurean teaching. The School was a caustic critic of all sorts of superstitious practice and belief, such as divination and astrology- a really substantial evil- and its record in this respect is in honorable contrast to that of Stoicism, which was only too ready to find adumbration's of truth in popular beliefs that were obviously not true.

So far as the world at large is concerned, then, nature means simply physics, the atoms out of which all things are made. So far as human beings are concerned, nature means self-interest, the desire of every man for his own individual happiness. All other regulation human action belongs to the class of conventions and is therefore meaningless for the wise man except in so far as a conventional rule may be serviceable in producing more happiness than men would get without it. There are, therefore, no intrinsic moral virtues and no intrinsic value of any sort except happiness.

There never was an absolute justice but only a convention made in mutual intercourse, in whatever region, from time to time, providing against the infliction or suffering of harm.[8]

The argument against intrinsic values is the variety of moral rules and practices which have prevailed in different times and places, an argument, which was originally exploited by certain of the Sophists and which had been noticed (and in intention refuted) by Plato in the discussion of justice in the *Republic*. At a later date it was vastly elaborated by the Skeptic Carneades against the Stoics.[9] The vital point in the argument is the view that the good is a feeling privately enjoyed and that social arrangements are justified, if at all, only as devices to secure the largest possible private good.

States, then, are formed solely for the sake of obtaining security, especially against the depredations of other men. All men are essentially selfish and seek only their own good. But in this way the good of everyone is jeopardized by the equally selfish action of all other men. Accordingly men enter into a tacit agreement with each other neither to inflict nor to suffer harm. The doing of injustice is not bad in itself, but suffering its consequences without protection is worse than any advantage to be gained. Since the state of affairs resulting from a general practice of injustice is intolerable, men adopt as a working compromise the plan of respecting the rights of others for the sake of obtaining an equal forbearance from them. In this way the state and the law come into existence as a contract to facilitate intercourse between men. If no such contract exists, there is no such thing as justice. Law and government exist for the sake of mutual security and they are effective solely because the penalties of the law make injustice unprofitable. The wise man will act justly because the fruits of injustice are not worth the risk of detection and punishment. Morality is identical with expedience.

It follows, of course, that what men regard as right and just conduct will vary with circumstances and with time and place.

Whatever in conventional law is attested to be expedient in the needs of mutual rising out of mutual intercourse is by its nature just, whether the same for all or not, and in case any law is made and does not prove suitable to the expediency of mutual intercourse, then this is no longer just. And should the expediency which is expressed by the law vary and only for a time correspond with the notion of justice, nevertheless, for the time being, it was just, so long as we do not trouble ourselves about empty terms but look broadly at facts.[10]

In general, no doubt, justice is largely the same among all peoples for human nature is much the same everywhere, but still it is easy to see that at least in its applications the principle of expedience will vary more or less according to the kind of lives men lead. Thus what is wrong for some peoples may be right for others. For similar reasons a law which was perhaps originally just because it facilitated human intercourse may become wrong if the conditions change. In any case test of law and of political institutions lies solely in expedience in so far as they meet the need for security and make mutual intercourse safer and easier they are just in the only intelligible sense of the word. It was not unnatural therefore that the Epicureans, while caring little about forms of government, should have had a general preference for the monarchy as being the strongest and therefore the securest of governments. They were drawn no doubt mainly from the propertied classes, for whom security is always a major political good.

The social philosophy of the Epicureans was backed up by a really impressive theory of the origin and development of human institutions upon purely materialistic principles. This has been preserved in the fifth book of Lucretius's poem *De rerum natura* but it presumably originated with Epicurus. All the forms of social life, its political and social institutions, the art and sciences, in short, all human culture, have come about without intervention of any intelligence other than man's. Living beings themselves are the result of purely physical causes, and Epicurus borrowed from Empedocles a theory that rather crudely suggests the modern hypothesis of natural selection. Man has no instinctive learning toward society and no implication other than the restless pursuit of his individual happiness. In the beginning he lived a roving and solitary life, seeking shelter in caves and struggling to maintain himself against wild beasts. The first step toward civilization was the accidental discovery of fire. Gradually he learned to shelter himself in huts and to clothe himself with skins. Language originated from the cries by which instinctively he expressed his emotions. Experience and the more or less intelligent adaptation of action to the conditions of nature in time produced the various useful arts, as well as the institutions and laws of organized society. Civilization is wholly the creation of natural human powers acting within the conditions set by the physical environment. Belief in the Gods arises from dreams; the beginning of wisdom lies in the realization that the Gods take no part in human affairs.

The full possibilities of such a theory of social evolution, and of a political philosophy based upon pure egoism and contract, could not be exploited until modern times. Then it was revived and the political philosophy of Hobbes – in its underlying materialism, its reduction of all human motives to self-interest, and in its constructions of the state upon the need for security – is remarkably like Epicureanism. In the ancient world the drift of thought was against its most vital element – its attack upon religion and superstition – for the importance of religion again among human interests was pretty steadily on the increase. It is true, however, that Epicureanism was on the whole a philosophy of escape. The charges of sensualism which gave its very name a bad meaning are mostly groundless, but it probably tended to foster a kind of bloodless aestheticism incapable of influencing, or of wishing to influence, the course of human affairs. For individual men it was a source of peace and consolation, but for the time being it had nothing to do with the progress of political ideas.

The Cynics

The Cynics also, perhaps held a philosophy of escape but of a very different kind. More than any other School they formulated a protest against the city-state and the social classifications upon which it rested, and their escape lay in the renunciation of everything that men commonly called the goods of life, in the leveling of all social distinctions, and in abandoning the amenities and sometimes even the decencies of social conventions. Apparently they were recruited from the ranks of the foreigners and exiles, that is, from those who already stood outside the citizenship of the state. The founder of the School, Antisthenes, had a Thracian mother; its most notorious member, Diogenes of Sinope, was an exile; and its most able representative, Crates, seems to have renounced his fortune to adopt a life of philosophic poverty as a wandering beggar and teacher. His wife, Hiparchia, was a woman of good family who was first his pupil and then the companion of his wanderings. The Cynics formed a somewhat vague and quite unorganized body of roving teachers and popular philosophers who adopted a life of poverty on principle and who suggested somewhat the mendicant friars of the Middle Ages. Their teaching was addressed for the most part to the poor; they taught contempt for all the conventionalities; and in their behavior they often affected a shocking rudeness and disregard for decorum. In so far as the ancient world produced such a phenomenon, the Cynic may be described as the earliest example of the proletarian philosopher.

The philosophical basis of their teaching was the doctrine that the wise man ought to be completely self-sufficing. This the Cynics take to mean that only what is within his power, his own thought and character, is necessary to a good life. Everything except moral character is a matter of indifference. Among things indifferent the Cynic includes property and marriage, family and citizenship, learning and good repute, and in short all the pieties and conventions of a civilized life. All the customary distinctions of Greek social life were thus subjected to an annihilating criticism. Rich and poor, Greek and barbarian, citizen and foreigner, freeman and slave, well-born and base-born are all equal, for they are all reduced to the common level of indifference. The equality of the Cynics, however, was the equality of nihilism. The School never became the medium for a social doctrine either of philanthropy or of amelioration, but learned always toward the ascetic and puritanical. For poverty and slavery were literally of no consequence in their eyes; true, the freeman was no better than the slave, but neither the one nor the other had any value in himself, nor would the Cynic admit that slavery was an evil or freedom a good. They appear to have been actuated by a real hatred of the social discriminations universal in the ancient world, but this hatred led them to turn their backs on inequality and to seek in philosophy the entrance into a spiritual realm where the abominations would not matter. It was hardly less a philosophy of renunciation than Epicureanism, but it was the renunciation of the ascetic and nihilist rather than of the esthete.

The result was that the political theory of the Cynics was utopian. Both Antisthenes and Diogenes are said to have written books on politics and both seem to have sketched a kind of idealized communism, or perhaps anarchy, in which property, marriage, and government disappeared. The problem was not one that, as the Cynic conceived it touched the lives of the great majority of men. For most men, of whatever social class, are in any case fools, and the good life is only for the wise man. Equally, a true form of society also is for the wise man only. Philosophy emancipates its votaries from the laws and conventions of the city; the wise man is equally at home everywhere and nowhere. He requires neither home nor country, neither city nor law, because his own virtue is a law to him. All institutions are equally artificial and equally beneath the notice of the philosopher, for between men who have attained moral self-sufficiency these things are all unnecessary. The only true state is that in which wisdom is the requirement for citizenship and this state has neither place nor law. All wise men everywhere form a single community, the city of the world, and the wise man is, as Diogenes said, a "cosmopolitan," a citizen of the world. This conception of world-wide citizenship involved important consequences and had a distinguished history in Stoicism, but this was due chiefly to the positive meaning which the Stoics gave it. What the Cynics emphasized was its negative side: primitivism, the abolition of civic and social ties and of all restrictions except those that arise from the wise man's sense of duty. The protest of the Cynic against social convention was a doctrine of the return to nature in the most nihilist sense of the term.

The chief practical importance of the Cynic School lay in the fact that it was a matrix from which Stoicism emerged. But the Cynics have an interest perhaps out of proportion to their importance. After an interval of more than two thousand years it is not easy to recover the obscurer elements of political thought and those not in accord with the more vocal classes in the state. The rise and spread of Cynicism shows that, even as far back as the time of Socrates, there were some upon whom the institutions of the city-state bore heavily and who saw in it by no means an object to be idealized. With Plato and Aristotle in opposition these men were bound to be minor prophets. Yet what they saw at the beginning of the fourth century of the declining importance of the city-state was only what all men saw by the end of the century.

NOTES

1. 372 d.
2. 7,3; 1325 a 16 ff.
3. *Politics*, 2,6; 1265 a 20
4. *Hellenistic Athens* (1911), pp. 1.ff.
5. W. W. Tarn, *Hellenistic* Civilisation (1927), p. 104.
6. Tarn, op. cit., p.81.
7. The school was founded by Epicurus at Athens in 306 and remained for centuries one of the four great Athenian Schools. IT was connected with Socrates through Apristippus.
8. Golden Maxims, See R.D. Hicks, *Stoic and Epicurean* (1910), pp.177 ff.
9. Carneade's argument is reviewed at length by Cicero, *Republic*, Bk.III, 5-20.
10. Golden Maxims, 37

REFERENCES

The Greek Atomists and Epocurus. By Cyril Bailey. Oxford, 1928. Ch. 10.

Titi Lucreti Cari De rerum natura Ed. With Prolegomena, Critical Apparatus, Translation and Commentary by Cyril Bailey. 3 vols. Oxford, 1947. Prolegomen, Section IV.

A History of Cynicism from Diogenes to the 6th Century A.D. By Donald R. Dudley. London, 1937.

Epicurus and His Gods. By A. M. J. Festugiere. Eng. Trans. By C.W. Chilton. Oxford, 1955.

Stoic and Epicurean. By R.D. Hicks. London, 1911. Ch. 5.

The Greek City from Alexander to Justinian. By A.H.M. Jones. Oxford, 1940.

Representative Government in Greek and Roman History. By J.A.O. Larsen. Berkeley, Calif., 1955.

The Social and Economic History of the Hellenistic World. By M. Rostovtzeff. Oxford, 1941

Diogenes of Sinope: A Study of Greek Cynicism. By Farrand Sayre. Baltimore, 1938.

The Greek Cynics. By Farrand Sayre. Baltimore, 1948.

Hellenistic Civilization. By W.W. Tarn. 3d ed. Rev. by the author and G.T. Griffith. London, 1952. Ch. 10.

5

Halifax and Locke

The final act in the drama of English politics in the seventeenth century came with climatic suddenness in the bloodless Revolution of 1688. The ill-judged efforts of James II to foster Catholicism touched Protestant opinion in England as the stupidities and degradation of Restoration government had not, for this question was settled. The bulk of Englishmen were unchangeably Protestant and after a brief experience with James were ready to decide that Protestant supremacy was essential. The speed and ease with which the "Glorious Revolution" was accomplished, though helped along by the incomparable fatuity of James, showed that more than Protestantism was settled. It laid the ghost of republicanism, if indeed that ghost was still able to walk, for no one worth mentioning wished to try again the sad experiment of the Commonwealth. England was to be a monarchy, but a monarchy controlled by parliament upon lines fixed by the results of the civil wars. After the settlement of the succession in William and Mary there could never again be a doubt that the crown was in the keeping of parliament, if it chose to expert itself. English government thus settled into the form which it kept for upwards of a hundred years, and without the reforms of representation which seemed inevitable in 1650. It was, indeed, a crass form of class-government, which in the course of the eighteenth century developed some of the worst abuses of class-government, but still it was after its fashion representative, and in comparison with any other European government it might be called liberal. The principles of this settlement were summed up by the two most enlightened Englishmen of their generation, the statesman George Savile, First Marquis of Halifax, and the philosopher John Locke.

Though the threat of a Catholic dynasty probably occasioned the Revolution, the settlement closed a chapter in the relations of religion and politics. Never again would the two be united as they had been since the Protestant Reformation. The Toleration Act was the only practicable basis for permanent peace between the churches, and though the Test Act survived to become a curiosity of English legislation, the injustice to Catholics and Dissenters war far different from persecution. Nothing is clearer in the political thought of Halifax and Locke then the recession of doctrinal and ecclesiastical questions from the position of dominant interest which they had held. Locke as a young man had hoped for a policy of "comprehension" in the English church itself, and when this hope was defeated he turned to a theory of almost universal toleration and of practical separation between church and state. Something not too remote from this was achieved in England by the Revolution, and more and more it became the accepted solution everywhere of this ancient problem. The whole intellectual temper of both Locke and Halifax was secular to a degree that would have been practically impossible fifty years before. The contrast even with Hobbes was striking. Though he had been perhaps as nearly non-religious as any man that ever lived, he had devoted half of Leviathan to the problem of *imperium and sacerdotium*. Locke, whose personal life was a distillation of the best qualities of Puritanism, was able to pass the whole question over except as it affected his argument for toleration. Both Halifax and Locke belonged in this respect to the eighteenth rather than the seventeenth century: they could meet theological dispute with the deadliest weapon, indifference. Personally religious and ethically Christian, Locke was profoundly reasonable and anti-dogmatic.

The same qualities of mind are discernible in the political theories of both Halifax and Locke. In both, common sense counts for more than logic. Both were cautions and willing to remain conservative where circumstances permitted. Both were in a marked degree pragmatic and compromising, not inclined to argue over much with what they took to be accomplished fact but inclined rather to accept and make the best of it. Halifax perhaps came nearer than any man in the seventeenth century to making this frame of mind a working political hypothesis. No man had a grater distrust of large generalizations or a prettier wit for pricking bubbles. With characteristic irony and perhaps with a shade of gentlemanly indifference to careful thinking, he let himself off the hard task of making a positive theory; he was enlightened and penetrating in the highest degree, but he was essentially an empiric and a skeptic. To a philosopher lie Locke this easy-going distrust of generalization was not possible. He too was an empiricist but with a large residue of philosophic rationalism and a firm belief in self-evident principles of right and wrong. Unfortunately common sense is a poor organ for synthesizing really opposed philosophical positions. The result in Locke was a series of compromises which always left the first principles unclear. It is true that his compromises satisfied nearly everyone for upwards of a half century and that by common sense he grasped firmly the fundamental ethical ideal of the English Settlement, that of individual rights. Yet his compromises went far to conceal the insufficiencies both of the ideal itself and of its realization in eighteenth-century England. As a consequence later political thought was related to Locke in a highly complex fashion.

Halifax

What chiefly impressed Halifax's[1] inquiring and skeptical mind is the fact that there are few if any general principles that hold good of government. It is, as he says, a "coarse thing," made up mostly of expedients and compromises, with hardly a propositions in it that is "not deceitful." A loud profession of principles is usually a pretense to cloak the pursuit of private or partisan advantage. What men choose to call "fundamentals," he says, is

> *A nail everybody would use to fix that which is good for them; for all men would have that principle to be immovable that serves their use at the time.*[2]

Fundamental is a word used by the laity, as the word sacred is by the clergy, to fix everything to themselves they have a mind to keep, that nobody else may touch it.[3]

Nothing is more certain than that every human institution will change and the so-called fundamentals of government with them. The divine right of kings, the indefeasible rights of property of persons, and laws which may mot be repeated or modified are all attempts to bind the future; they neither can nor ought to be effective. Laws and constitutions; he says, are made not once but a hundred times. In themselves they can do little and in the end they mean just what those who interpret and administer and enforce them intend them to mean. The common law, he says, with evident reference to Coke," hovers in the clouds," except as it is set in motion by a court or an executive, and then it becomes whatever the execution of the court's judgement makes of it. In the last resort law and government depend upon the intelligence and good will of the persons who conduct them. Abstractions count for something, but concrete interests and forces for much. Government as Halifax envisaged it was mainly the business of a ruling is to be a practicable compromise between and liberty, capable or expanding to meet and emergency, adaptable to changing, circumstances, strong enough to keep the peace but liberal enough to avoid repression.

Despite this emphasis on the personnel of government, Halifax had too much experience of affairs to imagine that a government could do as it liked. Behind the government is the nation, and nations make governments, not contrariwise. A people who loses its king is still a people, but a king who loses his people is no longer a king. There is in every nation a supreme power that alters the constitution as often as the good of the people requires. Some such principle of national life and self-preservation –which Halifax frankly admits he cannot define of forecast – is the nearest thing to a fundamental known to politics.

> *There is a natural reason of state, an undefinable thing, grounded upon the common good of mankind, which is immortal, and in all changes and revolutions, still preserveth its original right of saving a nation, when the letter of the law perhaps would destroy it.*[4]

This inherent power of self-development in a people will not and ought not to be curbed. The real power of a government depends upon its responsiveness to this internal drive. Without it neither constitutions nor force can long prevail. In this very general sense all government depends upon consent. A representative body is the best practicable device for giving voice to a nation's aspirations, but Halifax clearly regarded it as only a device. For practical purposes there must be room also for an indefinable power of leadership, a kind of omnipotence for great occasions, by which "a nation may at some critical times be secured from ruin."

It is upon this basis of expediency and national history that Halifax constructed his estimate of the crisis in England. Abstractly, he says in his *New Model at Sea*, there are three possibilities. One would be absolute monarchy –he was thinking of France-which, he admits, has some advantages in unity and speed of execution. But it destroys the "competent state of freedom" in which men ought to live, and in any event it is possible in England both because of the national tradition and because England's greatness must lie in trade, which is " the creature of liberty." A second possibility, which might be theoretically preferable to monarchy, would be commonwealth, but the invincible objection is that Englishmen do not like it. Monarchy is perhaps a thing of "bells and tinsel," but the fact remains that England's one experiment with a commonwealth ended in military dictatorship. The one remaining and the only real possibility, therefore, is a "mixed monarchy," a constitutional government divided between king and parliament. Halifax was well content with the choice, for such government, he thought, gives the best compromise between power and liberty. It is a mean between absolute monarchy and commonwealth:

> *We take from one the too great power of doing hurt, and yet leave enough to govern and protect us; we take from the other, the confusion, the parity, the animosities, and the license and yet reserve a due care of such a liberty, as may consist with men's allegiance.*[5]

Parliament may be troublesome but they give great strength to a wise administration.

In two respects, however, Halifax failed to understand the machinery of the two government. He did not see that ministers must become dependent on parliament and responsible to it, instead of being the personal choice of the monarch. Probably no one could have seen this until the course of parliamentary history made it plain, and Halifax died before the evidence was fairly in. Very naturally, therefore, he failed to see also that political parties had become an inherent part of parliamentary government. His judgement of parties was markedly hostile, an attitude due in part to his experience with the disreputable cabals of the Restoration and the intransigent factions of the revolutionary period, but also to a fastidiousness of temper that made it hard for him to cooperate when he could not control. A party he judged to be at the best a kind of conspiracy against the rest of the nation, the party discipline he felt to be incompatible with liberty of private opinion. This low estimate of political parties was typical until the publication of Burke's Present Discontents in 1770.

Halifax's political acumen surpassed that of every other English statesman of his age. Probably mist historians would now agree with Macaulay's assertion that "through frequent and violent revolutions of public feeling, he almost invariably took that view of the great questions of his time which has finally adopted." He had, to be sure, almost no political theory; almost he said that no political theory was possible. Certainly one was possible for him in terms of the absolute rights and obligations-the strong blacks and whites with no grays – that the seventeenth century characteristically loved. In this qualifying temper, this willingness to compromise, this readiness to judge in terms of expedience, lay the note of the eighteenth century. His on slaught on "fundamentals," side by side with Locke's attack on innate ideas, was the antecedent to Hume's empirical criticism of the theory of natural rights. His emphasis upon expedience as an ever-present factor in political adjustment was introductory to ethical and political utilitarianism, which was the only live social philosophy in England throughout most of the eighteenth century and which attained its mature influence only in the philosophical radicalism of Bentham and the Mills. Thus, Halifax, though he would not have been flattered by being called a philosopher, displayed and intellectual temper which became an integral part of philosophy.

Locke: The Individual and the Community

The political philosophy of John Loke wore the guise of an occasional performance. It was contained in two essays published in 1690 with the avowed purpose of defending the Revolution,[6] and of these essays the first, which was devoted to the refutation of Filmer, had no permanent importance. In fact, however, the second treatise war far from being merely a tract for the times; it reached back into the past, right across the whole period of the civil wars, and joined hands with Hooker's *Ecclesiastical Polity*, which had summed up the political thought of England at the close of the Reformation and before the break between parliament and the king. Through Hooker, Locke was joined with the long tradition of medieval political thought, back to St. Thomas, in which the reality of moral restraints on power, the responsibility of rulers to the communities which they ruled, and the subordinate of government to law were axiomatic. It was not that Locke was in any sense an antiquarian. The chief mark of his genius was neither learning nor logic but an incomparable common sense by which he gathered together the chief convictions, in philosophy, politics, morals, and education, that the experience of the past had generated in the more enlightened minds of the generation. By giving to these a simple and sober yet persuasive statement, he passed them on to the eighteenth century, where they became the matrix from which grew the later political philosophy both of England and the Continent. The medieval tradition, which Loke tapped through Hooker, was an indispensable part of the constitutional ideals of the Revolutions of 1688. The years of the civil wars had changed but had no destroyed it. Loke's problem, therefore, was not to reproduce historically the thought of Hooker but to gather together anew the abiding elements of that thought and to restate them in the light of what had happened in the intervening century.

Of all the figures in this intervening century incomparably the most important for the development of a consistent political theory had been Thomas Hobbes. Hobbes, with his clear-cut proof that political absolutism can be deduced from rigidly individualist principles, was the opponent whom Loke should have undertaken to refute if he were to give an equally penetrating defense of constitutional government. Unfortunately, he did not assume this obligation in his second treatise but continued his refutation of Filmer. In view of Loke's controversial purpose this is understandable, for his royalist opponents were far from identifying themselves with Hobbes, who was unpopular with both sides. Moreover, they had revived Filmer and had thus made him an obvious target. Filmer had the merit, also, for controversial purposes, of being in some respects absurd and of seeming more absurd than he was. Locke failed to discriminate Filmer's absurdities from his solid arguments, which were largely derived from Hobbes. Since Locke intended his treatises for popular tracts, he made the obvious choice, but it detracted seriously from their philosophical incisiveness. They never came to terms with the hardest problems. This is indeed characteristic of is philosophy generally. Like most philosophies that lean heavily on common sense, it is often lacking in analytic thoroughness and therefore fails to get back to first principles.

So far as concerns his political philosophy, the gist of the issue may be stated as follows. The medieval tradition that reached Locke through Hooker, and the constitutional ideals followed in the settlement of 1688, held that government –the king specifically but not less parliament itself and every political agency-is responsible to the people or the community which is governs; its power is limited both by moral law and by the constitutional traditions and conventions inherent in the history of the realm. Government is indispensable and its right is therefore in a sense indefeasible, but it is also derivative in the sense that it exists for the well-being of the nation. This argument clearly presumes the corporate or social reality of the community, not a difficult assumption in an age when society was regulated by custom and in any event a settled principle of the medieval Aristotelianism which inspired Hooker. The main result of Hobbes's analysis, however, had been to show that a community as such a pure fiction, that it has no existence except in the cooperation of its members, that this cooperation is always due to advantages enjoyed by its members individually, and that it become a community only because some individual is able to exercise sovereign power. Upon this analysis Hobbes had based his conclusion that subjection is unavoidable in any form of government, and that ideas such as contract, representation, and responsibility are meaningless unless backed by a sovereign's power. Hence they are valid within the state but not for the state but not for the state.

The logical opposition between these two points of view is extreme. The first is stated in terms of functions. It conceives both individual and institutions as doing a socially valuable work, regulated by government for the good of all, and within the framework of the law which makes the group a community. The second is stated in terms of individual self-satisfaction. It conceives society as composed of persons actuated by selfish motives, looking to law and government for security against their equally selfish fellows, and seeking the largest amount of private good consistent with keeping the peace. If Locke could have adopted either point of view and rejected the other, he would have been more consistent than he was. The circumstance under which he wrote required him to adopt both, and this ought to have entailed an examination of principles and a synthesis of the highest order, It was in fact a task that exceeded Locke's powers. His defense of the Revolution was practically upon the lines marked out by Hooker and already adopted in substance by Halifax. It assumes that the English people forms a social group persisting continuously through the changes of government required by its political evolution and setting moral standards which it rulers must respect. On the other hand, there were urgent reasons why Locke had to adopt into his social philosophy a large part of Hobbes's premises. With or without Hobbes's systematically egoistic psychology a theory of society in term of individual interests was in Locke's day a foregone conclusion. The whole drift of the theory of natural law was in this direction and to this tendency Locke made no small contribution. For he interpreted natural law as a claim to innate, indefeasible rights inherent in each individual. Of such rights that of private property is the typical case. Consequently his theory was by implication as egoistic as that of Hobbes. Both government and society exist to preserve the individual's rights, and the indefeasibility of such rights is a limitation on the authority of both. In one part of the Locke's theory, therefore, the individual and his rights figure as ultimate principles; in another society itself plays this part. There is nothing which adequately explains how both can be absolute.

The Natural Right to Property

Though Locke was not directly criticizing Hobbes, he attacked some ideas more typical of him than of Filmer, notably the theory that the state of nature is a war of all against all. Locke held that the state of nature is one of "peace, good will, mutual assistance and preservation." This is defended on the ground that the law of nature provides a complete equipment of human rights and duties. The defect of the state of nature lies merely in the fact that it has no organization, such as magistrates, written law, and fixed penalties, to give effect to the rules of right. Everything that is ever right or wrong is so eternally; positive law adds nothing to the ethical quality of different kinds of conduct but merely provides an apparatus for effective enforcement. In the state of nature every man must protect his own as best he can, but his right to his own and his duty to respect what is another's are as complete as ever they can become under government. It will be noted that this is exactly the ground that Thomas had taken centuries before Locke. Locke was merely repeating Hooker and through him the medieval tradition about the relation between law and morals. If the fiction about a state of nature be laid aside, this can mean only one thing, namely, that moral rules are broader in their application than the rules of positive law and are valid whether governments observe them or not. Just what gives morality its force remains a question. It might depend upon divine will, or it might be rationally self-evident, or it might depend on the fact that society is more deeply ingrained in human nature than government and so sets standards that governments cannot defy. In any case Locke emphatically held that moral rights and duties are intrinsic and prior to law; governments are obligated to give effect by their law to what is naturally and morally right.

It is evident, then, that Locke's whole theory dependent upon explaining exactly what was meant by the law of nature upon which his pre-political condition of mutual assistance rested and in accordance with which political society arose. At least it was incumbent on him to show why it was binding even without administration or enforcement. In fact he never gave any careful analysis of it at all, his most explicit treatment of it being merely incidental to his discrimination –following Aristotle and directed against Filmer- of paternal from political power. Because it was traditional to discuss property in connection with the family. This had the effect of uniting his treatment of natural law with his theory of the origin of his private property. Before discussing the general question of the validity which Locke attributed to natural law, therefore, it will be better to present his theory of the right to private property, for he constantly assumes that this is the type to which all natural rights are analogous.

In the state of nature, Locke believed, property was common in the sense that everyone had a right to draw subsistence from whatever nature offers. Here again he was bringing ideas from a far distance past. In the Middle Ages it had be not uncommon to suppose that common ownership is a more perfect and hence a more "natural" state than private ownership, the latter being attributed to the effects of sin upon human nature after the fall of man. In the Roman law also there existed the very different theory that private property beings with the appropriation of things which before had a common use though no communal ownership. Locke departed from both theories by asserting that a man has a natural right to that with which he has "mixed" the labour of his body, as for example by enclosing and tilling land. Apparently he was generalizing from the example of colonists in a new land like America, but it is probable that he was influenced also by a strong sense of the superior productivity of private agricultural economy as compared with the communal tillage of a more primitive system. Locke believed that greater production would raise the standard of living throughout the community. In the eighteenth century the enclosure of land did in fact increase the yield, but the capitalist landlord took advantage of his strategic position to sequestrate the benefits. Whatever the origin of Locke's theory may have been, his argument was that the right to private property arises because by labour a man extends, so to speak, his own personality into the objects produced. By expending his internal energy upon them he makes them a part of himself. In general their utility depends upon the labour expended upon them, and thus Locke's theory led to the later labour-theories of value in classical and socialist economics.

From Locke's theory of the origin of private property it follows that the right is prior even to the primitive society which he described as the state of nature. As he himself said, property is "without any express compact of all the commoners."[7] It is a right which each individual brings to society in his own person, just as he brings the physical energy of his body. Hence society does not create the right and except within limits cannot justly regulate it, for both society and government exist, in part at least, to protect the prior private right of property. This account of property, though introduced almost casually, had a profound effect on Locke's whole social philosophy. He never said, and almost certainly did not believe, that there was no natural right except property. The expression which he most commonly used to enumerate natural rights was "life, liberty, and estate." Frequently, however, he used "property" where he seems to have meant any right, and since property was the only natural right which he examined at length, it was inevitable that it should stand out as the typical and important right. In any case, he conceived all natural rights on the same lines as property, that is to say, as attributes of the individual person born with him, and hence as indefeasible claims upon both society and government. Such claims can never justly be set aside, since society itself exists to protect them; they can be regulated only to the extent that is necessary to give them effective protection. In other words, the "life, liberty, and estate" of one person can be limited only to make effective the equally valid claims of another person to the same rights.

Philosophical Ambiguities

This theory, in all its social and political implications, was as egoistic as that of Hobbes. It is true that Locke drew a different picture of the state of nature. The war of all against all no doubt seemed to his common sense to be overdrawn, but like Hobbes he was saying in substance that society exists to protect property and other private rights which society does not create. As a result the psychology which in the eighteenth century grew out of Locke's theory of mind was fundamentally egoistic in its explanation of human behavior. It ran in terms of pleasure and pain, and not like Hobbes's in terms of self-preservation – a doubtful improvement – but the calculation of pleasure was exactly as self-centered as the calculation of security. Hobbes's better logic had its way in spite of Locke's better feeling. By a strange and undersigned cooperation the two men fastened on social theory the presumption that individual self-interest is clear and compelling, while a public or a social interest is thin and unsubstantial. Perhaps the influence of Locke, precisely because it was less aware of its principles, was the more insidious. He left standing the old theory of natural law with all its emotional connotations and almost religious compulsions, but he completely changed without knowing it, the meaning which the term had in writers like Hooker. Instead of a law enjoining the common good of a society, Locke set up a body of innate, indefeasible, individual rights which limit the competence of the community and stand as bars to prevent interference with the liberty and property of private persons. Like later liberals he assumed that the two things-preservation of the common good and protection of private rights-come to the same thing. In the existing state of politic$ and industry perhaps this was measurably true, but there was no logical ground for it except the vague assumption that in the harmony of nature "somehow good will be the final goal of ill." This sentimental trust in nature, quite unwarranted by anything that modern science or modern philosophy knew about it, ran right across the history of political and economic theory in the eighteenth century.

It is exceedingly difficult to understand exactly what Locke believed to be the philosophical justification for his theory of natural rights, or in other words to see how he meant to unite his political theory with his general philosophical position. That all individuals are endowed by their creator with a right to life, liberty, and estate, aside from all reference to their social and political associations, is certainly not a proposition for which any empirical proof can be given. There seems to be no way whatever to prove it; it must stand, as Thomas Jefferson said, simply as self-evident, an axiom from which social and moral theorems can be deduced but which in itself is more obvious than any other ethical principle. Probably this is what Locke believed. The tendency to regard natural law in moral and legal science as analogous to axioms in geometry was well settled in seventeenth-century thought after Grotius. But even if some moral values are admitted to be self-evident, it is far from obvious that they must take the form of innate individual rights. Probably Locke never really faced this question, since he seems not to have been aware how greatly his own theory of natural rights differed from the older versions of the theory.

If this latter question be put aside, however, it is still hard to see how Loke's philosophical position warranted him in believing that an apparently self-evident proposition, in ethics or any other subject, is for that reason true. The first Book of the *Essay concerning Human Understanding* was devoted to showing that no idea is innate, that is, so fundamentally a part of the mind that belief in it is warranted apart from evidence. For practical purposes this is the same as saying that self-evidence is not reliable, since even a false proposition, because of custom or habit, may appear to be obvious. Undoubtedly Locke meant his attack on innate ideas to be a solvent for all kinds of prejudice, in morals and religion as well as in science. His own belief, that ideas come from the senses, he regarded as affording a basis for knowledge quite different from the spurious test of innateness.

In accord with this empirical theory of the origin of ideas, Locke gave up the belief that any empirical science –one which depended on the report of the senses about physical existences-could be demonstrably true. Yet he retained the current belief that any fully reliable science must be demonstrable. He supposed that reason was able to perceive necessary "agreements and disagreements" between some ideas and that these sufficed to support a few demonstrable sciences such as mathematics, and he supposed also that ethics was included among these. Hence he believed that his political theory was supported by the self-evident truths of a demonstrable science of ethics. Thus his philosophy as a whole presented the anomaly of a theory of the mind which was in general empirical, joined with a theory of the sciences and a procedure in political science which was rationalist. The curious result in his social philosophy was a theory markedly tolerant and critical in defending religious freedom and capable of being highly dogmatic in defending rights of property.

In philosophy the weight of Locke's influence was on the side of empiricism, that is, on the side of a psychology in which human knowledge and behavior are explained from the senses and in which the rules of conduct claim the validity of generalizations from experience. It was manifest that natural rights –indefeasible claims to liberty of action inherent in human beings whatever their social relationships or without social relationships—could not be verified in this way, nor could they pass unchallenged as axioms after his refutation of innate ideas. Thus it happened that his English successors in the first half of the eighteenth century (following suggestions in the *Essay*) rapidly developed a theory of behavior in terms of pleasure and pain, the first operating as a force of attraction and the second as one of repulsion, and a theory of value in which the greatest net sum of pleasures, after deducting the pains as negative quantities, was set up as the socially valuable end of conduct. At first a mainly academic psychology allied to a theological ethics, this theory passed through a French medium into the hands of Bentham and the philosophical radicals. Logically, as Hume showed, it eliminated altogether Locke's natural rights and fictions about the state of nature and a contract. It remained egoistic, however, both in its psychological explanation of behavior and in its theory of value – ethical, political, and economic - and merely assumed the coincidence of individual freedom with the greatest public good. The individualism of all social theory between Locke and John Stuart Mill depended less on logic than on its agreement with the interests of the class that mainly produced it.

The Contract

Having describe the state of nature as a condition of peace and mutual aid and having defined natural rights, on the analogy of property, as prior even to society, Locke next proceeded to derive civil society from the consent of its members. This part of his theory suffered inevitably from the inherent contrariety of what he took from Hooker and what agreed with Hobbes. Civil power he had defined as "the right of making laws with penalties ... for the regulating and preserving of property, and of employing the force of the community, in the execution of such laws... all this only for the public good."[8] Such a power can arise only by consent, and though this may be tacitly given, it must be the consent of each individual for himself. For civil power can have no right except as this is derived from the individual right of each man to protect himself and his property. The legislative and executive power used by government to protect property is nothing except the natural power of each man resigned "into the hands of the community," or "resigned to the public," and it is justified merely because it is a better way of protecting natural rights than the self-help to which each man is naturally entitled. This is "original compact" by which men "incorporate into one society"; it is a bare agreement "to unite into one political society, which is all the compact that is, or needs be between the individuals, that enter into, or make up a commonwealth."[9]

The difficulty with this theory is that Locke is nowhere clear as to what precisely does arise by the "original compact." Is it society itself or only government? That the two are different he emphatically asserted at a later point in the second *Treatise*, where he argued that a political revolution which dissolves a government does not as a rule dissolve the community which that government rules. Moreover, the individual resigns his natural right to the community or the public, which presumably must be some kind of entity if it can receive a grant of power. On the other hand, right is lodged, necessarily according to Locke's theory, only in the hands of individuals until they resign it. Yet he regarded this surrender of individual right as conditional against both society and government, for individual power is resigned "only with an intention in everyone the better to preserve himself his liberty and property," and society itself is "obliged to secure everyone's property."[10] To clarify this problem those Continental writers like Althusius and Pufendorf, who had elaborated the theory of compact most carefully, had postulated two contracts, the one between individuals giving rise to a community and the other between the community and its government. Some such position Locke tacitly assumes, though he nowhere states. The twofold contract, of course, explains nothing, since the propriety of using the same concept to cover the two cases is really the doubtful point, but it does give formal clarity to the theory. Formal clarity was not a quality which Locke greatly valued and hence he contended himself with a conflation of two points of view. The older theory which he got from Hooker assumed a community capable of holding its magistrates morally responsible; this he mainly followed in his defense of the Revolution as a justifiable effort to make English government serve the needs of English society. The newer theory, most clearly stated by Hobbes, assumed only individuals and their private interests, and this also Locke followed in so far as he made both society and government agencies for protecting life, liberty, and estate.

The two phases of Locke's theory are united – very precariously, it must be admitted – by the hypothesis that an act of the community is constituted by the agreement of a majority of its members. The consent by which each person agrees with others to form a body politic obligates him to submit to the majority; as Pufendorf had argued, the fiction of a social contract must be helped out with the further fiction of unanimous consent. And the agreement of a majority is identical with an act of the whole society.

> *That which acts any community, being only the consent of the individuals of it, and it being necessary to that which is one body to move one way; it is necessary the body should move that way whether the greater force carries it, which is the consent of the majority.*[11]

This way of solving the difficulty, however, is open to objection from both sides. If an individual's rights are really indefeasible, it is no better for him to be deprived of them by a majority than by a single tyrant; apparently it did not occur to Locke that a majority could be tyrannous. Nor is there any good reason why an individualist should resign his private judgement merely because those who disagree with him are numerous. On the other hand, if the "public" or the "community" really has a unitary quality of its own there is no a *priori* reason why its decision must always be made by a numerical majority. Older theories of popular sovereignty, such as Marsilio's had commonly held that the "prevailing part" of a community may be weighted for quality as well as for quantity. In general it cannot be said that the principle of majority-rule has any such obvious validity as Locke imputed to it.

Society and Government

On the whole Locke regarded the setting up of a government as a much less important event than the original compact that makes a civil society. Once a majority has agreed to form a government, "the whole power of the community is naturally in them." The form of the government depends upon what disposition the majority, or otherwise the community, makes of its power. It may be retained or it may be delegated to a legislative body of one form or another. Following the experience of the English Revolution, Locke assumed that the legislative power is supreme in government, though he admitted the possibility that the executive may share in lawmaking. Both powers, however, are limited. Legislative power can never be arbitrary, for even the people who set it up had no such power; it cannot rule by extemporary decrees, since men unite to have known law and judges; it cannot take property without consent, which Locke interprets to mean by majority-vote; and it cannot delegate its legislative power, since this is unalterably in the hands where the community has placed it. In general, its power is fiduciary, since the people have supreme power to alter the legislature when it acts contrary to the trust reposed in it. The executive is further limited by a general dependence on the legislature and also because the prerogative is limited by law. For the sake of freedom it is important that legislative and executive power should not be in the same hands. Every detail of Locke's account of the relation between legislatures and executives reflects some phase of the controversy between the king and the parliament.

The power of the people over government, however, is still not quite as complete in Locke as it came to be in later and more democratic theories. Though he called the power of the legislature fiduciary and a delegation from the majority that acts for the community, he retained the older view that the grant of the community divests the people of power so long as the government is faithful to its duties. In this respect his theory was logically somewhat arbitrary, as Rousseau later pointed out. For if government is merely the trustee of the people, it is hard to see why the principal should have bound his hands by executing the trust. The people's legislative power is in effect limited to a single act (through Locke admits that a democracy is conceivable), namely, that of setting up a supreme legislature. Even if the community resumes its power for good cause, it cannot do so "till the government be dissolved." A democrat like Rousseau naturally considered this to be an unwarranted limitation on the perpetual power of the people to govern itself as it saw fit. Probably several causes united to fix Locke in his opinion. He was a cautious and sober-minded man, in no wise willing to encourage licence even though he had to defend a revolution. Besides, he rightly regarded democratic government, at least in England, as an academic question. More important than these reasons, probably, was the persistence in his mind of the tradition which he derived from Hooker and which had governed the thought of Coke and Sir Thomas Smith. The right of a community to govern itself had not been thought inconsistent with a kind of indefensibility in the right of its king and other governing organs, which after all had a status or a vested interest in their places. This phase of Locke's theory persisted in the Whig liberalism of the eighteenth century, which regarded government, while responsible for the common well-being, a balance between the great interests of the realm, such as crown, nobility, church and commonalty. With Edmund Burke this conception became a starting-point for the theory of modern conservatism. The English Revolution did not break violently the tradition of English government, and similarly Locke, it philosophical exponent, was the most conservative of revolutionists. Locke's ideas in France in the eighteenth century had quite a different history.

At whatever date his treatises were written, Locke's purpose was to defend the moral right of revolution; hence at the end of his second treatise he discussed the right to resists tyranny. His most effective arguments depended on principles taken from Hooker. In substance it amounts to this: English society and English government are two different things. The second exists for the well-being of the first, and a government which seriously jeopardizes social interests is rightly changed. This argument is supported by a rather lengthy examination of the right which can be gained by conquest. Locke here distinguished between just and unjust warfare. A mere aggressor gains no right, and even a conqueror in a just war can never establish a right which contravenes the right of the conquered to their liberty and property. The argument is directed against any theory that a government can derive a just power merely from conquest or from success in the use of force. The principle of Locke's argument is essentially the same as that later developed by Rousseau, that moral validity and force are two distinct things, the latter being incapable of giving rise to the former. Consequently a government which beings in force can be justified, as all governments are justified, only by its recognition and support of the moral rights inherent in persons and communities. In other words, the moral order is permanent and self-perpetuating, and governments are only factors the in moral order. In this sense natural law meant for Locke substantially what it had meant for Cicero and Seneca and the whole of the Middle Ages.

A government, as distinct from a society, is dissolved either by a change in the location of legislative power or by a violation of the trust which the people have reposed in it. Locke contemplated two cases, both drawn from English experience in the preceding fifty years. He wished to show that the king had been the real author of the Revolution by attempting to stretch the prerogative and to rule without parliament; this was a dislocation of the supreme legislative power vested by the people in their representatives. He had also retentive memory for the his misbehavior of the Long Parliament and accordingly he had no thought of leaving the legislature unfettered. Any invasion of the life, liberty, or property of subjects is *ipso facto void*, and a legislature which attempts these wrongs forfeits its power. In this case power reverts to the people, who must provide by a new act of constitutional legislation for a new legislature. As in all such arguments, Locke created a considerable, and perhaps needless, confusion by his use of the word "lawful." He continually speaks of unlawful acts of the executive or legislature when he well knows that there is no legal remedy, and of lawful resistance to tyranny when he means resort to an extra-legal but morally defensible remedy. Broadly speaking he used lawful as synonymous with just or right and made no distinction between what is morally just and what is legally actionable. This usage grew from and perpetuated the traditional belief that law- natural, positive, and moral –is all of a piece, and that there are therefore "fundamental" laws not made even by the supreme legislature. The reality of such rules in English law disappeared with the very Revolution which Locke was defending, though the belief in moral limitations on parliament persisted. Perhaps the American practice of discriminating between constitutional and statutory law, and between ordinary legislation and extraordinary legislation by referendum, was closer to Locke's ideas.

The Complexity of Locke's Theory

Locke's political philosophy can hardly be represented in a simple and straightforward exposition because of the logical difficulties which it reveals when it is subjected to analysis. In spite of the simplicity which it seems on the surface to possess and which made it the most popular of political philosophies, it is in reality involved. This was due to the fact that Locke saw with great clarity a multitude of issues involved in the politics of the seventeenth century and tried conscientiously to combine them all. But this theory had no logical structure elaborate enough to contain so complicated a subject-matter. Though circumstances made him the defender of a revolution, he was by no means a radical, and in intellectual temperament he was the least doctrinaire of philosophers. Perhaps something is explained by the fact that his mature life fell in a generation when the results of civil war were accomplished but not acknowledged. His principles he mainly inherited and he never examined them very thoroughly. But he was extraordinarily sensitive to realities and absolutely candid in trying to face them. The mid-period of the seventeenth century had changed enormously both English politics and English thought, and yet it had not broken continuity with the days before the civil wars. Locke's political philosophy was an effort to combine past and present and also to find a nucleus of agreement for reasonable men of all parties, but he did not synthesize all that he combined. As he combined diverse elements from the past, so from his political philosophy emerged diverse theories in the century following him.

The defects of logical structure in Locke's political theory arose from the fact that he never made up his mind what exactly was fundamental and what was derivative. There are in fact no less than four levels in his account of civil society, and the last three are represented as successfully derivative from the first. Yet Locke never hesitated, if it was convenient, to impute a kind of absoluteness to each of the four. The foundation of the whole system was represented as being the individual and his rights, especially that of property. On the whole this must be regarded as the most significant phase of his political theory, which made it primarily a defense of individual liberty against political oppression. Second, men are also members of a community, and though Locke described society as depending on tacit consent and as meaning effectively a majority, he constantly spoke of the community as a defined unit and the trustee of the individual's rights. Third, beyond society there is government, which is trustee for the community, somewhat as the latter is for the individual. Finally, within government the executive is less important and less authoritative than the legislature. Yet Locke certainly did not regard the king and his ministers as merely a committee of parliament. In the defense of liberty and property the legislature controls the executive, and the community controls government. Only in the remote event that society itself is dissolved, a contingency which Locke never seriously contemplated, does the defense of liberty revert to self-help. Society, the legislature, and even the king were all treated as having a kind of vested right, or permanent authority, only to be forfeited for cause, though the individual rights of property and liberty were the only rights which Locke declared to be absolutely indefeasible. The plausibility of Locke's theory was greatly increased by not trying to show too precisely how the actual power of institutions is derived from the equal and inalienable rights of individuals.

The actual complexity of Locke's political thought, concealed beneath its apparent simplicity of statement, makes difficult an estimate of its relations to later theories. What was immediately grasped included its most obvious but also its least important consequences. The enormous vogue which he enjoyed during the earlier part of the eighteenth century was probably due precisely to the deceptive simplicity of his thought, which has always commended his philosophy to common sense. Such liberal thought as survived the success of the Revolution carried on the spirit of Locke's philosophy most truly in respect to religious toleration, which had real vitality in eighteenth century England despite the political disqualification of Catholics and Dissenters by the continuation of the Test Act. The supremacy of parliament was no longer a controversial issue and party differences about the power of the crown had little importance. With some lip- service to Locke Whiggism in the eighteenth century represented quite subsidiary elements of his *Treatise*: that the powers of government remain indefeasible in the organs where they have once been placed, unless one tries to invade the province of another, and that government is at bottom a balance of the vested interests of the realm: crown, landed aristocracy and corporations.[12] In this almost nothing of Locke's theory of individual rights remained but much of what Ire ton, in his dispute with the Levelers, had called the "permanent fixed interests" of the kingdom. This made it possible for the myth of a separation of powers to persist to the end of the century. As Black-stone said,

> *Every branch of our civil polity supports and is supported, regulates and is regulated, by the rest: for the two houses naturally drawing in two directions of opposite interest, and the prerogative in another still different from them both, they mutually keep each other from exceeding their proper limits; while the whole is prevented from separation, and artificially connected together by the mixed nature of the crown, which is a part of the legislative, and the sole executive magistrate.*[13]

The monopoly of power by the landowning class was contrary not only to Locke's theory of individual rights but also to his theory of the importance of property in general.

The greatest importance of Locke's philosophy, therefore, lay beyond the contemporary English settlement in the political thought of America and France which culminated in the great revolutions at the end of the eighteenth century. Here Locke's defense of resistance in the mane of inalienable rights of personal liberty, consent, and freedom to acquire and enjoy property had their full effect. Because all these conceptions were in germ must older than Locke and had been the birthright of all European peoples since the sixteenth century, it is impossible to attribute their existence in America and in France to him alone, but he was known to everyone who gave any attention to political philosophy. His sincerity, his profound moral conviction, his genuine belief in liberty, in human rights, and in the dignity of human nature, united with his moderation and good sense, made him the ideal spokesman of a middle-class revolution. As a force in propagating the ideals of liberal but not violent reform Locke probably stands before all other writers whatsoever. Even his more doubtful ideas, such as the separation of powers and the inevitable wisdom of majority-decisions, remained a part of the democratic creed.

In the course of the eighteenth century the system of natural law, which provided the logical basis for Locke's political philosophy, receded gradually from the dominating position which it held in the scientific thought of the seventeenth century. This was due in part to a general progress of empirical method both in the natural sciences and in social studies, but in no small degree to the development of those parts of the Locke's philosophy which stressed the importance of a natural history of human understanding. This development followed lines already suggested by Locke himself. It greatly expanded the psychological explanation of behavior, making it depend upon the pursuit of pleasure and the avoidance of pain as its sole motives. In place of the rational standard of inherent good sought by the theory of natural law it put a utilitarian theory of moral, political, and economic value.

About the middle of the century Hume showed that this development, if logically carried through, made it possible to dispense with the theory of natural law altogether. The internal structure of Locke's political philosophy was thus completely destroyed. Yet most of its practical purposes and much of its inward spirit passed over to utilitarianism. Though less explicitly a defense of revolution, it continued Locke's spirits of cautions but radical reform. Its programme continued the same idealization of individual rights, the same beliefs in liberalism as a panacea for political ills, the same tenderness for the rights of property, and the same conviction that public interests must be conceived in terms of private well-being.

NOTES

1. Halifax's works have been edited by Walter Raleigh, Oxford, 1912; they are printed also in H. C. Foxcroft's *Life and Letters of Sir George Savile, Bart., First Marquis of Halifax*, 2 vols., London, 1898. His most important essays are "The Character of a Trimmer," written in 1684 and first printed in 1688; "A Rough Draught of a New Model at Sea," published in 1694 from an essay first written much earlier; and "The Anatomy of an Equivalent," 1688. All were occasional pieces.
2. Foxcroft, Vol. II, p. 492
3. *Ibid.*, p.497
4. *Trimmer* (ed. By Raleigh), p. 60.
5. *Ibid.*, p.54
6. *Two Treatises of Government;* probably written in 1681. See P. Laslett, "The English Revolution and Locke's Two Treatises of Government," *Camb. Hist. J.*, XII (1965), pp. 40 ff. Locke published three letters *Concerning Toleration* in 1689, 1690, and 1692.
7. *Of Civil Government* (Book II), sect. 25.
8. *Ibid.*, sect. 3.
9. *Ibid.*, sect. 99.
10. *Ibid.*, sect. 131
11. *Ibid.*, sect. 96
12. See the accounts of Whig principles in Burke's *Appeal from the New to the Old Whigs.*
13. *Commentaries*, Bk.1. ch.2, sect.2.

REFERENCES

Locke on Peace and War. By Richard Cox. New York, 1960.

John Locke, A Biography. By M.W. Cranston. London, 1957.

Life and Letters of Sir George Savile, Bart., First Marquis of Halifax. By H.C. Foxcroft. 2 vols. London, 1898.

A Character of the Trimmer: Being a Short Life of the First Marquis of Halifax. By H.C. Foxcroft. 2 vols. Cambridge, 1946.

John Locke's Political Philosophy. By J. W. Gough. Oxford, 1950.

The Social Contract. By J.W. Gough. 2nd ed. Oxford, 1957. Ch. 9.

Religious Toleration in England." By H.M. Gwatkin. In the *Cambridge Modern History,* Voll. V. (1908), ch.1.

The Library of John Locke. By John Harrison and Peter Laslett. Oxford 1965.

The Social and Political Ideas of Some English Thinkers of the Augustan Age, A.D. 1650-1750. Ed. By F.J. C. Hearnshaw, London, 1928. Chs. 3, 4.

John Locke and the Doctrine of Majority-rule. By Willmoore Kendall. Urbana, III., 1941.

The Moral and Political Philosophy of John Locke. By Sterling P. Lamprecht. New York, 1918.

Property in the Eighteen Century, with Special Reference to England and Locke. By Paschal Larkin. London, 1930.

Political Thought in England from Locke to Bentham. By Harold J. Laski. London, 1920.

"The English Revolution and Locke's Two Treatises of Government." By Peter Laslett. *In the Cambridge Historical Journal,* Vol. XII (1956), pp. 40-55

John Locke: Essays on the Law of Nature. Ed. By W. von Leyden. Oxford, 1954.

John Locke, A Critical Introduction. By John D. O'Connor. Baltimore, 1952.

Locke's Theory of the State. Pollock, Sir Frederick, In: *Essay in the Law.* London, 1922. Ch. 3.

Smith, Arthur Lionel, English Political Philosophy in the Seventeenth and Eighteenth Centuries." In: *The Cambridge Modern History,* Vol. VI (1909), ch.23.

Vaughan. C.E., *Studies in the History of Political Philosophy before and after Rousseau.* By . 2 vols. Manchester, 1925. Vol. 1, Ch. 4

Yolton, John W., "Locke on the Law of Nature." In: *The Philosophical Review,* Vol. LXVII (1959), pp. 477-498.

Koelln, Fritz C. A., and James P. Pettegrove, *The Philosophy of the Enlightment.* Ernst Cassirer. Eng. Trans. By . Princeton, N. J., 1951.

Courtney, C.P., *Montesquieu and Burke.* By . Oxford, 1963.

Montesquieu and English Politics (1750-1800). By F.T.H. Fletcher, London, 1939.

The Faith of Reason: The Idea of Progress in the French Enlightenment. By Charles Frankel. New York, 1948.

Condorcet on the Progress of the Human Mind. By Sir James George Frazer. Oxford, 1933.

Voltaire's Politics: The Poet as Realist. By Peter Gay. Princeton, N.J., 1959.

Turgot. By C.J. Gignoux. Paris, 1945

The Social and Political Ideas of Some Great French Thinkers of the Age of Reason. Ed. by F.J. C. Hearnshaw. London, 1930. Chs. 5, 6, 8.

"The Age of Reason." Diderot." by Harold J. Laski. In *Studies in Law and Politics*. London, 1932.

The Rise of European Liberalism: An Essay in interpretation. By Harold J. Laski. London, 1936. Ch. 3.

The Political Doctrine of Montesquieu's Esprit des lois. By Lawrence M. Levin. New York, 1936.

French liberal Thought in the Eighteenth Century: A Study of Political Ideas from Bayle of Condorcet. By Kingsley Martin. 2nd ed. Rev. London 1954.

Voltaire: *Man of Justice*. By Adolph Meyer. London, 1952.

Natural Rights: *A Criticism of Some Political and Ethical Coriceptions*. By David G. Ritchie. London, 1895.

The *Pioneers of the French Revolution*. By Marius Roustan. Eng. trans. by Frederic Whyte. Boston, 1926.

Voltaire and the State. By Constance Rowe. New York, 1955.

Progress in the Age of Reason. By R.V. Sampson, Canbridge, Mass., 1956.

Condorcet and the rise of Liberalism. By J. Salwyn Schapiro. New York, 1934.

Montesquieu: A Critical Biography. By Robert Shacleton. New York, 1961.

Montesquieu in America, 1760-1801. By Paul M. Spurlin. University, Louisiana, 1940.

Baron d' Holbach: A Prelude to the French Revolution. By W.H.. Wickwar. London, 1935.

6

The Rediscovery of the Community: Rousseau

Between the writers most characteristic of the French Enlightenment and Jean Jacques Rousseau is fixed a great gulf. Its existence was patent to everyone concerned; its exact nature has never been finally settled. Diderot described it as "the vast chasm between heaven and hell" and said that the very idea of Rousseau disturbed his work "as if I had a damned soul at my side." Rousseau in turn said that any man who could doubt his honest "deserved the gibbet." All Europe resounded with the quarrel and the bitterness on both sides passes belief. Even the elementary question of personal honest is still debated, though probably few now believe that Diderot was anything but an upright man or that Rousseau was really a hypocrite. Thomas Carlyle once said that he differed from Sterling only in his "opinions." Rousseau differed from his contemporaries in everything but his opinions; even when he used the same words he meant something different. His character, his outlook on life, his scale of values, his instinctive reactions, all differed essentially from what the Enlightenment regarded as admirable. The twelve years from 1744 to 1756 that he spent in Paris brought him into close association with the circle that wrote the *Encyclopaedia* but they only produced on both sides the conviction that Rousseau did not belong there.

This opposition, and indeed all that Rousseau wrote on philosophy and politics, grew in some devious way from his complex and unhappy personality. His *Confessions* gives a clear picture of a deeply divided personality, in which morbidities both of sex and religion played a large part. "My tastes and thoughts," he says, "always seemed to fluctuate between the noble and the base." His relations with women, both real and imaginary, display a violent sensuality failing alike of animal satisfaction or effective sublimation, but issuing in a riot of sentimental fancy and introspective attitudinizing. For him the discipline, intellectual or moral, characteristic of Calvinism in its more vital forms had never existed. But he continued to be bedevilled by a Puritan conscience, a sense of sin, and the fear of damnation. It had little effect perhaps on what he did but it produced, by way of compensation, a fine crop of moral sentiments. "I easily forget my misfortunes, but I cannot forget my faults, and still less my virtuous sentiments." Rousseau's passionate belief that men are naturally good, which he once said was the fundamental principal of his ethical writings, was less an intellectual conviction than a reversal of his innate fear that he was bad. By throwing the fault on society he was able at once to satisfy his need for condemnation and to shelter himself in a comfortable myth.

This conflict in Rousseau's personality between the noble and the base, the ideal and the real, robbed him of all satisfaction in his work or confidence in its value. The inception of an idea was like a light from heaven, resolving "all the contradictions of our social system." The expression conveyed not one-quarter of the vague but glittering vision. In social relations he labored under a painful sense of inadequacy, stupidity, and self-distrust. He seems never to have been comfortable except with women and in relationships practically devoid of intellectual content. By inclination he was parasitic and during considerable periods he lived in a state of semi-dependence, but he could never accept dependence gracefully. Instead, he built around himself a myth of pseudo-Stoicism and fictitious self-sufficiency, which expressed itself most definitely in suspicion of those who tried to be-friend him and in the discovery of elaborate plots, probably imaginary, to ruin and betray him. Before the end of his life these suspicions became well-defined delusions of persecution. Despite his years of not uncongenial vagabondage, he represented in taste and morals the sentimentality of the lower middle class. Essentially he was interested in homely things, was terrified of science and art, distrusted polished manners, sentimentalized commonplace virtues, and enthroned sense above intelligence.

The Revolt Against Reason

More than most men Rousseau projected the contradictions and maladjustments of his own nature upon the society about him and sought an anodyne for his own painful sensitivity. For this purpose he adopted the familiar contrast between the natural and the actual, current in all the appeals to reason. But Rousseau did not appeal to reason. On the contrary he turned the contrast into an attack upon reason. Against intelligence, the growth of knowledge, and the progress of science, which the Enlightenment believed to be the only hope of civilization, he set amiable and benevolent sentiments, the good will, and reverence. What gives value to life is the common emotions, perhaps one might say instincts, in respect to which men differ hardly at all and which he imagined to exist in a purer and less perverted form in the simple uneducated man than in the enlightened and sophisticated. "A thinking man is a depraved animal." All his moral valuations turned upon the worth of these common feelings: the affections of family life, the joy and beauty of motherhood, the satisfactions of the homely arts like tilling the soil, the universal feeling of religious reverence, above all, the sense of a common lot and the sharing of a common life—all that men learned after him to call the "realities" of everyday living. By contrast science is the fruit of idle curiosity; philosophy is mere intellectual frippery; the amenities of polite life are tinsel.

The hero of Rousseau's primitivism was not the noble savage; it was the irritated and bewildered bourgeois, at odds with a society that despised and looked down on him, conscious of his own purity of heart and the greatness of his own deserts, and profoundly shocked at the badness of the philosophers to whom nothing was sacred. By some queer logic of the motions, therefore, he joined in an equal condemnation both the social order that oppressed him and the philosophy which had attacked the foundations of that society. Against both he set up the pieties and the virtues of the simple heart. The truth is that Rousseau first made vocal a newly awakened fear, the fear that rational criticism, having demolished the more inconvenient pieties like the dogmas and disciplines of the church, might not be made to stop before the pieties which it still seemed judicious to retain.

These vain and futile declaimers [the philosophers] go forth on all

> *sides, armed with their fatal paradoxes, to sap the foundations of our faith, and nullify virtue. They smile contemptuously at such old names as patriotism and religion, and consecrate their talents and philosophy to the destruction and defamation of all that men hold sacred.*[1]

In short, intelligence is dangerous because it undermines reverence; science is destructive because it takes away faith; reason is bad because it sets prudence against moral intuition. Without reverence, faith, and moral intuition there is neither character nor society. This was a note which the Enlightenment could not easily understand—unless it were a covert defense of revaluation and the church, as in fact it was not—for the Enlightenment was accustomed to center its faith and its hope in reason and science. The enormous importance of Rousseau lies in the fact that, broadly speaking, he carried philosophy with him against its own tradition. Kant acknowledged that Rousseau had first revealed to him the surpassing value of the moral will as compared with scientific inquiry, and Kant's philosophy, if not the beginning of a new age of faith, at least began a new division between science on the one side and religion and morals on the other. In this new alignment philosophy was less the ally of science than the protector of religion. Science must be carefully confined to the phenomenal world, where it can do no harm to the verities of the heart, to religion and the moral law. To say that science knows only appearances at least suggests that there is some other way of knowing realities. Philosophy, once released from science, did not always walk soberly with the moral law. Sometimes it sought the higher truth by ways non-rational and irrational, by faith, by the light of genius, by metaphysical intuition, or in the will. The distrust of intelligence was written large over the philosophy of the nineteenth century.

A political philosophy which, like Rousseau's, began by magnifying the moral sentiments against reason, might be carried out in a variety of ways but it was bound to be contrary to the traditional liberalism either of natural rights or of utility. Both Rousseau and Kant denied that rational self-interest is a reputable moral motive and excluded prudence from the list of moral virtues. The outcome might be a more radical doctrine of equality that could be defended on grounds of reason and individual rights, since Rousseau supposed that the moral virtues exist in the greatest purity among the common people. As he said in *Emile*:

> *It is the common people who compose the human race; what is not the people is hardly worth taking into account. Man is the same in all ranks; that being so, the ranks which are most numerous deserve most respect.*[2]

A democracy of this sort, however, need imply very little personal liberty because it attaches only slight importance to individual preeminence. An ethics that identifies morality with rational self-interest as least presumes freedom of private judgement, but an ethics of sentiment, especially if it stresses sentiments that are equally native to all men, need not do so. In the end what it is most certain to inoculate is reverence for the authority of tradition and custom. The morality of the plain man, however much of the good will it may embody, is inevitably the morality of his time and place. Its standards are rather those of the group than of the individual, and such a morality always teaches submission to the group and conformity to its customary duties. This being so, there is no assurance that they will turn out in the end to be democratic at all. It was more or less an accident that Rousseau put a high estimate on a simple society with no marked differences of rank. The virtues of loyalty and patriotism, which he chiefly admired, and the glory of finding happiness in the welfare of the group, need have no special reference to democracy. It is hard to say whether Rousseau belonged more truly to Jacobin republicanism or to a conservative reaction.

Man as Citizen

It is convenient to distinguish between two periods of Rousseau's political writing, a formative period dated about 1754-55, in which he gave shape to his own ideas in opposition to Diderot,[3] and the period in which the final version of the *Social Contract* was prepared for publication in 1762. Many critics have felt a fundamental logical discrepancy between the works of these two periods, described by Vaughan as "the defiant individualism of the *Discours sur l'inegalite* and "the equally defiant collectivism of the *Contrat social.*" It is certain that Rousseau himself felt no such opposition; in the *Confessions* he says that "every strong idea in the *Social Contract* had been before published in the *Discourse on Inequality.*" In general Rousseau's opinion was correct, though it is also true that incompatible ideas abound throughout his writings. Much that seems like "defiant individualism" persisted in the *Social Contract*, and none of his works can be reduced to a consistent system. The difference between the earlier works and the *Social Contract* is merely that in the former he was writing himself free from an uncongenial social philosophy and in the latter he was expressing, as clearly as he could, a counter-philosophy of his own.

The social philosophy from which Rousseau had to disentangle himself was the systematic individualism which, by the time he wrote, was attributed to Locke. It held that the value of any social group consists in the happiness or self-satisfaction which it produces for its members, and especially in the protection of their inherent right to own and enjoy property. Human beings are led to cooperate by enlightened self-interest and a nice calculation of individual advantage. A community is essentially utilitarian; in itself it has no value though it protects values; the motive on which it rests is universal selfishness; and it contributes mainly to the comfort and security of its members. Quite rightly Rousseau attributed this philosophy as much to Hobbes as to Locke. Against Hobbes he brought the pertinent objection that the state of war attributed to individual men in a state of nature really belongs to "public persons" or "moral beings called sovereigns."[4] Men fight not as detached individuals but as citizens or subjects.

The writer who did most to release Rousseau from this individualism was Plato. With Rousseau there begins, in fact, a new era of classical influence in political philosophy, which was extended through Hegelianism and which was more genuinely Greek than the pseudo-classicism of the eighteenth century. What Rousseau got from Plato was a general outlook. It included, first, the conviction that political subjection is essentially ethical and only secondarily a matter of law and power. Second and more important, he took from Plato the presumption, implicit in all the philosophy of the city-state, that the community is itself the chief moralizing agency and therefore represents the highest moral value. The philosophy to which Rousseau stood opposed began with fully formed individuals; to them it imputed a full complement of interests and the power to calculate—a desire for happiness, the idea of ownership, the power to communicate with other men, to bargain with them, to make an agreement, and finally to make a government that will give the agreement force. Plato stimulated Rousseau to ask, Where do individuals get all these capacities except from society? Within a society there may be individuality, freedom, self-interest, respect for covenants; outside it there is nothing moral. From it individuals get their mental and moral faculties and by it they become human; the fundamental moral category is not man but citizen.

To this conclusion Rousseau was led also by his own citizenship in the city-state of Geneva. It is difficult to see in his early life that this ever exerted any tangible influence on him while he was subject to it, but afterward he rationalized and idealized it. This may be seen in the dedication which he placed before the *Discourse on Inequality*, written at a time when he planned to make Geneva his home. This idealization of the city-state was one reason why his political philosophy never articulated closely with contemporary politics. In formulating a theory he never envisaged a state on a national scale, and in writing on concrete questions, his views had little to do with his theories. Rousseau himself was in no sense a nationalist, though his philosophy contributed to nationalism. By reviving the intimacy of feeling and the reverence connoted by citizenship in the city-state, he made it available, at least as an emotional coloring, to citizenship in the national state. The cosmopolitanism implied by natural law he chose to regard as merely a pretext for evading the duties of a citizen.

During the two years in which his political ideas were forming, Rousseau was largely concerned with the meaning of conventional expressions such as the "state of nature" or the "natural man," which were obviously incompatible with his own idea that men have no moral qualities outside a community. A difference of opinion on this subject with Diderot began the life-long quarrel between the two men. The volume of the *Encyclopaedia* published in 1755 contained an article on Natural Law by Diderot and one on Political Economy by Rousseau: about the same time he wrote a criticism of Diderot's article for the *Social Contract* but later excluded it from the final draft.

Diderot's article was a rhetorical flourish with conventional ideas: Man is rational; his rationality subjects him to the law of natural equity; the test of morals and government is the general will of the race, embodied in the law and practices of civilized peoples. Its very conventionality made it the proper object for Rousseau's attack; he dissented from every article of the accepted creed. In the first place, the society of the whole human race is a "veritable chimera"; a race is not a society because mere likeness of kind creates no real union, while a society is a "moral person" arising from a real bond (*liaison*) uniting its members. A society must have common possessions, such as a common language and a common interest and well-being, which is not a sum of private goods but the source of them. The human race as a whole has nothing of this sort in common. In the second place, it is absolutely false that reason by itself would ever bring men together, if they were concerned only with their individual happiness, as the conventional theory supposes. The whole argument is fictitious because all our ideas, even of self-interest, are drawn from the communities in which we live. Self-interest is not more natural or more innate than the social needs that draw men together in communities. Finally, if there is any idea of a general human family, it arises from the little communities in which men live instinctively; an international community is the end and not the beginning.

> *We conceive a general society according to our particular societies; the establishment of little states makes us think of large ones; and we begin properly to become men only after we have become citizens. This shows what we should think of those pretended cosmopolitans who, in justifying their love for their country by their love for the human race, make a boast of loving all the world in order to enjoy the privilege of loving no one.*[5]

Nature and the Simple Life

The argument of the *Discourse on Inequality,* which was published at about the same time, was seriously clouded by the arresting attack on private property for which the work has been mainly known. Obviously if there are no rights of man, property is not one; in his *Plan for a Constitution of Corsica* Rousseau even said that the state ought to be the sole owner. But certainly he was not a communist. In the article on Political Economy he referred to property as "the most sacred of all the rights of citizenship" and even in the *Discourse* itself he treated it as a quite indispensable social right. It is true that the half-century before the Revolution produced in France schemes of utopian communism which bear about the same relation to middle-class radicalism as Winstanley's communism to the political doctrine of the English Levellers. Meslier before Rousseau and Mably and Morelly after him sketched "natural" schemes of society in which goods, especially land, were to be owned in common and the produce shared, and in the revolutionary era itself Marechal's *Manifesto of Equals* and Babeuf's communist uprising in 1796 carried on the idea that political freedom is a superficial remedy without economic equality. To this body of communist ideas Rousseau's attack on private property in the *Discourse* may be said vaguely to belong. But he had no serious idea of abolishing property and no very definite idea about its place in the community. What Rousseau contributed to socialism, utopian or other, was the much more general idea that all rights, including those of property, are rights within the community and not against it.

As a whole the *Discourse* was meant to deal with the same question as the chapter in criticism of Diderot's article on Natural Law. It was this which Rousseau put into the Preface as the problem of the book: What really is natural and what is artificial is human nature? In general terms his answer is that, over and above self-interest, men have an innate revulsion against suffering in others. The common basis of sociability is not reason but feeling; except to the perverted man suffering anywhere is directly painful. In this sense men are "naturally" good. The calculating egoist of the theories exists not in nature but only in a perverted society. The philosophers "know very well what a citizen of London or Paris is but not what a man is."[6] What then is the truly natural man? The answer cannot be drawn from history because if natural men ever exited, they certainly do not now. If one tries to make a hypothetical picture, the answer is certain: Natural man was an animal whose behaviour was purely instinctive; any thought whatever is "depraved." He wholly lacked language, unless in the form of instinctive cries, and without language any general idea is impossible. Consequently the natural man was neither moral nor vicious. He was not unhappy but neither was he happy. Obviously he had no property, for property resulted from ideas, foreseen wants, knowledge, industry, which were not intrinsically natural but implied language, thought, and society. Selfishness, taste, regard for the opinion of others, the arts, war, slavery, vice, conjugal and paternal affection all exist in men only as they are sociable beings who live together in larger or smaller groups.

This argument was quite general: it proved merely that the natural egoist is a fiction, that some kind of community is inevitable, and that no society is purely instinctive. Rousseau intertwined with it, however, another argument that was logically irrelevant. His early writings far more than the *Social Contract* are filled with a kind of pessimism, probably the result of irritation induced by his residence in Paris, which made him believe that existing French society was little more than an instrument of exploitation. Grinding poverty in one class contributes merely to parasitic luxury in another; the arts fling "garlands of flowers over men's chains" because they are beyond the reach of the masses on whose labour they are supported; and economic exploitation issues naturally in political depostism. Against this perverted society Rousseau chose to set an idealized simple society which is in a just mean between primitive indolence and civilized egoism. Evidently the conclusion that existing societies are perverted and should be simplified has nothing to do with the prior conclusion that some kind of society is the only moralizing force in human life. If society as such were a perversion, the conclusion would be that it ought to be abolished: Rousseau has been accused of timidity for not drawing it. In fact this was not his conclusion. The simple society that he chose to admire is very far removed, as he was at pains to show, from natural instinct. For this reason it is not very clear just what practical consequences, if any, do flow from his criticism of the state of nature. It all depends on the nature of the society in which the individual is to be imbedded. A national state, a militant working-class, or ultramontane Catholicism might all claim, as easily as the city-state that Rousseau affected, to represent the ultimate value to which men ought to give their loyalty. The implications can be conservative quite as easily as radical.

Of the early works that which stated Rousseau's political theory most clearly is the article on Political Economy in the fifth volume of the *Encyclopaedia*. It was evidently in some sense a companion-piece to Diderot's article on Natural Law in the same volume. Rousseau's most characteristic political idea, the "general will," appeared in both, and it is uncertain whether he or Diderot invented the term. Certainly Rousseau made it his own. His article touched briefly on most of the ideas developed later in the *Social Contract*—the theory that a community has a corporate personality or *mol commun*, the organic analogy for a social group, the doctrine that the general will of the corporate self sets the moral standards valid for its members, and the implied reduction of government to a mere agent of the general will. The general principle behind the argument is that already mentioned, that mere likeness of kind does not make men into a society but only a psychological or spiritual bond—"the reciprocal sensibility and internal correspondence of all the parts"—analogous to the vital principle of a living organism.

> *The body politic, therefore, is also a moral being possessed of a will; and this general will, which tends always to the preservation and welfare of the whole and of every part, and is the source of the laws, constitutes for all the members of the state, in their relations to one another and to it, the rule of what is just or unjust.*[7]

The tendency to form societies is a universal trait; wherever individuals have a common interest they form a society, permanent or transient, and every society has a general will which regulates the conduct of its members. Larger societies are composed not directly of individuals but of smaller societies, and each more inclusive society sets the duties of the smaller societies that compose it. Thus Rousseau still left standing the "great society," the human race, of which natural law is the general will, but as a society rather than as a race. The bonds of this society, however, are obviously weak. In effect Rousseau sets up patriotism as the supreme virtue and the source of all other virtues.

> *It is certain that the greatest miracles of virtue have been produced by patriotism: this fine and lively feeling, which gives to the force of self-love all the beauty of virtue, lends it an energy which, without disfiguring it, makes it the most heroic of all passions.*[8]

Human beings must be made citizens before they can be made men, but in order that they may be citizens, governments must give liberty under the law, must provide for material welfare and remove gross inequality in the distribution of wealth, and must create a system of public education by which children are "accustomed to regard their individuality only in its relation to the body of the state." The general problem of a political philosophy Rousseau stated almost in the form of the paradox with which he opened the *Social Contract*:

> *By what inconceivable art has a means been found of making men free by making them subject?*[9]

The General Will

The *Social Contract* was published in 1762. By Rousseau's account it was a part of a much larger work which he had projected but was not able to finish. The plan of this larger work is unknown, but in view of the arrangement of subject-matter in the *Social Contract* itself, he probably began by stating abstractly his theory of the general will and then went on to make observations at large about history and politics. The latter part of the book as published retains traces of the reading of Montesquieu, as did also Rousseau's published plan for a constitution of Corsica and his *Considerations sur le gouvernement de Pologne*. The *Social Contract*, in its theoretical part, is excessively abstract; when Rousseau writes on current questions it is usually difficult to see what the theory that has to do with his proposals or the proposals with the theory. It is safe to say, therefore, that nothing was lost when he abandoned his more extended work. The general will and the criticism of natural right comprised everything of importance that he had to say. The practical uses to which that theory might be put were various, and Rousseau had neither the knowledge nor the patience to explore them. His belief that a small community like the city-state is the best example of the general will made it impossible for him to discuss contemporary politics with much point.

The development of the theory of the general will in the *Social Contract* was involved in paradoxes, partly because of the cloudiness of Rousseau's ideas but partly, it seems, because he had a rhetorician's liking for paradox. Manifestly, in view of his criticism of the natural man, he ought to have avoided the notion of contract altogether as both meaningless and misleading. Seemingly he retained the phrase because he liked its popular appeal, and in order not to make the inconsistency too glaring, he deleted the criticism of the state of nature which he had written against Diderot. Not content with this complication, after introducing the contract he explained it away, so far as any definite contractual meaning was concerned. In the first place, his contract has nothing to do with the rights and powers of government, since the latter is merely the people's agent and is so devoid of independent power that it cannot be the subject of a contract. In the second place, the imaginary act by which a society is produced is not even remotely like a contract, because the rights and liberties of individuals have no existence at all except as they are already members of the group. Rousseau's whole argument depended upon the fact that a community of citizens is unique and coeval with its members; they neither make it nor have rights against it. It is an "association" not an "aggregation," a moral and collective personality. The word contract was about as misleading as any that Rousseau could have chosen.

> *The social order is a sacred right which is the basis of all other rights.*[10]
>
> *The problem is to find a form of association which will defend and protect with the whole common force the person and goods of each associate, and in which each, while uniting himself with all, may still obey himself alone, and remain as free as before.*
>
> *Each of us puts his person and all his power in common under the supreme direction of the general will, and, in our corporate capacity, we receive each member as an indivisible part of the whole.*[11]

Another paradox lay in the fact that Rousseau could not persuade himself to give over trying to prove that men individually gain more by being members of society than they would by remaining isolated. This is implied in the famous sentence with which the *Social Contract* opened and in which he proposed to explain what can make the bondage of society "legitimate." This way of putting the question implied that Rousseau was going to show, as Holbach or Helvetius might, that being a member of society is on the whole a good bargain. Of course he was going to do nothing of the sort, if the state of nature was a chimera and all the values by which the bargain might be judged were non-existent except in a society. Similarly, the assertion that man "is everywhere in chains" implied that society is a burden for which individuals need to be compensated, whereas Rousseau was going to argue that they are not human at all except as members of a community. A bad community might impose chains on its members, but Rousseau was logically bound to hold that it did so because it was bad and not because it was a community. The question, what justifies the existence of communities, should have been treated by him as non-sensical. The question, what makes one community better than another, is of course legitimate; it would involve a comparison of communities in terms of the social and individual interests that each conserves, but not a comparison between a community and its absence. Again, an individual might be better off in one community than in another, but the question whether he would be better or worse off in no community ought to have been ruled out as unmeaning. For it was society, he said, that "substituted justice for instinct and gave men's actions the morality they had formerly lacked." "Instead of a stupid and unimaginative animal, it made him an intelligent being and a man." Apart from society there would be no scale of values in terms of which to judge well-being.

The general will, therefore, represented a unique fact about a community, namely, that it has a collective good which is not the same thing as the private interests of its members. In some sense it lives its own life, fulfills its own destiny, and suffers its own fate. In accordance with the analogy of an organism, which Rousseau had developed at some length in the article on Political Economy, it may be said to have a will of its own, the "general will" (*volonte generale*):

> *If the state is a moral person whose life is in the union of its members, and if the most important of its cares is the care for its own preservation, it must have a universal and compelling force, in order to move and dispose each part as may be most advantageous to the whole.*[12]

The rights of individuals, such as liberty, equality, and property, which natural law attributed to men as such, are really the rights of citizens. Men become equal, as Rousseau says, "by convention and legal right," not, as Hobbes had said, because their physical power is substantially equal.

> *The right which each individual has to his own estate is always subordinate to the right which the community has over all.*[13]

In the community men first gain civil liberty, which is a moral right and is not merely the "natural liberty" which by a figure of speech might be attributed to a solitary animal.

The Paradox of Freedom

So far this is perfectly true and a fair reply to the extravagances of contemporary speculation about the state of nature. Just what it entails, however, about the rights of men in society is far from obvious, and Rousseau's account of the matter sometimes contradicted itself within the limits of a single page. For example:

> *The social compact gives the body politic absolute power over all its members.*
>
> *Each man alienates, I admit, by the social compact, only such part of his powers, goods and liberty as it is important to the community to control; but it must also be granted that the sovereign is sole judge of what is important.*
>
> *But the sovereign, for its part, cannot impose upon its subjects any fetters that are useless to the community.*
>
> *We can see from this that the sovereign power, absolute, sacred, and inviolable as it is, does not and cannot exceed the limits of general conventions, and that every man may dispose at will of such goods and liberty as these conventions leave him.*[14]

In fact, Rousseau moved back and forth at will between his own theory of the general will and the indefeasible individual rights which ostensibly he had abandoned. In itself the mere fact that rights of any sort require social recognition and can be defended only in terms of a common good signifies nothing about what individual rights a well-regulated community will give to its members. Since Rousseau believed as a matter of course that social well-being itself dictates some liberty of individual choice and action, wherever he meets this sort of case he sets it down as a limitation upon the general will. Logically it is nothing of the sort, if liberty itself is one of the things that the general good requires. On the other hand, Rousseau was quite capable of arguing that because there are no indefeasible rights in defiance of the general good, there are no individual rights at all. This again was a logical confusion, unless one argues, as Rousseau certainly did not mean to do, that all liberty is contrary to the social good. The truth is that the general will is so abstract—asserting merely that rights are social—that it justified no inference at all about the extent to which individuals might wisely be left to their own devices within society. At the same time the general position was of course valid against a theory of natural rights that left social well-being entirely out of account. This confusion in Rousseau's argument gave rise to another paradox which is especially important and especially irritating, the paradox of freedom. He began by assuming a burden that was incumbent on egoistic theories but not upon him, provided he meant really to reject egoism, namely, to prove that in society a man "may still obey himself alone." Consequently he undertook nothing less than to show that real coercion never occurs in society and that what is taken to be coercion is only apparently so, a paradox of the worst sort. Even a criminal wills his own punishment!

> *In order then that the social compact may not be an empty formula, it tacitly includes the undertaking . . . that whoever refuses to obey the general will shall be compelled to do so by the whole body. This means nothing less than that he will be forced to be free. . . . This alone legitimizes civil undertakings, which, without it, would be absurd, tyrannical, and liable to the most frightful abuses.*[15]

In other words, coercion is not really coercion because when a man individually wants something different from what the social order gives him, he is merely capricious and does not rightly know his own good or his own desires.

This kind of argument, in Rousseau and after him in Hegel, was a dangerous experiment in juggling with ambiguities. Liberty had become what Thorstein Veblen called an "honorific" word, the name for a sentiment with which even attacks on liberty wished to be baptized. It was perfectly legitimate to point out that some liberties are not good, that liberty in one direction may entail loss of liberty in another, or that there are other political values which in some circumstances are more highly esteemed than liberty. Straining language to show that restricting liberty is really increasing it, and that coercion is not really coercion, merely made the vague language of politics still vaguer. But this was not the worst of it. What was almost inevitably implied was that a man whose moral convictions are against those commonly held in his community is merely capricious and ought to be suppressed.

This was perhaps not a legitimate inference from the abstract theory of the general will, because freedom of conscience really is a social and not merely an individual good. But in every concrete situation the general will has to be identified with some body of actual opinion, and moral intuitionism usually means that morality is identified with standards which are generally accepted. Forcing a man to be free is a euphemism for making him blindly obedient to the mass or the strongest party. Robespierre made the inevitable application when he said of Jacobins, "Our will is the general will."

> *They say that terrorism is the resort of despotic government. Is our government then like despotism? Yes, as the sword that flashes in the hand of the hero of liberty is like that with which the satellites of tyranny are armed. . . . The government of the Revolution is the depotism of liberty against tyranny.*[16]

The general will, as Rousseau said over and over again, is always right. This is merely a truism, because the general will stands for the social good, which is itself the standard of right. What is not right is merely not the general will. But how does this absolute right stand in relation to the many and possibly conflicting judgments about it? Who is entitled to decide what is right? Rousseau's attempts to answer these questions produced a variety of contradictions and evasions. Sometimes he said that the general will deals only with general questions and not with particular persons or actions, thus leaving the application to private judgement, but this conflicted with his assertion that the general will itself determines the sphere of private judgement. Sometimes he tried to make the general will equivalent to decision by a majority, but this would imply that the majority is always right, which he certainly did not believe. Sometimes he spoke as if the general will registered itself automatically by making differences of opinion cancel each other. This opinion cannot be refuted but neither can it be proved. It amounted to saying that communities—states or nations—have an inscrutable faculty for discerning their well-being and proper destiny. Rousseau originated the romantic cult of the group, and this was the fundamental difference between his social philosophy and the individualism from which he revolted. The rationalist centered his scheme of values in the culture of the individual, in intellectual enlightenment and independence of judgement and enterprise. Rousseau's philosophy emphasized the aggrandizement of a group, the satisfactions of participation, and the cultivation of the non-rational.

In Rousseau's intention the theory of the general will greatly diminished the importance of government. Sovereignty belongs only to the people as a corporate body, while government is merely an agent having delegated powers which can be withdrawn or modified as the will of the people dictates. Government has no vested right whatever, such as Locke's theory of the contract had left to it, but has merely the status of a committee. Rousseau conceived this to exclude any form of representative government, since the sovereignty of the people cannot be represented. The only free government is therefore a direct democracy in which the citizens can actually be present in town-meeting. Just why the general will should be restricted to this one form of expression is not very clear, apart from Rousseau's admiration for the city-state. Doubtless it was his belief that the theory of popular sovereignty diminished the power of the executive but this was an illusion. For though "the people" have all power and all moral right and wisdom, a corporate body cannot as such express its will or execute it. The ore the community is exalted the more authority its spokesmen have, whether they are called representatives or not. Even parties and factions, which Rousseau thoroughly detested, are more likely to be strengthened than weakened by the idea of corporate sovereignty. A well-regimented minority, whose leaders are persuaded of their own inspiration and whose members "think with their blood," has proved an almost perfect organ for the general will.

Rousseau and Nationalism

Rousseau's political philosophy was so vague that it can hardly be said to point in any specific direction. In the age of the Revolution probably Robespierre and the Jacobins owed most to him, for his theory of popular sovereignty and his denial of any vested right in government made, as Gierke said, a kind of doctrine of "permanent revolution" which was very suitable to the purposes of a radical democratic party. Moreover, there was really nothing in the conception of the general will that required it to be shared consciously by the whole people or to be expressed only in a popular assembly. Rousseau's enthusiasm for the democratic city-state was an anachronism. The small community with a prevailingly rural economy, loosely federated with other similar communities, which would perhaps have represented his ideals most literally, had no importance in Europe and only a passing importance in America. Though Rousseau believed that free citizenship was impossible in any form of larger state, it was inevitable under the circumstances that the sentiment which he aroused should result mainly in idealizing national patriotism. Thus in his essay on Poland he might advise a policy of decentralization, but the only effect of the work must lie in its appeal to Polish nationalism. On the other hand, he persistently libelled the humanitarian and cosmopolitan ideals of the Enlightenment as a mere lack of moral principle.

> *Today there are no longer Frenchmen, Germans, Spaniards, or even Englishmen; there are only Europeans. . . . They are at home wherever there is money to steal or women to seduce.*[17]

The net effect was a very uncritical adaptation of the ideal of citizenship as it had been in a city-state to the modern national state, which is an almost wholly different kind of social and political unit. Thus the state was idealized as including all the values of national civilization, much as the Greek city had overlapped nearly all phases of Greek life, though in fact no modern state did anything of the sort. Thus without being himself a nationalist, Rousseau helped to recast the ancient ideal of citizenship in a form such that national sentiment could appropriate it.

Nationalism, however, was not a simple force acting in a single direction or with a single motive. It might mean democracy and the rights of man, as in general it did in the age of the Revolution, but it might mean also an alliance between the landowning gentry and the new middle-class aristocracy of wealth. It might sweep away the remnants of feudal institutions only to build in their place new institutions that would rely no less heavily on traditional loyalties and the subordination of classes. Inevitably nationalism in France and England, where there was no doubt of political union, would be quite different from nationalism in Germany, where the aspiration for a national government commensurate with the unity of German culture would soon overtop all other questions. Rousseau's idealizing of the moral feelings of the plain man found an immediate echo in the ethics of Kant. Its full significance, especially his idealizing of the collective will and of participation in the common life, appeared in German philosophy with the idealism of Hegel. Rousseau's collectivism, however, required a drastic revaluation of custom, tradition, and the accumulating heritage of the national culture, without which the general will was nothing but an empty formula. This, in turn, amounted to a thoroughgoing revolution in philosophical values. Since the time of Descartes custom and reason had by common consent been set in contrast to one another. The proper work of reason had been to release men from the bondage of authority and tradition, in order that they might be free to follow the light of nature. This was the meaning of the whole imposing system of natural law. This the sentimentalism of Rousseau tacitly set aside. The idealism of Hegel tried to weave reason and tradition into a single unit—the expanding culture of a national spirit or consciousness. In effect reason was to be bent to the service of custom, tradition, and authority, with a corresponding emphasis on the values of stability, national unity, and continuity of development.

Hegel's philosophy conceived the general will as the spirit of the nation, expanding and embodying itself in a national culture and creating its organs in an historical constitution. Apart from the incoherence of Rousseau's presentation of it, the obvious defect of the general will as he left it was the extreme abstractness of the conception. It was the mere idea or form of a community, as Kant's categorical imperative was the mere form of a moral will. Nothing but historical accident, so to speak, attached it to the sense of membership in a nation and the idealizing of national citizenship. Rousseau's position as an alien in French national life, his moral incapacity to ally himself with any social cause, and the state of French politics when he wrote, all conspired to prevent him from giving to the general will any concrete embodiment. This want, however, was at once supplied by Edmund Burke. For Burke the conventions of the constitution, the traditional rights and duties of Englishmen, the living presence of a rich national culture growing from generation to generation were not abstractions but real existences, suffused with the warmth of ardent patriotism and the glow of moral sentiment. In the later years of his life the shock and horror of the French Revolution forced him to break the habit of a lifetime and to state in general terms the philosophy upon which he had always acted. The result was at once a contrast and a supplement to Rousseau. In Burke the corporate life of England became a conscious reality. The general will was released from temporary bondage to Jacobinism and made a factor in conservative nationalism.

Throughout the eighteenth century the tradition of philosophical rationalism and the system of natural law which was its most typical creation was in a state of gradual decadence. Rousseau's denial of it was largely a matter of feeling; he lacked the intellectual penetration and the steadiness of intellectual application to criticise the system in place of which he set up the autonomy of sentiment. But this criticism already existed, the work of David Hume. From the time of Locke, the growth of the empirical philosophy and the increasingly empirical practice of social studies had caused a steady infiltration of incongruous ideas into the system of natural law. Perhaps it would be truer to say that the system of natural law itself had included from the start, under the name of reason, a variety of factors which for the sake of clearness needed to be discriminated and which grew steadily more incongruous as social studies advanced. The breaking apart of the old system was due mainly to the analytic genius of Hume. His negative limitation of reason was really a logical precondition both of the value which Rousseau attributed to moral sentiment and of that which Burke attributed to a growing national tradition.

NOTES

1 *The Arts and Sciences*, Eng. trans. by G.D.H. Cole, *The Social Contract and Discourses* (Everyman's Library), p. 142.

2 Quoted by Morley, *Rousseau* (1886), Vol. II, pp. 226 f.

3 The chief works were the *Discours sur l'inegalite* (1754), the article in the *Encyclopaedia* on 'Economie politique" (1755), a suppressed chapter, "De la societe generale du genre humain" (I, ii), of the first draft of the *Contrat social*, and several unpublished fragments. The best edition is C.E. Vaughan's *Political Writings of Jean Jacques Rousseau*, 2 vols., Cambridge, 1915. The published works are translated by G.D.H. Cole, *The Social Contract and Discourses* (Everyman's Library).

4 The fragment on *L'etat de guerre*, Vaughan, Vol. I, p. 293.

5 Vaughan, vol. I, p. 453.

6 *L'etat de guerre*, Vaughan, Vol. I, p. 307.

7 Vaughan, Vol. I, pp. 241 f; Eng. trans. by G.D.H. Cole, p. 253.

8 Vaughan, Vol. I, p. 251; Eng. trans. by G.D.H. Cole, p. 263.

9 Vaughan, Vol. I, p. 245; Eng. trans. by G.D.H. Cole, p. 256.

10 *Social Contract*, I, i.

11 *Ibid.*, I, vi.

12 *Ibid.*, II, iv.

13 *Ibid.*, I, ix.

14 *Ibid.*, II, iv.

15 *Ibid.*, I, vii.

16 To the National Convention, February 5, 1794; *Moniteur universel*, 19 Pluviose, l' an 2, p. 562.

17 *Considerations sur le gouvernement de Pologne*, ch. 3; Vaughan, Vol. II, p. 432.

REFERENCES

Rousseau and Romanticism. By Irving Babbitt. Boston, 1919.

Rousseau: A Study of His Thought. By J.H. Broome. London, 1963.

The Question of Jean-Jacques Rousseau. By Ernst Cassirer. Eng. trans. and ed. by Peter Gay. New York, 1954.

Rousseau-Totalitarian or Liberal? By John W. Chapman. New York, 1956.

Rousseau and the Modern State. By Alfred Cobban. London, 1934.

The Early Rousseau. By Mario Einaudi. Ithaca, 1967.

Rousseau and the Idea of Progress. By Frederick C. Green. Oxford, 1950.

Jean-Jacques Rousseau: A Critical Study of His Life and Writings. By F.C. Green. Cambridge, 1955. Ch. 7.

Jean-Jacques Rousseau: Discours sur les sciences et les arts. Ed. by George R. Havens. New York, 1946. Introduction.

The Social and Political Ideas of Some Great French Thinkers of the Age of Reason. Ed. by F.J.C. Hearnshaw. London, 1930. Ch. 7.

Jean-Jacques Rousseau, Moralist. By Charles W. Hendel. 2 vols. London, 1934.

The Idea of Nationalism: A Study in Its Origins and Background. By Hans Kohn. New York, 1944. Ch. 5.

The Political Philosophy of Rousseau. By Roger D. Masters. Princeton, 1968.

Rousseau and the French Revolution. By Joan McDonald. London, 1965.

Rousseau and Burke: A Study of the Idea of Liberty in Eighteenth-century Political Thought. By Annie M. Osborn. New York, 1940.

La pensee de Jean-Jacques Rousseau: essai d' interpretation nouvelle. By Albert Schinz. Paris, 1929.

The Rise of Totalitarian Democracy. By J.L. Talmon. Boston, 1952.

The Political Writings of Jean-Jacques Rousseau. Ed. by C.E. Vaughan. 2 vols. Cambridge, 1915. Introduction.

The Political Tradition of the West: A Study in the Development of Modern Liberalism. By Frederick M. Watkins. Cambridge, Mass., 1948. Ch. 4.

"Rousseau's Political Religion," *Review of Politics* (October, 1965). By Fred H. Willhoite, Jr.

The Meaning of Rousseau. By Ernest H. Wright. London, 1929. Ch. 3.

7

Liberalism: Philosophical Radicalism

The reaction against the philosophy of natural rights which began with Rousseau and Burke and received its first systematic statement from Hegel by no means superseded the tradition of individualism which formed the main strand of political thinking throughout the seventeenth and eighteenth centuries. On the contrary this philosophy produced its chief practical consequences in the nineteenth century. Its history was an example of the paradox of which Hegel was so fond, that a philosophy is fully developed in its details and applications only when its main principles have come to be taken for granted and, to that extent, have become retarded in their speculative development. The principles of the Revolutionary Era, first clearly stated by Locke and embodied in great political manifestoes like the American declaration of Independence and the French and American bills of rights, summed up political ideals which in the nineteenth century seemed certain of progressive realization in the politics of all countries where the culture of Western Europe prevailed and might probably come to be realized throughout the world. These ideals included the civil liberties-freedom of thought, of expression, and of association-the security of property, and the control of political institutions by an informed public opinion. Everywhere, as it seemed, these ends were to be practically realized by the adoption of the forms of constitutional government, by the acceptance of the rules that government must work within the limits set by law, that the center of political authority should fall within representative legislatures, and that all branches of government should be responsible to an electorate that tended to include the entire adult population. These ideals, and this type of political agency for realizing them, had been defended in the name of natural rights and they continued to sum up the purposes and, broadly speaking, the achievements of nineteenth-century liberalism. At the core of this mode of political thought was a fundamental postulate about the nature of value, viz., that all value inheres ultimately in the satisfactions and the realizations of human personality. It was this postulate which Kant had expressed in his famous dictum that morality consists in treating persons as ends and not as means, and which Jefferson had affirmed when he said that governments exist to protect and realize the inalienable rights of man.

Yet between the philosophy of natural rights in the Revolutionary Era and the liberalism of the nineteenth century there was a profound difference of temper and spirit. The philosophy of natural rights was in essence a revolutionary creed; it could brook no compromise where a fundamental right was invaded. But the French Revolution bred in many quarters a reaction against revolution. On the Continent the imperial ambitions of Napoleon left the constitutional traditions of every western nation in ruins. Even in England, where this was not the case, the progress of parliamentary reform was checked by reaction and was resumed only with difficulty after 1815. Everywhere the Revolution produced, as revolutions are wont to do, a revulsion against its excesses, and it became the fashion to attribute these excesses to the *philosophes* and the rights of man. Chateaubriand expressed the temper of liberalism everywhere when he said, "We must preserve the political work which is the fruit of the Revolution . . . but we must eradicate the Revolution from this work." At a later date the same idea was expressed by idealizing evolution as the antithesis of revolution.

In part this moderating of the liberal attitude was due to philosophical reasons. The ethical theory upon which the philosophy of natural rights had depended was necessarily institutional. There is no way to defend a theory of imprescriptible individual rights except to affirm, as both Locke and Jefferson had done, that such rights are self-evident. But the drift of science in general and of social thought in particular was pretty steadily toward empiricism, and therefore away from the faith that a proposition may be taken as axiomatic because it appears to be obvious. In short, the authority of rationalism steadily diminished, and the theory of natural rights had always been an element of philosophical rationalism. More influential than any theoretical consideration, however, were no doubt the changes that naturally occurred in the outlook of the commercial and industrial middle class as its position and influence became more assured. This class everywhere formed the spearhead of liberal political reform in the nineteenth century, and the trend of industrial and commercial development made the expansion of its political power a foregone conclusion. Correspondingly, the influence of the landed gentry was relatively declining, and wage earners, at least during the first half or two-thirds of the century, had as yet attained little political self-consciousness and no effective organization. It is a gross exaggeration to say, as Marxian critics of liberalism often do say, that the ideals of constitutional government and personal liberty represented nothing but the interests of the middle class. It is a fact, however, that in the beginning this class was the main spokesman for these ideals and it is also a fact that the social position of this class made it progressively less revolutionary in its outlook and methods. When Francis Place could assure the passage of the Reform Bill of 1832 by threatening a run on the Bank of England, he was clearly not addressing a class which must exert its influence at the barricades.[1] It was also true as time went on that liberal political reform passed more and more out of the region of ideology and into that of institutional reconstruction. The modernizing of administration, the improvement of legal procedure, the reorganization of the courts, the creation of sanitary codes and factory inspection-all characteristic liberal reforms-were effected not by revolutionary enthusiasm but by hard, matter-of-fact research and the careful drafting of legislation. The ideals of liberalism were an aftermath of the Revolutionary Era but its achievements were largely the outcome of a high level of practical intelligence applied to specific problems. Its theory was still rationalistic but its rationalism was qualified by the realization that ideals have to be made effective in a multitude of concrete cases. Very naturally its philosophy tended to become utilitarian instead of revolutionary.

Political liberalism as a whole was a massive movement that made itself felt in all the countries of Western Europe and in

America but its most characteristic development took place in England. In Germany liberal philosophy remained for the most part academic, not deeply rooted in popular thought, and in 1848 the cause of parliamentary government and ministerial responsibility was definitely lost. The issue of liberal constitutionalism was overshadowed in the minds of Germans by the issue of national unification, and this was accomplished under the non-liberal auspices of Bismarck and the Hohenzollerns. Only in the German judicial system were such liberal values realized as security of property and a considerable measure of civil liberty, and German liberal theory was accordingly juristic rather than political. In France the most significant social consequence of the Revolution was perhaps the creation of five or six million peasant proprietors who were politically inert, except in their power to obstruct, and who felt their interests to be identical with those of the bourgeoisie. In opposition to both there grew up for the first time in Europe a proletarian working-class movement that was socialist and radical in its political outlook rather than liberal, a social development of momentous importance that was at once incorporated in Marx's theory of the class struggle. French liberalism, therefore, far more than English, tended to be the social philosophy of a class, rather aristocratic in its attitude toward "the masses," and mainly critical in function, since it could hardly aspire to carry through a national policy.[2] Only in England, which throughout the nineteenth century was the most highly industrialized country in the world, did liberalism achieve the status at once of a national philosophy and a national policy. Here, contrary to the expectation implied by Marxism, it provided the principles for an orderly and peaceful transition, first to complete freedom for industry and the enfranchisement of the middle class and ultimately to the enfranchisement of the working class and their protection against the most serious hazards of industry. This was possible because the cleavage between social and economic classes in England never coincided exactly with the lines between political parties. Even in its earlier stage, when its economic theories in particular represented clearly the interest of industrialists, English liberalism in intention at least was always a theory of the general good of the whole national community. In its later stages this intention became conscious and explicit, when it became apparent that other interests, especially those of labour and agriculture, had to be considered along with those of industry and commerce.

As an effective political movement liberalism in England was composed of many elements which learned to cooperate for specific purposes without insisting upon ideological agreement. Most striking of all, perhaps, was what Graham Wallas called "the tradition of a working alliance" between Evangelical Christianity and the non-religious radicalism of Jeremy Bentham and the Philosophical Radicals. The disparity of their philosophical beliefs was more than offset by the essential similarity of their moral and social purposes. The backbone of political liberalism, as Gladstone remarked, was the nonconformist religious sects.[3] At the start they had every motive to safeguard and extend their religious liberty and their participation in political rights. Though sometimes deficient in intellectual enlightenment they provided an element of Christian charity and humanitarianism which was lacking in the grim egoism of utilitarian ethics and of the classical economics. Moreover, the nonconformists as a body were not at all revolutionary or even radical in their political views. Because it held in suspension these and other groups with diverse ideologies, political liberalism was from the start less doctrinaire than its theory, and with time the conciliation of many interests became an overt part of its philosophy. It was the Philosophical Radicals, however, who provided the intellectual structure of early liberalism and therefore its programme. They were at all times a group of intellectuals rather than a political party, but their influence was never measured by their numbers. As so often happens in politics the intellectuals provided ideas which politicians used piecemeal, or sometimes not at all, according to the exigency of circumstances.

For the purpose of emphasizing this conciliatory and synthesizing phase of English liberal philosophy it is desirable that it should be divided into two periods and yet that the historical continuity of the two periods should be kept clearly in view. For the distinguishing characteristic of its history was its development from a philosophy which at the start could not unjustly be branded, as its critics generally have branded it, as the ideology of middle-class interests, into the philosophy of a national community whose ideal was to protect and conserve the interests of all classes. The development was possible because the criticism, though not unjust, was never wholly true. The early liberals, though they were often provincial and doctrinaire, were also profoundly and sincerely public-spirited men who turned a defective social philosophy to purposes which in a large measure were socially beneficent and were never in intention merely exploitative. It was for this reason that liberalism could transform itself into all intellectual bridge between the individualism of its earlier period, which was its heritage from the philosophy of the Revolutionary Era, and a recognition of the reality and the value of social and communal interests, which tended in general to put themselves forward in anti-liberal forms. Thus the purpose of later liberalism could become at once the conservation of the political and civil liberties which individualism embodied and the adaptation of them to the progressive changes of industrialism and nationalism that bred philosophies which threatened to nullify them. Acknowledging political freedom as an addition of permanent value to modern culture, liberalism could still accept the task of making it a good more accessible to a larger number of persons and hence a genuine social good. The division of liberalism into two periods is, therefore, somewhat more than an expository convenience. It is intended to suggest a change of great importance coupled with a continuity of equal importance. The dividing line can best be drawn, perhaps, at John Stuart Mill because his philosophy stood curiously on both sides of the line. Accordingly this chapter will deal with the classical version of liberalism, that of the Philosophical Radicals, the next with the revision and modernization of liberalism.

The Greatest Happiness Principle

The social philosophy of the Philosophical Radicals was in essence a programme of legal, economic, and political reforms connected as they supposed by the fact that they are all derivative from the principle of the greatest happiness of the greatest number. This principle they held to be the only rational guide both to private morals and to public policy, and the more theoretical part of their philosophy was designed to make this principle more accurately applicable to practical problems. In point of fact no member of the group, including Bentham himself, was in any way remarkable for philosophical originality or even for a very firm grasp of philosophical principles. The formal and deductive manner of presentation which they affected gave an appearance of system to their thought that turns out upon analysis to be deceptive. The order in which the several parts of the system appeared is significant of the fact that their relationship was practical rather than logical. Originally and indeed until he was nearly sixty years old Bentham was interested wholly in legal reforms, and he expected that these would be accomplished sooner by enlightened despotism than by political liberalism. Accordingly, after the publication of the *Principles of Morals and Legislation* in 1789, he preferred to address himself to a Continental public by publishing his later works on jurisprudence in French. It was not until the 1820s that his ideas came home to England by the translation of his French works or by the publication of new works such as the *Rationale of Judicial Evidence*, which John Stuart Mill edited from his manuscripts and published in 1827. In the meantime, about 1808, James Mill convinced Bentham that legal reform in England depended on the liberalizing of representation in Parliament, and it was only then that he abandoned the Tory politics in which he had been reared. The change was in no sense due to the logical dependence of liberalism upon the greatest happiness principle but solely to the hope that it might prove a more practicable agency of legal reform than aristocracy or enlightened depotism.

In a somewhat similar manner the economic theory of the Philosophical Radicals, which was mainly the work of Ricardo and was developed without any close relation to the legal reforms that interested Bentham, was directed from the start toward the practical purpose of freeing commerce from the restrictions imposed on it by a protective tariff on foodstuffs and by the navigation laws. These reforms also, like legal reform, could be achieved only by breaking down the political monopoly enjoyed by the English landowning class. It was not until practical purposes such as these were by way of being realized that James Mill undertook a theoretical examination of the psychological and philosophical principles upon which the group had always professed to rely. His *Analysis of the Phenomena of the Human Mind* was published in 1829, when he was already fifty-six years old. This book, which logically should have been the cornerstone of the system, was in truth little more than a systematization, in a deductive and highly dogmatic manner, of the associational psychology developed eighty years before by David Hartley, by the English moralists of the eighteenth century, and by French thinkers like Condilac and Helvetius. To this psychology Mill contributed little that was original and nothing that tended to bring it into line with a realistic study of human behavior based upon observation. The alleged empiricism of the Utilitarians was in fact filled with unexamined presumptions. The greatest happiness principle in ethics might have been adopted, as it often had been in the past, without the hedonistic psychology which was supposed to support it, and the reforms advocated in the name of the greatest happiness were implied only if the principle was supplemented by a large number of premises unrelated to the system.

The general outline of utilitarian thinking, apart from economics, was announced in Bentham's earliest work, the *Fragment on Government*, which he published 1776. This was a criticism of Blackstone's *Commentaries* and through him an attack upon the whole legal profession and upon the Whig conception of English government. Bentham thus announced his major interest, the cause of legal reform, and presented in outline the point of view which he was later to develop in a long series of books on jurisprudence. Blackstone's account of English law, he said, is at best merely expository-it describes the law as it is-or at worst it is an apology for the *status quo* disguised as an exposition. The true function of jurisprudence is "censorial," the criticism of the legal system with a view to its improvement. For such criticism a standard of value is required, and that can be supplied only by the principle of utility. "It is the greatest happiness of the greatest number that is the measure of right and wrong." This insight Bentham attributed to Hume; when he had first read Hume's ethical works, he said, he felt as if the scales had fallen from his eyes. Hume's criticism demolished the whole apparatus of indefeasible rights and contractual limitations on the power of government by showing them to be either meaningless or else confused references to the clear principle of utility. The basis of government is not contract but human need, and the satisfaction of human needs is its sole justification. In consequence, Bentham concluded, relying perhaps as much on Hobbes as on Hume, Blackstone's glorification of the British

Constitution and its supposed division of powers moves in the realm of myth. Legal power by its very nature cannot be legally limited, and somewhere in every political society authority must head up in some person or persons whom others are accustomed to obey. This holds true, Bentham argued, of free as well as of despotic governments. The two are indeed different in respect to the responsibility of rulers for their acts, the liberty of subjects to criticize and to combine for political purposes, and in the freedom of the press, but not in respect to the power they exercise. The *Fragment on Government* thus laid down the chief ideas that actuated the Philosophical Radicals: the greatest happiness principle as a measure of value, legal sovereignty as an assumption necessary for reform by legislative process, and a jurisprudence devoted to the analysis and "censure" of the law in the light of its contribution to the general happiness.

The *Fragment on Government* was in the main critical but Bentham proceeded at once to construction. The *introduction* to the *Principles of Morals and Legislation*, privately printed in 1780 and published in 1789, united psychology, ethics, and jurisprudence upon the lines already suggested by Helvetius. Pleasure and pain, Bentham argued, provide not only the standard of value needed for a "censorial" jurisprudence but also the cause of human behavior by which the skillful legislator can control and direct it.

> *Nature has placed mankind under the governance of two sovereign masters, pain and pleasure. It is for them alone to point out what we ought to do, as well as to determine what we shall do. On the one hand the standard of right and wrong, on the other the chain of causes and effects, are fastened to their throne.*[4]

Accordingly Bentham now included in his theory a somewhat lengthy and highly schematic account of pleasure and pain as motivating forces, designed to show how a calculation of their amount and influence is possible. He assumed, as had commonly been done by the hedonist moralists, that pleasure and pain are commensurable, a given amount of the one offsetting a like amount of the other, and also that they can be added, so that a sum of pleasures maybe calculated, which will define the greatest happiness both of an individual and a group of individuals. In this calculation four "dimensions" or phases of a pleasure or pain must be considered: its intensity, its duration, the certainty with which it will follow a given kind of action, and the remoteness of the time at which it will occur. Since one pleasure or pain is likely to induce another, this tendency also must be taken into account, and in any social calculation the number of persons affected must be considered. Usually Bentham spoke as if he believed that human beings really do act in accordance with some such mental parallelogram of forces as this, though occasionally he acknowledged that the notion of adding pleasures, and especially the pleasures of different persons, is fictitious. What is certainly true was that he considered the fiction to be "a postulatum without the allowance of which all political reasoning is at a stand." He had in fact no skill in psychological observation and no interest in it for its own sake. But he aspired to be the "Newton of the moral sciences" and he considered his psychological fictions to be no more violent than some that had proved serviceable in the science of mechanics.

The theory of pleasure and pain, and also the sensationalist psychology associated with it, had for Bentham another value besides that of enabling him to calculate the effects of legislation. He believed that by using this psychology he could track down and neutralize the "fictions" which he saw everywhere in social studies and in political reasoning. Bentham's theory of knowledge was rigidly nominalist, a quality which it probably owed to Hobbes more than to Hume. Now a name is the name of something, and that something must in the end be a concrete bit of sensuous experience. The meaning of a name is determined by the experience to which it points, its "referent," as it would now be called. Consequently, in so far as names refer to real entities, they are, so to speak, "masses of proper nouns"; as general terms they run the risk at least of becoming fictitious if this fact is overlooked. Fictitious entities are indeed necessary for "convenience of discourse" ("relation," for example, instead of "objects related"), but clarity requires that the factual reference should be precisely known. "Lamentable have been the confusion and the darkness produced by taking the names of fictitious for the names of real entities."[5] It must always be possible to put one's finger on the tangible experience referred to. As William James said many years later, for an empiricist every difference must make a difference. For Bentham, the utility of this theory of fictions lay chiefly in the spheres of politics and legislation. Both are filled with fictions, and legal fiction, he was convinced, "has never been employed to any purpose but the affording a justification for something which otherwise would be unjustifiable." Terms like rights, property, the crown, the general welfare, are all liable to fictional use, and usually for defending vested interests. From Bentham's point of view any corporate body, such as society or the state, is evidently fictitious. Whatever is done in its name is done by someone, and its good, as Bentham said, is "the sum of the interests of the several members who compose it." The utility of the greatest happiness principle, therefore, consists in the fact that it is the great solvent of fictions, for it means that the real significance of a law or an institution must be judged in terms of what it does, and so far as possible by what it does to specific individuals. It is of course not possible, as Bentham knew, to trace out in all cases just where the effects fall, but anything short of this is a makeshift. Since value is identical with pleasure, and pleasure can occur only in the experience of some individual human being, the worth of law and government must lie in their effects upon the lives and fortunes of actual men and women. Some such principle is a postulate of any liberal philosophy, but it does not, of course, imply accepting the crudities of Bentham's psychology.

Bentham's Theory of Law

The greatest happiness principle, as Bentham believed, placed in the hands of the skillful legislator a practically universal instrument. With it he can "rear the fabric of felicity by the hands of reason and law." For it provides a theory of basic human nature, both its valuations and its motivations, which Bentham supposed to be applicable at all times and all places. The legislator needs to know only the special circumstances of time and place that have produced peculiar customs and habits, and he can then control behavior by allocating pains and penalties to produce the most desirable results. The only limitations upon the method which Bentham recognized were psychological and ethical, fixing on the one hand what the law can do and on the other what it can wisely try to do. In the nature of the case, he believed, there can be no legal limitations upon it. Even the massive limitation imposed by long established custom or long accepted institutions were construed by Bentham as psychological, since he regarded custom and institutions as merely habits. Like all habits they contain many threats to an intelligent adjustment of means to ends; they are the source of the technicalities and fictions which the greatest happiness principle was designed to obviate. This distrust of custom and its complete subordination to legislation were among the principal characteristics of Bentham's jurisprudence. With them was connected an indifference to, or rather a contempt for, history as a factor in social studies. From Bentham's point of view history was for the most part a compendium of the crimes and follies of mankind. This temper of mind was perhaps the principal reason why his social philosophy seemed antiquated in the second half of the nineteenth century. Even his own disciple, John Stuart Mill, came to regard it as a weakness, and certainly it was often responsible for a superficial understanding of the profound differences between men reared in different cultural heritages.

Bentham's jurisprudence, which was not only the greatest of his works but one of the most remarkable intellectual achievements of the nineteenth century, consisted in the systematic application of the point of view just sketched to all branches of the law, civil and criminal, and to the procedural law and the organization of the judicial system.[6] In all cases its purpose was critical rather than descriptive, "censorial" rather than expository, as he had urged at the start against Blackstone. In all branches of jurisprudence, therefore, he distinguished what he called a natural method from a technical method. The latter consists in taking at their face value the classifications and technical procedures accepted by the law and embodied in its customary terminology, its writs, and processes. The effect of such a jurisprudence is at most to reduce legal concepts to some sort of formal order. A natural method, on the contrary, conceives of all legal prohibitions and all procedures for giving them effect in terms of their utility, as means to the greatest happiness of the greatest number. A juristic problem is essentially the correct allocation of penalties to produce desirable results.

In the field of the civil law this method required an analysis of legal rights and obligations in terms of the help or hindrance that their enforcement causes in the exchange of goods and services upon which utility depends. In the nature of the case every legal obligation must impose a limitation upon the freedom of such exchanges. A right in one person implies that his freedom of action is guaranteed by a penalty which prevents another person from invading it, and this can be justified only by the relative utility of such a limitation in comparison with what would happen if the acts of both persons were left to voluntary choice. In all cases the utility of legislation is to be measured in terms of its effectiveness, the costliness of its enforcement, and in general by its consequences in producing a system of exchanges which on the whole is advantageous to most members of the community. Utility is the only reasonable ground for making action obligatory. Property rights are justified in general by the need for security, for making the consequences of action calculable, and for avoiding the frustrations that follow uncertainty and disappointment, certainly a limited conception of social security. In Bentham's judgement security of property is a major condition of achieving the greatest happiness, but it is, as he perceived, a highly conservative principle. It implies the legal protection of the distribution of property which at any given time exists. As a matter of policy he was convinced that the law should aim at a comparatively equal distribution of property, or at least not at the creation of arbitrary inequalities. In practice it must strike some kind of workable balance between security and equality. Similarly the sanctity of contract, which Bentham believed had been treated by jurisprudence as a kind of incantation, like transubstantiation in theology, is really justified only because it contributes to the maintenance and reliability of commercial transactions.

In the field of the criminal law the principle of utility provided, as Bentham believed, a natural method for arriving at a rational theory of penalties. The technical method starts from the assumption that crime "deserves" punishment, but the concept of desert is essentially indefinable except in terms of existing practices and ideas. The natural method, on the contrary, starts from the principle that punishment is always an evil, since it causes pain, and is justified only in so far as it either prevents a greater future evil or repairs an evil already done. Criminal jurisprudence must provide a realistic classification of crimes, not in terms of the customary categories of the law, which Bentham justifiably regarded as contradictory and largely unintelligible, but in terms of the injury that certain modes of action inflict and the incidence of these injuries on assignable individuals or on classes and on the general public. It must provide also an analogous classification of punishments in order to apportion the penalty to the crime and prevent or redress the injury as effectively as possible. In general the rule is that the pain occasioned by a punishment must exceed the profit gained by committing the offense but must exceed as little as possible the evil caused by the offense. This part of Bentham's work was much like the conclusions already reached by Beccaria, another follower of Helvetius, though it was more systematic and rather curiously did not repeat Beccaria's sound conclusion that certainly of punishment is a more effective deterrent than severity. It is true, however, that in practice Bentham was favourable to proposals, like those of Sir Samuel Romilly, for eliminating the savage and quite ineffective penalties that disfigured English criminal law at the beginning of the nineteenth century. In his criminal jurisprudence, as in most of Bentham's reformatory projects, it appears that he was more moved by a love of order and efficiency than by humanitarian motives, though it is only fair to say that he expended large amounts both of his time and his private fortune to bring about the improvement of prisons. The driving force of his personality was enlightenment, and he was more concerned about the interests of the general public than about the interests of the unfortunate or the reformation of delinquents.

It was in his theory of legal procedure and judicial organization, perhaps, that Bentham developed his most characteristic ideas, and it was certainly here that he departed farthest from the liberal tradition as it had been before him. In his desire to simplify procedure and improve the efficiency of the courts he proposed to abandon almost entirely the checks and safeguards which had been deemed necessary to protect the subject's rights. Bentham here extended to procedural law the principles which he had already adopted relative to constitutional law in the *Fragment on Government*. He pointed out correctly that legal formalism and artificial rules about the admissibility of evidence were largely predicated upon a belief that the substantive law is bad and that government is dangerous, and he argued that, if this belief is indeed true, the reasonable remedy is to improve the law, not to weaken the courts. Formality, obscurity, and technicality in the law, he urged, result in a maximum of expense, delay, and vexation to litigants, in withholding justice from great numbers of persons, and in rendering the outcome of legal processes capricious and uncertain. This technical system, as Bentham called it, he regarded as nothing short of a conspiracy on the part of the legal profession to mulct the public. Even in the *Fragment on Government* he had paid his respects to lawyers and he pursued them throughout a long life with a reformer's rancor.

> *A passive and enervate race, ready to swallow anything, and to acquiesce in anything; with intellects incapable of distinguishing right from wrong, and with affections alike indifferent to either; insensible, short-sighted, obstinate; lethargic, yet liable to be driven into convulsions by false terrors; deaf to the voice of reason and public utility; obsequious only to the whisper of interest, and to the beck of power.*[7]

Bentham's ideal was "Every man his own lawyer." To this end he urged the substitution for formal pleading of informal proceedings before an arbiter who would aim at conciliation, the universal admissibility of any kind of relevant evidence, and a large measure of judicial discretion, rather than rigid rules, to exclude irrelevance. In respect to the organization of the courts Bentham attacked especially the practice of paying judges and other officers of the courts by fees rather than salaries; the divided, overlapping, and contradictory jurisdictions of the existing English courts; and the jury system, which he thought enjoyed a quite unmerited popularity.

Bentham's theory of law established the point of view of analytic jurisprudence, which was almost the only system of the subject generally known to English and American lawyers throughout the nineteenth century. This School is usually associated with the name of John Austin, but in fact Austin did little more than bring together systematically ideas that were scattered through Bentham's voluminous and not always very readable works.[8] In political theory the chief effect of Austin's work was to attach an exaggerated importance to the theory of sovereignty, which was in fact incidental to Bentham's plan for reforming the courts by Parliamentary control. Clarity of organization does indeed imply that responsibility should be definitely located somewhere, but Bentham's idea that a government is merely certain determinate persons set apart to rule, and toward whom subjects have merely a habit of obedience, is grossly inadequate to explain the part that institutions play in politics. Of vastly more historical importance than the theory of sovereignty was the fact that Bentham's work on jurisprudence provided the plan according to which the administration of justice in England was completely revised and modernized in the course of the nineteenth century. It is true that Bentham's ideas were never systematically adopted and put into effect at a single time and also that some of his ideas, notably a general codification of English law, were never adopted. But in a long succession of acts a thoroughgoing reform of the law and the courts was brought about, and in an astonishing number of cases the reforms followed the direction that Bentham's criticisms had indicated.[9] Sir Frederick Pollock has said rightly that every important reform of English law during the nineteenth century can be traced to the influence of Bentham's ideas.

It is certainly true, however, that Bentham's jurisprudence was not so completely determined by the principle of utility as he supposed. In fact utility is an utterly indefinite word until one specifies utility for what and for whom. The liberal elements in Bentham's philosophy resided largely in its tacit premises. When he said that "One man is worth just the same as another man," or that in calculating the greatest happiness each person is "to count for one and no one for more than one," he was obviously borrowing the principle of equality from natural law. He did not in fact rely merely on the unprovable assumption that one man's pleasure is like another man's. Behind his love for order and efficiency there were genuinely liberal postulates, particularly the value of a humane form of living for all persons, that efficiency or the greatest happiness principle did not cover. It is also true that his jurisprudence, by reason of its individualism, had an unintended bias. The rule that a law must be judged by the incidence of its effects on human beings, and so far as possible on assignable individuals, was a sound liberal principle, but it was vastly easier to apply in some types of law than in others.

The restriction of a property right is apparent, but the precise consequences of a law to protect public health cannot easily be shown in the better health of any single person. As was to become apparent, the extension of freedom of contract to as many private relations as possible resulted in quite specious senses of freedom. The connotations of Bentham's jurisprudence no doubt made social legislation more difficult. Far more than he realized his thought was influenced by *ad hoc* considerations, especially by the fact that legal reform in his day was so largely a matter of getting rid of obsolete practices. Nevertheless, despite obvious inadequacies in his thought, there are few thinkers in the history of social philosophy that have exercised so wide and so beneficent an influence as Bentham.

The Economic Theory of Early Liberalism

The liberal philosophy of law was almost wholly inspired by Bentham. Its economic theory-the so-called classical economics or the theory of *laissez faire*-formed another strand of liberal thought which owed little to Bentham but was similar in purpose and point of view. Like Bentham's own views on economic subjects it was derived from Adam Smith's *Wealth of Nations*. To this had been added the work of a generation of English writers, as well as that of the French successors to Quesnay and the Physiocrats. The classical economics received its most important statement in David Ricardo's *Principles of Political Economy* (1817), which incorporated the theory of population associated with the name of T.R. Malthus and also the theory of economic rent which Malthus had stated and to which Ricardo's own name has been attached. Thus economics emerged as an independent social study beside Bentham's jurisprudence and beside the study of politics. Like these it was conceived to depend upon the general laws of human nature stated by the associational and hedonistic psychology that Bentham had used. Hence it purported to state the laws of any economic society irrespective of time and place and without reference to prescriptions set up by systems of law or government. In its intellectual temper and point of view, therefore, the classical economics was quite in accord with the philosophy of Bentham. It was a kind of social Newtonianism which regarded institutions and their history as scientifically irrelevant, because they are reducible to habits of thought and action which can be fully explained by rather simple laws of individual behavior. This assumption that economics and government are mutually independent, or are only indirectly related through individual psychology, was one of the most characteristic elements in the point of view of early liberalism. It is also the characteristic which now makes the classical economics appear most seriously antiquated. This is due not only to the fact that the associational psychology itself was thoroughly inadequate, or to the fact that the policy of *laissez faire* espoused by liberal economists became progressively impossible in the latter part of the nineteenth century, though both these statements are true. The fundamental fact, made progressively clearer by social psychology and anthropology, is that both political and economic institutions are always related factors in a culture, and that the institutions of a culture shape from birth the innate characteristics of the individuals who compose it. Whatever the laws of human behavior turn out to be, they will certainly be far too general to correlate with the practices of any given time or place.

Though the classical economics aspired to be a science and therefore to be independent of the particular social and political circumstances in which it originated, it was marked, like Bentham's jurisprudence, by the practical reformatory purposes of its creators. The peace of 1815 produced a serious depression in the market for English manufactured goods both at home and abroad. It accordingly brought to the surface the radical disparity of interests between English landowners and English manufacturers which had been kept under cover by the crisis of the Napoleonic Wars. English agriculture had long enjoyed a market protected by the tariff on grain, while the interests of English merchants and manufacturers were all on the side of cheap food. The manufacturers themselves, having a technology superior to that of any other country, were for the time being without any need of governmental support. Under the circumstances a policy of free trade was clearly in their interest, and the stringency that followed the close of the War touched off a controversy that brought bout the reform of Parliament in 1832 and culminated in the repeal of the Corn Laws in 1846. The outcome was the emergence of England as the first of the modern industrial nations, committed to the typical liberal policies of unrestricted trade, the extension of representative government at home, and the ideal of an international concert of nations all alike liberal in politics and all following their national self-interest in an international division of labour. Richardo's economics was characteristic of the years of controversy in which his theories were formulated.

Though the classical economics purported to be a rigidly logical system, it in fact embraced two points of view that were diverse and that issued in very different ideas of economic society.[10] This diversity reflected two conceptions of nature that had been implicit in modern philosophy from the start. On the one hand was a belief that the natural order is inherently simple, harmonious, and beneficent, on the other the belief that it is devoid of ethical attributes and that its laws have no relation to justice, reason, or human welfare. Even in Bentham's jurisprudence, as has already been said, there were rudiments of natural right which contrasted with the pure naturalism or utilitarianism that he derived from Hume and professed to follow. In the case of Ricardo's economics the contrast was between what he called the static theory and the dynamic. From the point view of social statics economic science is the theory of the exchange of goods in a freely competitive market in which prices are fixed by the condition of the market itself, unobstructed by any forces other than the choices of the individuals involved. An economic society is conceived to be composed of individual producers each bringing his products and exchanging them with other producers, each buying as cheaply as possible and selling for the best price he can get. From the point of view of social dynamics, however, economics is a theory of the distribution of total product among the producers-as Ricardo puts it, "an enquiry into the laws which determine the division of the produce of industry amongst the classes who concur in its formation." The chief components of this part of the science are the theories of rent, profits, and wages, these being the principal kinds of income into which the product of industry must be divided. From this point of view an economic society consists of classes rather than of individuals.

The difference between these two points of view is in fact very considerable. For a free market, relieved of all factors of monopolistic restraint, was conceived, in the long run at least, to serve the interests of all alike and therefore the greatest good of the greatest number. By what Adam Smith had called "the simple principle of natural liberty," the operations of the market continually tend to produce prices as low as is consistent with maintaining the service and yet yielding a fair return for the effort expended. In short, complete freedom of exchange produces automatically a natural harmony of interests, which only needs to be let alone in order to produce as much economic advantage to everyone as the circumstances permit. The picture is, however, extremely different when one considers the laws of distribution. Not only do these laws run in terms of a system of economic classes in which the fate of any individual is largely determined by the portions of wealth which economic forces allot to his class, but they also make it logically inevitable, as Ricardo believed, that the interests of each class must in general always be adverse to the interests of the other classes. From this point of view the state of an economic society is typically one of class conflict. Moreover, the direction in which Ricardo expected the dynamic laws to carry a developing economy was by no means toward a natural harmony of interests.

The first of these two contrasting points of view depended upon the labour theory of value, the supposition that in a free market the value of a commodity is fixed by the amount of labour necessary to produce it. By Ricardo this theory was probably intended to provide an absolute economic standard behind the confusing array of prices that occur in an actual market. In general, as he supposed, prices would fluctuate around value according to temporary conditions of supply and demand. This purpose was not achieved, as Ricardo regretfully admitted, because the argument was in effect circular: prices are themselves the only thing that gives a definite measure of the amount of labour in a commodity. But a strictly naturalistic meaning of this sort was far from the connotations that had usually been attached to the labour theory of value. Locke had used it in an ethical sense to justify the right of property which a man acquires when he "mixes" his labour with the goods he produces, and Adam Smith had used the theory to develop the concept of a "natural" price, which in general he regarded as a just price. For if goods are exchanged according to the amount of labour that produces them, it seems to follow that in general (temporary aberrations being neglected) buyers and sellers must put in and take out equivalent amounts of value. On the whole everyone would keep a value equivalent to the amount of labour he had expended, and in effect he would retain the whole value that he had produced. Perfectly free exchange would therefore produce a system of "natural" justice. There is no doubt that the labour theory of value commended itself to Ricardo's disciples, J.R. MacCulloch, for example, less because of its use in economics than because it provided an ethical justification for free trade and an argument against "artificial" obstructions to it by legislation. The free play of human motives, all in themselves egoistic, works out to the greatest good of the community and the nearest practicable approach to justice for all its members. As Ricardo himself said, paraphrasing Adam Smith's famous expression about the "unseen hand," "The pursuit of individual advantage is admirably connected with the universal good of the whole."

This argument was not, however, utilitarian and it was glaringly at odds with Bentham's use of pleasure and pain in his jurisprudence. Utility, according to Bentham, does indeed require a harmony of interests and the greatest happiness of all, but such a condition is not natural. It can be produced only by legislation, and the significance of pleasure for a jurist is that, in addition to providing a standard of value, it makes possible the control of human behavior. Moreover, Bentham had consistently refused to name liberty as the object of law, because law exists solely to force men to do what they would not do voluntarily. From Bentham's point of view social harmony is produced by legislative coercion; from the economists' point of view the harmony of economic interests is produced by the absence of legislation. There can be no doubt that, for a utilitarian, Bentham's position was the more consistent, though possibly, in an effort to secure the repeal of a tariff, the economists' argument was the more persuasive. For even though coercion is always an evil, as Bentham believed, it is a necessary evil, and the limits of its use are set only by its power to prevent a greater evil. It is of course possible to argue on utilitarian grounds against particular restraints of trade, but some legal regulation of it is inevitable, and the principle of utility can justify any amount of "interference" with trade, provided only it does less harm than good. *Laissez faire*, however, was often defended on the ground that any legal control is intrinsically productive of inequalities of exchange, and this argument apparently assumes that the condition which prevails in the absence of regulation is one of natural liberty and natural equality.

The dynamic laws which govern the distribution of the social product presented a picture very different from the harmony and justice implied by the system of natural liberty. The distribution is between social classes, and the interests of the classes are in general antagonistic. The dynamic laws, moreover, are laws of social evolution, and the normal expectation which they establish for an expanding economy is, as Ricardo described it, very far from optimistic. The crucial factor among the dynamic forces is the property which Malthus had attributed to population in his *Essay*, first published in 1798[11] Malthus's point was that human fecundity, if uncontrolled, sets an inevitable limit to the possibility of social progress anticipated by Condorcet and in England by William Godwin. Any improvement in the standard of living results is an increase of population which nullifies the improvement, and since in general population increases faster than the production of food, population tends always to press hard upon the means of livelihood. Apart from temporary fluctuations, therefore, the standard of living for the mass of mankind will stand at about the level of subsistence. It cannot, of course, permanently fall below this minimum, but neither can it permanently rise higher, for a further increase of population will always overtake any increase in the supply of food. The economic consequences of this sociological law were formulated in the second dynamic law, the law of rent, which Malthus had stated and which Ricardo elaborated. Food is the product of land, and land is peculiar in that it is limited in amount and differs in its productivity. Clearly a cultivator can afford to pay a higher rent for fertile than for infertile land, since larger crops can be produced at equal cost. If land produced enough barely to pay the costs of production no rent could be paid for it; for more fertile land the rent which the owner can exact will be greater as the productivity rises. Rent therefore, is the differential between the productivity of any given piece of land and that of land which, at prevailing prices of food would just fail to pay the cost of using it.

From these two laws of population and rent Ricardo deduced important consequences. It follows in the first place that the landlord is a monopolist, or indeed a kind of economic parasite, who can collect a tribute from all other economic classes, since rent contributes in no way to production. As Ricardo said, "The interest of the landlord is always opposed to the interest of every other class in the community." Moreover, any increase in the price of food, because it brings less fertile land under cultivation, will increase rents, and an increase of population will increase prices. In the second place, the laws of rent and population imply a law of wages, viz., that except temporarily wages cannot rise above or fall below the level of subsistence. As Ricardo said, the "natural price of labour is that price which is necessary to enable the labourers, one with another, to subsist and perpetuate their race, without either increase or diminution." Finally, since the total product of industry is in general distributed as rent, wages, or profits, it follows that any increase in the first two is subtracted from the portion that goes to the capitalist. The normal tendency of a progressive economy, therefore, in which production is rising, will be for landlords to receive a larger share, though they contribute nothing to progress, for capitalists to receive a smaller share, and for labour to receive as always only so much as will replace the labour force. Even the most determined optimist would hardly describe this as a system of natural justice. In Ricardo's dynamic laws nature figures merely as the brute instinct of procreation without regard for consequences.

What held together the idea of a naturally harmonious economic society and the idea of naturally conflicting classes was not logic but the fact that both appeared to converge on a policy of free trade and more specifically on the repeal of the tariff on grain. This conclusion would follow obviously from the theory that economic society is naturally self-regulating by competition. On the other hand, if rent is an unproductive drain on the economy, it would follow that rent ought not to be increased by legislation that artificially raises the price of food. This concentration on the immediately practical purpose of repealing a single kind of taxation had the effect of narrowing the interest of the classical economics in a manner that depended very little upon the logic of the system. Any taxation is bound to affect the economy in some way, and from a purely utilitarian point of view there is no reason why a legislator should not direct taxation to increasing the general welfare, provided only that his measures would work.

James Mill, for example, admitted that it might be directed to increasing capital, though he believed the attempt would probably not succeed. Moreover, there are many forms of economic rent besides the rent of land, and even if the state were to confiscate them all, the legislation, according to the theory, would in no way hamper production. Henry George's *Progress and Poverty* (1879), which affected so powerfully the young Englishmen who were about to found the Fabian Society, reflected a change of interest more than a change of theory, namely, a desire to explore the possibilities, within existing economic theory, of using legislation to regulate the economy for general good. The opposition of many of the classical economists to all forms of social legislation, possibly excepting the public support of education, reflected their concern with a single problem of the English economy and an unconscious bias in favor of the class they represented. The alleged impossibility of improving the lot of wage earners by legislation depended on Malthus's sociological law of population, which turned out to be the least reliable part of the system. The opposition to social legislation was never shared by humanitarian liberals. The English legislation of the 1820s began the removal of restraints on trade, but it included also the beginning of the factory acts and of the removal of limitations on the right of labour to organize. It is true, however, that the emphasis of liberal legislation, until after the middle of the century, was on the side of *laissez faire*.

The extent to which liberal economics was controlled by practical considerations rather than by logic is curiously illustrated by the ease with which Karl Marx turned its arguments to a quite different purpose. Ricardo had emphasized the antagonism of the landlord's interest to the interest of labour and capital, but it was equally easy to argue that the interests of the capitalist were similarly antagonistic to those of labour, since whatever share of the product went to profits was withdrawn from wages. And if the landlord could exact rent because he monopolized land, it could equally well be held that the capitalist in an industrialized economy monopolizes the means of production and that his profits are a kind of surplus value or, in essence, an economic rent, as the Fabians argued. Moreover, it is far from obvious that Ricardo's laws for a developing economy are the only ones or the correct ones. Richardo might pessimistically expect that capitalists would be impoverished in the interest of landlords, but it was equally open to an optimist to hope that they might be expropriated in the interest of wage earners. The truth is that the classical economics provided Marx with a ready-made picture of the exploitation of labour. The economist, to be sure, imagined that he was describing a system that was rooted in the nature of things. But having the Hegelian dialectic in hand, Marx could readily think of it as rooted in history and ascribe the exploitation to the capitalist system.

The Political Theory of Early Liberalism

The political theory of Benthamite radicalism was less significant than Bentham's jurisprudence or the classical economics. In part this was due to the fact that the dogma of a self-regulating economy left to government a role of very restricted importance. In part it was due to the fact that the direction which liberal political reforms must take in England had long been evident and that such reforms were long overdue. Quite evidently the political monopoly of the landed interests in Parliament must be broken, if either legal or economic reform was to be possible. James Mill, in an article contributed to the newly founded organ of the radicals, the *Westminster Review*,[12] estimated that effectively the House of Commons was chosen by some two hundred families, to which the clergy of the Established Church and the legal profession were substantially adjuncts. Between the two existing political parties there was, he said, practically no difference except that the one in opposition was bent on securing the patronage enjoyed by the one in power, without changing the monopoly by which both profited. English government, he charged, was absolutely an organ of class interests. Both parties represent a small ruling class, mostly landowners, with some small infiltration of influence by moneyed interests mostly through bribery. The remedy, as he naively supposed, consisted simply in extending representation to the whole community and especially tot he industrial middle class. "In the grand discovery of modern times, the system of representation, the solution of all difficulties, both speculative and practical, will perhaps be found."[13]

The original parts of the early utilitarian political theory were all suggested by Bentham's jurisprudence and had indeed been outlined in the *Fragment on Government*. They consisted in an extension to constitutional law of the same ideas which he used in this plans for the reorganization of the judicial system.[14] The fundamental principle is that liberal government cannot be equated with weak government. Devices for legal limitations on sovereignty, such as bills of rights, the separation of powers, and checks and balances, Bentham regarded as confused in theory and self-defeating in practice, like the building up of formality and technicality in the law. Accordingly he accepted the complete legal sovereignty of Parliament and the need for relying upon an enlightened public opinion to insure responsibility. Ultimate political sovereignty, he believed, should in here in the people, since only so can the interest of government be made to coincide with the general interest. To make the interest of the people effective he believed in universal suffrage, with only temporary disqualifications until education can produce an enlightened electorate. And to make Parliament responsive to the electorate he would have reduced its legal life to a year. The significance of these political ideas lies not so much in the fact that they were more radical than any scheme of reform that was practicable in Bentham's lifetime as in the fact that he jumped, so to speak, quite over the stage of liberal thought that regarded constitutional limitations as the chief guaranties of freedom. Conceptions of government, which he had originally applied to enlightened despotism he applied forthwith to liberalism. His belief in enlightenment was such that he had no misgivings about the possible tyranny of a majority. As John Stuart Mill later said, the early utilitarians were liberals not so much because they believed in liberty as because they believed in good government. Bentham was, no doubt, inclined to underestimate the importance of institutional safeguards for political and civil liberty, and this was of a piece with his deficient sense of the reality of institutions in culture. At the same time his position was sound in so far as it depended on the principle that liberal government need not be defended by accepting its inefficiency.

James Mill's ideas of government and reform differed in no important respect from those of Bentham, but his *Essay on Government* exposed somewhat more clearly the philosophical basis of those ideas. In particular it showed that the political thought of the Benthamite liberals depended more on Hobbes than on Hume. Like Hobbes, Mill believed that all men are driven by a restless desire for power which institutional limitations cannot check. Like Bentham he rejected, for liberal as well as for autocratic governments, any conception of the division or balancing of powers, though he asserted broadly that the only difficult questions in government have to do with restraining the power which rulers must have. The problem, as he supposed, could only be solved by securing a legislature whose interests are identical with those of the country, so that its members have no motive for using their power otherwise than in the general interest, and by giving the legislature control over the executive. As has been said, he imagined, rather fatuously, that such a result would automatically be brought about by a representative system with universal suffrage and short terms of office. In spite of his tendency to state every argument as if it embodied a universal and eternal principle, Mill's political thinking was in fact dominated by the immediate purpose which he considered important, namely, the enfranchisement of the industrial middle class. This class he described quite frankly as "the wisest part of the community," and he supposed that the "lower classes" would always be guided by it. He never contemplated the possibility that the middle class might itself use political power for its own advantage.

Like classical economics, Mill's political thought united in an uneasy combination an egoistic theory of individual motivation with a belief in the natural harmony of human interests. His argument for universal suffrage depended upon the premise that all human beings, at least with a moderate amount of education, can be brought to a clear sighted understanding of their interests and that, understanding their interests, they will infallibly act in accordance with them,. It depended also on the tacit assumption that, if all men reasonably seek their individual interests, the greatest good of the greatest number will result. In short he succeeded, after some manner known only to a doctrinaire, in combining a rather pessimistic estimate of human nature with some remnant of that sublime faith in reason which had made revolutionary radicals like Condorecet and Godwin look forward to limitless human progress. John Stuart Mill described his father's point of view quite accurately as follows:

> *So complete was my father's reliance on the influence of reason over the minds of mankind, whenever it is allowed to reach them, that he felt as if all would be gained if the whole population were taught*

> *to read, if all sorts of opinions were allowed to be addressed to them by word and in writing, and if by means of the suffrage they could nominate a legislature to give effect to the opinions they adopted. He thought that when the legislature no longer represented a class interest, it would aim at the general interest, honestly and with adequate wisdom.*[15]

Manifestly a belief such as this could have been logically supported only upon the assumption that reasonable action issues naturally in social harmony and could never have been reached on empirical or utilitarian grounds.

The liberalism of the Philosophical Radicals was an intellectual force of enormous practical importance in nineteenth-century politics. Without themselves attaining the proportions of a political party, they disseminated ideas in the light of which a vast amount of antiquated political lumber was swept away, and legislation, administration, and judicial process were made both more efficient and more democratic. The reform of Parliament, the repeal of obsolete restrictions on trade and industry, and the reorganization of the judicial system were the most conspicuous examples of this process but they were not the only ones. The reform of Parliament in 1832 amply justified Bentham's belief that liberal reform would not limit the power of government but would invigorate its action. Parliamentary reform initiated within a few years a long series of administrative reforms in which men trained in the ideas of Bentham played an important though not always a conspicuous part. Almost at once a centralized administration for the Poor Law was begun, and the moving spirits were Edwin Chadwick and George Grote. The organization of services for protecting public health and of centralized administration for the county police and the inspection of factories followed soon, and again Chadwick played a leading part. In 1840 J.A. Roebuck and other Benthamites secured the passage of an inadequate but still substantial bill looking to a universal system of primary education. Lord Durham's Report in 1839, prepared in part by Charles Buller and Edward Gibbon Wakefield, began a revision of colonial policy and introduced in Canada a liberal constitution which was the first constitution granted to a colony. This, with Wakefield's plan for the colonization of Australia, was in effect the inception of the British Commonwealth of Nations.[16] In the patient drudgery of these utilitarian the faith in reason which they inherited from the Enlightenment was combined with an ideal of professional competence which they learned from Bentham, and the two together issued in reforms that made government both more liberal and more efficient.

The criticisms commonly passed upon Philosophical Radicalism and given currency even by liberal successors like John Stuart Mill were that it neglected institutions and their historical growth and that it worked with a falsely schematic conception of human nature and motives. Both criticisms were true. Often however they were taken to imply that it was clear, rigidly logical and systematic, and merely based on premises too narrowly limited. This was not true. Its fundamental weakness was rather that as a philosophy it was never clear and never critical of its assumptions or its deductions. In certain respects it was a system of "nature" like the rationalist philosophies of the seventeenth century, but it had no theory of knowledge that made an appeal to nature intelligible. It claimed to be empirical but it made little effort to check its premises by observation, and in effect its empiricism stopped with a crude from of sensationalism that had been derived from Locke two generations before. Hence it easily fell a victim to criticism as soon as it faced thinkers less impressed than Mill with its characteristic dogmas. Philosophical Radicalism was in truth largely an *ad hoc* philosophy, and it was also largely the spokesman for a single social interest which it identified, hastily though not hypocritically, with the well-being of the whole community. The consciousness of this fact, together with a perception of the intolerable consequences of its social policy, tended to discredit it as a social philosophy, even before the legal reforms for which it stood were accomplished. Its weakness as a social philosophy can be summed up by saying that it had no positive conception of a social good, and that its egoistic individualism made it look with suspicion on the validity of any such conception, at a time when the total welfare of the community was becoming a principal object of concern. Its weakness as a political philosophy was that its theory of government was almost wholly negative, at a time when it was becoming inevitable that government should assume a larger responsibility for the general welfare. In a long view of political evolution, therefore, Philosophical Radicalism tended to be carried by inertia instead of projecting itself upon the growing lines of development. Its importance as an agent of political obsolescence was inestimable but by limiting itself to that function it dated itself as the organ of a period.

NOTES

1 Graham Wallas, *Life of Francis Place* (1898), pp. 309 ff.

2 On Continental liberalism see Guido de Ruggiero. *The History of European Liberalism*, Eng. trans. by R.G. Collingwood, 1927.

3 On the importance of nonconformity in the political life of England early in the century see Elie Halevy, *A. History of the English People in 1815*, especially Vol. I, Book III. Eng. trans. by E.I. Watkin (1924).

4 Ch. 1, Sect. 1.

5 See *Bentham's Theory of Fictions*, edited by C.K. Ogden (1932), with Ogden's Introduction.

6 See Elie Halevy, *The Growth of Philosophic Radicalism*, Eng. trans. by Mary Morris (1928), especially Part 1, ch. 2, and Part III, ch. 2.

7 Preface; ed. by F.C. Montague (1891), p. 104.

8 His lectures on jurisprudence were delivered between 1828 and 1832 at University College, London, then newly founded under Benthamite auspices. They were published in the *Province of Jurisprudence Determined*, 1832, which was later incorporated in the more extended *Lectures on Jurisprudence*, 1861-63. Selections edited with notes by W. Jethro Brown under the title, *The Austinian Theory of Law*, London, 1906.

9 See the essay of Sir Charles Synge Christopher Bowen on "The Administration of the Law, 1837-1887" in *The Reign of Queen Victoria* (1887), ed. by T.H. Ward, Vol. 1, p. 281; reprinted in *Select Essays in Anglo-American Legal History*, edited by a Committee of the Association of American Law Schools, Vol. I (1907), p. 516. For a contemporary appreciation of Bentham as a legal reformer see Lord Brougham's speech "On the Present State of the Law," February 7, 1828, and the Introduction, in Speeches (1838), Vol. II. p. 287.

10 This disparity is developed by Halevy, *The Growth of Philosophic Radicalism*, especially Part III, ch. 1.

11 In fact, so many earlier writers had approximated Malthus's conclusions that his originality consisted chiefly in his pseudo-

mathematical statement of the principle. See Halevy, *op. cit.*, pp. 225 ff.

12 Vol. I (1824), p. 206; on the *Edinburgh Review.*

13 The article on Government in the Supplement to the *Encyclopaedia Britannica*, 1820; reprinted in *Essays on Government*, etc., 1825.

14 The principal work is the *Constitutional Code* (1830), *Works* (ed. by Bowring), Vol. IX.

15 *Autobiography* (1873), p. 106.

16 See B.W. Richardson, *The Health of Nations, a Review of the Works of Edwin Chadwick* (1887), especially the Biographical Dissertation and Vol. II, Parts I and II. J.A. Williamson, Short History of British Expansion (2nd ed., 1930), Part V. chs. 3 and 4.

REFERENCES

Bentham and the Ethics of Today. By David Baumgardt. Princeton, N.J., 1952.

The Austinian Theory of Law. By W.J. Brown. London, 1906.

The Politics of English Dissent: The Religious Aspects of Liberal and Humanitarian Reform Movements from 1815 to 1848. By R.G. Cowherd. New York, 1956.

Political Thought in England: The Utilitarians from Bentham to J.S. Mill. By William Davidson. New York, 1916.

Jeremy Bentham. By Charles W. Everett. London, 1966

The Growth of Philosophic Radicalism. By Elie Halevy. Eng. trans. by Mary Morris. New ed. New York, 1949.

The Social and Political Ideas of Some Representative Thinkers of the Revolutionary Era. Ed. by F.J.C. Hearnshaw. London, 1931. Ch. 7.

Jeremy Bentham: An Odyssey of Ideas, 1748-92. By Mary P. Mack. New York, 1963.

The Social Problems of an Industrial Civilization. By Elton Mayo. Boston, 1945. Ch. 2.

Bentham's Theory of Fictions. By C.K. Ogden. London, 1932. Introduction.

"Benthamism in England and America." By P.A. Palmer. In the *Am. Pol. Sci. Rev.*, Vol. XXXV (1941), p 855.

Three Criminal Law Reformers: Beccaria, Bentham, Romilly. By Coleman Phillipson. London, 1923. Part II.

The English Utilitarian. By John P. Plamentz. 2d ed. rev. Oxford, 1958. Chs. 4-7.

A History of European Liberalism. By Guido de Ruggiero. Eng. trans. by R.G. Collingwood. Oxford, 1927.

French Politica. Thought in the Nineteenth Century. By Roger Soltau. New York, 1959.

The English Utilitarians. By Leslie Stephen. 3 vols. London, 1900.

The Life of Francis Place, 1771-1854. By Graham Wallas. 4th ed. London, 1925.

Select Essays in Anglo-American Legal History. Compiled and edited by a Committee of the Association of American Law Schools. 3 vols. Boston, 1907-1909, Vol. I, Part IV.

8

Marx and Dialectical Materialism

Liberal political thought developed largely as an elaboration of two fundamental social or moral ideas, that politics is distinctively an art of reaching non-coercive adjustments between antagonistic interests and that democratic procedures are the only effective ways for making such adjustments. Consequently, though its later history undertook to take into account Hegel's valid critique of individualism, it never accepted the two major assumptions in Hegel's social philosophy. These were, first, that society is a moving balance of antithetical forces which generate social change by their tension and struggle, and second, that social history is annternal or quasi-logical evolution of the forces themselves. These elements of Hegel's though, however, played a large part in the political theory of the nineteenth century and later. This was due in the main to the transformation of Hegel's philosophy effected by Karl Marx. Marx removed from Hegel's theory the assumption that national cultures are the effective units of social history—an assumption that never had any close logical relation to his system—and replaced the struggle of nations with the struggle of social classes. Thus he took away from Hegelianism its distinctive qualities as a political theory—its nationalism, its conservatism, and its counter-revolutionary character—and transformed it into a new and very powerful type of revolutionary radicalism. Marxism became the progenitor of the more important forms of party socialism in the nineteenth century and ultimately, with very important modifications to be sure, of present-day communism.

In important respect, however, Marx's philosophy was continuous with Hegel's. In the first place he continued to believe that the dialectic was a powerful logical method uniquely capable of demonstrating a law of social development, and in consequence his philosophy, like Hegel's was a philosophy of history. For both men the ground of any social change is its necessity or "inevitability," and this term was as ambiguous in Marx as it had been in Hegel, combining as it did the concepts both of casual explanation and of moral justification. Though Marx construed his philosophy as a form of materialism, he still used the dialectic to support a theory of social progress in which higher moral values are necessarily realized. In the second place, for Marx as for Hegel the driving force of social change is struggle, and the determining factor in the last resort is power. The struggle is between social classes rather than nations, and the power is economic rather than political, political power being in Marx's theory a consequence of economic position. But for neither Marx nor Hegel was the struggle for power amenable to peaceful adjustment for the mutual advantage of the contending parties. Marx shared with Hegel a profound skepticism about the ability of human foresight or good intentions to modify the action of social forces, and both temperamentally and by reason of his social philosophy he had almost no belief in the power of legislation to remedy economic abuses. It is true that Marx hoped and expected that his revolutionary radicalism would issue in a form of socialism, in social equality and a genuine liberty, which would complete the equality and liberty of political democracy. But in fact he offered no good reason to believe that the power politics of radicalism would prove to be less authoritarian in practice than the power politics of conservative nationalism. His social philosophy, therefore, harbored a discrepancy between his democratic aspirations and the internal logic of the system. In Marx's lifetime this remained latent, because the social revolution he envisaged was never a practical political issue. It became explicit in the communist version of revolutionary Marxism.

The Proletarian Revolution

Marx's social philosophy depended upon and first clearly brought into the focus of attention a social change of absolutely first-rate importance which occurred in the nineteenth century: the rise to political self-consciousness and finally to political power of an industrial working class. This, as was said in the preceding chapter, became responsible for changing the course of liberal thought, but Marx perceived its importance far sooner than the liberals. Especially in the historical studies which formed an integral part of his philosophy he presented capitalism for the first time in what might be called its human aspect, as an institution that had produced and was continually enlarging a class of men who must live wholly from wages and who were therefore related to their employers only by a cash-nexus. Their power to work is a commodity, the only economically valuable commodity they have, which must be sold in a competitive market where the only obligation of the purchaser is to pay the current price. The relationship of employer and employee in industry tends thus to be stripped of human significance and of moral obligation and becomes simply one of power. Marx rightly saw in this situation potentially the most revolutionary fact in modern history—on the one hand a class defined by its ownership of the means of production and motivated chiefly by the necessity of creating profits, on the other an industrial proletariat having no power except through the pressure of well-organized masses and obliged to set as its end not political liberty but the maintenance or improvement of its standard of living. Understanding this as an historical fact, Marx was aware of capitalism as an institution, not the result of timeless economic laws but a phase in the evolution of modern society. Starting therefore from the fact of divergent class interests, already made abundantly clear by the classical economists, he set himself both to interpret political liberalism as the ideology characteristic of the middle class and also to create a social philosophy for the rising proletariat, suitable for its use in the struggle for power.

This project, like Hegel's theory of the state, depended upon an estimate of the historical importance of the French Revolution. Like Hegel, Marx believed that the Revolution had signaled the collapse of feudal society, but while Hegel believed that the Revolution would be consummated in the emergence of national states, Marx regarded it as preliminary to a more drastic and thoroughgoing revolution. The Revolution, he believed, had been at once fundamentally important and yet in a sense superficial. It was important because it realized a necessary stage in the development of civilization, and yet it was superficial in the sense that it merely opened the way to a higher stage. The abolition of feudalism meant for Marx the rise to power of the middle class and the creation of a political system which made its power effective. In its most developed form, as yet only partially reached, this system would be the democratic republic. The French Revolution, therefore, had been essentially a political revolution. It had transferred social dominance from the nobility and the clergy to the industrial and commercial middle class; it had created the state as a typical organ of middle-class repression and exploitation; and its philosophy—the system of natural rights in politics and economics—was the ideal justification and rationalization of the middle-class right to exploit the worker. The manifest next step beyond the political revolution was a profounder social revolution. This must be the work of the rising proletarian class of workers, which must displace the middle class from power as the middle class had displaced the older feudal class. The rising class, too, must have its philosophy, and as the philosophy of the middle class was in substance a claim to the natural rights of property, so a proletarian philosophy must be a socialist claim to the human rights of men without property. But just because the proletariat lay at the bottom of the social structure, with no class below it to be exploited, a proletarian revolution would not merely transfer the power to exploit but would abolish exploitation. It would be the first step to a society without distinctions of social class and a true beginning of history as a record of full human self-realization. This was the grandiose mission which Marx's philosophy set for itself.

In intention, therefore, Marx's philosophy was profoundly practical, as indeed Hegel's had been. Both men believed that effective political action depended on understanding the general direction in which history is moving—what Marx called "the natural phases of evolution"—and upon accepting the tasks imposed by one's position in it. Whereas Hegel had supposed that European history culminates in the rise of the Germanic nations including the Germans, the Swedes, the Norwegians, the Danes, the Dutch, and the English: Marx believed that social history had culminated in the rise of the proletariat, and he looked forward to the advance of that class to a dominant place in modern society. In Hegel's philosophy of history the driving force was a self-developing spiritual principle that embodied itself successively in historic cultures, in Marx's it was a self-developing system of productive forces that embodied itself in basic patterns of economic distribution and in the social classes consequent thereto. For Hegel the mechanism of progress was warfare between cultures; for Marx it was antagonism between social classes. Both men regarded the course of history as rationally necessary, a pattern of stages unfolding according to a logical plan and advancing toward a predetermined goal. This majestic march of human civilization invites men to co-operate and to serve. Both philosophies were powerful incitements to action and most effective forms of moral exhortation. While Hegel appealed to national patriotism, Marx appealed to the fidelity of workers to their fellow workers. In both cases the appeal was quite different from the individualism of liberal political philosophies. It was addressed to loyalty rather than to self-interest, to duties rather than to rights; and it offered no reward except the hope that one's private life would gain meaning through service to a cause greater than oneself. Marx's philosophy was conceived by him as providing a plan and a motive for a social revolution that should free the workers from poverty and exploitation.

This union in Marx of a programme of revolutionary action with a philosophical theory of the "necessary" course of social development is unintelligible unless one understands the peculiar sense which the dialectic imparts to words like "necessary" and "inevitable." If they meant merely the relation of cause and effect, human cooperation with the course of history would be meaningless; its implication would be political quietism. But obviously neither Marxian communists nor Hegelian nationalists have been quietists; on the contrary they have been determined or even ruthless activists, often at the cost of their private interests. The distinction that commentators have often drawn between Marx the social philosopher and Marx the organizer of party socialism is one which no Marxist—indeed no Hegelian—would ever draw. The "necessity" which both men attributed to history calls for participation and active cooperation; it is a goad to action and to self-dedication. It has less affinity with scientific cause and effect than with the predestination which Calvinists attributed to the will of God. Like the latter, History provides the Marxian revolutionist with his vocation, with his assurance of ultimate success, and perhaps with absolution for the crimes he commits in History's name. Historical necessity, therefore, means not merely cause and effect, or desirability, or moral obligation, but all three at once—a kind of cosmic imperative which creates and guides human interest and human calculation and makes them its servants. But while Calvinists called this theology, Hegelians and Marxists call it science.

Marx's social philosophy fell into two periods divided roughly at about 1850 or a few years thereafter. To the earlier period belongs the plan of the system, an outgrowth of Marx's study of Hegel at the University of Berlin. But this time (some five years after Hegel's death) the school was divided into an idealist wing, largely concerned with religious apologetics, and a materialist wing led by Ludwig Feuerbach. In later years Marx described Feuerbach as a small figure compared with Hegel but epoch-making after Hegel, because he freed Hegelianism from its idealist "mystifications" and thus, as Marx believed, both relieved it of its conservative implications and brought it into line with science. When Marx left Germany for Paris he was already deeply involved with French socialism, which was part of the whole revolutionary ferment that culminated in 1848. This convinced Marx that socialist theory had been superficial because it lacked understanding of the dynamics of social evolution, which, he believed, was supplied by Hegel's dialectic. The product of this line of thought was dialectical or economic materialism—the theory that social development depends upon the evolution of the forces of economic production. This theory was sketched in a variety of works, largely occasional and controversial, of which the *Communist Manifesto* (1848) was the most notable, but neither then nor later was it stated systematically or freed from vagueness or ambiguity.

With the cessation of revolutionary outbreaks after 1848 Marx's life as an active revolutionist ended and the remainder of his life was spent as an exile in England. Here he devoted himself to the writing of his great work *Capital*, the first volume of which he published in 1867; the second and third volumes were put together from his papers by his friend Friedrich Engels after Marx's death in 1883. *Capital* took economic materialism for granted but here too the theory was never developed. Marx had now conceived the idea of underpinning his philosophy with a thoroughgoing critique of Classical Economics, which he took to be a valid theory of a capitalist economy. Against this Marx set his own theory of "surplus value," designed to show dialectically that a capitalist system is inherently self-contradictory. In consequence discussion of Marxism in the latter part of the nineteenth century turned almost wholly on Marx's economics; his earlier revolutionary pamphlets tended to be overlooked, and economic materialism hardly began to be much discussed until after Marx's death. Thus it happened that Marx's social philosophy was never systematically expounded by him and it contained in a few very compact pronouncements in occasional writings, while the systematic theorizing in *Capital* (as distinguished from the historical chapters) can hardly count today as more than economic scholasticism. Yet it can hardly be denied that Lenin was right when he said that economic materialism is "the central point around which the entire network of ideas, expressed and discussed, turns." The theory of surplus value may therefore be left to the history of obsolete economic theories. Considered as a social philosophy, Marxism depends upon the meaning and the validity of Marx's main thesis: that the evolution of economic production in a society determines its institutional and ideological superstructure.

The sources for the study of economic materialism fall into two groups. First, there are several works by Marx written before 1852. These are polemic writings written while he was formulating his theory of social revolution and occasional pamphlets analyzing the failure of revolutionary movements in France. Second, there are several works by Engels, including a number of important letters written after Marx's death, explaining the theory and criticizing what he regarded as distortions of it by younger socialist writers in Germany toward the close of the century. Since an interval of more than twenty-five years separated these two groups of works, it is desirable to deal with each by itself. While it is certain that Engels never intentionally departed from Marx's meaning, his explanations were sometimes rather different.

Dialectical Materialism

Marx's first statements of dialectical materialism were made in a group of works written between 1844 and 1848 under the stimulus of Feuerbach's materialist interpretation of Hegel and as incidents in Marx's career as a revolutionary socialists.[1] It should be noted that Marx used the word "materialism" in a specialized sense that may be misleading, since the word already had, and after Marx retained, a meaning quite different from Marx's. Pre-revolutionary French works like Holbach's *System of Nature* had used "materialism" to mean a philosophy which purported to depend on physics and chemistry, and which held that the mechanical explanations given by these sciences could be extended to all subject matters, vital, mental, and social. This conclusion was not at all shared by Marx, and in his *Holy Family* he distinguished his materialism sharply from the French materialism of the eighteenth century. For Marx the qualification "dialectical" was the essence of the matter. Like Hegel he regarded mechanical explanation as suitable to physics and chemistry because these sciences deal with subject matters which involve no problems of historical development; Marx never believed their methods could be adopted by social studies. The dialectic he regarded as a logical method uniquely capable of dealing with a continuously developing subject matter and of revealing the "necessity" of its development. Like Hegel, Marx also regarded mechanical explanation as belonging to a lower form of logic because it deals with a lower stage of reality. At a later date, to be sure, after the publication of Darwin's *Origin of Species*, Marx sometimes claimed for his theory of social development an affinity with organic evolution, and there is in fact a superficial similarity between the class struggle and natural selection. What impressed Marx on a first reading of Darwin's book was "the crude English method of development" and this was indeed a characteristic reaction for a Hegelian.[2] For Darwin's theory of evolution was strictly an empirical generalization—a causal theory of change with no implication of progress—while the dialectic was for Marx as for Hegel a law of logic. It provided an a *priori* theory of progress which was at once a principle of explanation and an evaluation. Marx's materialism in no way displaced the Hegelian assumption of a n underlying force which is the hidden reality behind a multiplicity of more or less ephemeral manifestations and appearances. The metaphysical model appropriate to it was not mechanism but a kind of naturalistic vitalism.

At the same time there were several implications of "materialism" which were important for Marx. In the first place he tended to equate the word with "scientific," and though he had no belief that social studies could imitate physics, he did believe that they could be made equally precise and certain. Hence he was readily convinced by Feuerbach that Hegelian notions like "Absolute Spirit" or the "Spirit of Age" were merely imaginary, and that the real motive forces in the history of a society are its material conditions. Marx wholly lacked the contemptuous arrogance toward science that Hegel occasionally displayed. Indeed, one gains the impression that the native bent of Marx's mind was essentially matter of fact and empirical; few politicians have buttressed their policies with a body of historical and economic scholarship equal to Marx's. Perhaps it was this quality of mind that imparted a kind of vagueness to the sweeping generalizations of Marx's philosophy. Sometimes expressions like "tendencies that work out with an iron necessity toward an inevitable goal" (which occurs in the Preface to *Capital*) are used as if they were sheer dogmas, but again they may be used as if they were suggestive working hypotheses. Sometimes he speaks as if dialectical materialism were a formula that could be applied mechanically to any period of history, but at other times he protested violently against this way of using it. And though he might be very free in making predictions, he was also free in making exceptions to them. Thus he could say that revolution was inevitable but also that it might not occur in England or the United States; or he could assert that capitalism was a necessary stage of social development but he could also entertain the idea that perhaps in Russia socialism might grow directly from the village communities. In general the dialectic imparted a looseness to Marx's logic that prevented him from distinguishing between probability and rigid implication, or from recognizing that necessary statements are characteristically conditional.

In the second place materialism implied for Marx a radical rejection of religion, indeed a militant atheism. Since religions unquestionably one of the great conservative social forces, materialism had for Marx, as for many others, a connotation of radicalism. The dissident Hegelianism with which Marx was allied had already produced, in 1835, David Friedrich Strauss's *Life of Jesus*, in its day regarded as a scandalous book because it construed the Scriptural story as merely myth. And though the implications of Hegel's philosophy had been in general conservative, Marx was convinced that its correct implication is revolutionary. For the dialectic can be taken as a solvent of every supposed absolute truth and every transcendent value, since it shows them to be relative—social products that grow up in the life of a community in the course of its temporal and historical evolution. All such so-called truths, Marx concluded, are fictitious supports for whatever class controls a society and exploits its subordinate classes. Religion supplies imaginary or "fantastic" satisfactions that misdirect any rational effort to find real satisfaction. Thus Christianity, with its distinction of soul and body, imparts to men a double life and offers the imaginary joys of heaven as a solace for the real miseries of this life. It is "the opium of the people," a soporific that prevents the oppressed from making any effort to better their lot by resisting their exploiters. Materialism meant for Marx, as it has continued to mean for Marxists, an anti-religious secularism regarded as the precondition of any thorough-going social reform.

The third meaning that materialism and the dialectic had for Marx was the suggestion of a new and more far-reaching revolution. The French Revolution had indeed abolished feudalism, as Hegel said, but the natural rights of man which the revolutionists claimed as its consequents are no more absolute than the dogmas of religion. Nor can Hegel's spiritualized state be the ultimate synthesis that the dialectic requires. Beyond the freedom of the democratic republic, though this is indeed the highest form of middle-class society, and beyond the state as it has yet evolved, is a higher form of society in which the state will be superseded, and to reach this higher stage a new revolution is required, a social revolution as contrasted with the political revolution that has already occurred. In the past, revolutions have transferred power from one class to another but they left the fundamental abuse, the power to dominate and exploit. Like Christianity the political revolution leaves men still with a double life, imaginary freedom and real servitude. For the root of servitude is not political; it lies in a system of production which permits one class to monopolize the means of production and in the division of labour which private ownership entails. Beyond the political revolution, therefore, there is the social revolution which by socializing production will wholly unite the man with the citizen and will once for all uproot the sources of exploitation and of social inequality. And as the middle class was the active force that produced the political revolution, so the proletariat, the product of middle-class dominance and the final class below which no exploited class remains, is the force which by freeing itself will free society, and by abolishing social inequality can create a classless society.

> *The division of labour implies the contradiction between the interest of the separate individual or the individual family and the communal interest of all individuals who have intercourse with one another. . . . For as soon as labour is distributed, each man has a particular, exclusive sphere of activity, which is forced upon him and from which he cannot escape . . . while in communist society, where nobody has one exclusive sphere of activity but each can become accomplished in any branch he wishes, society regulates the general production and thus makes it possible for me to do one thing today and another tomorrow.*[3]

Thus in the last resort materialism had for Marx an ethical meaning: the root of social inequality is economic; by comparison all political reform is superficial, leaving the source of inequality untouched; and only by abolishing private ownership can any substantial change be made; and by this change the whole inequitable structure of society will be changed at once. The classless society is both the final goal of social development and also the logical next step beyond the middle-class freedoms already achieved by the middle-class revolution. For Marx, as for Hegel, the unlimited relativism which the dialectic seems to impose on history is crowned by a last and absolute end to which his philosophy will show the way.

Economic Determinism

Feuerbach's claim that the motive forces in social history are material meant for Marx that these forces are economic. The economic, moreover, meant for him the method of economic production, for he was convinced that any system of production carries with it a corresponding way of distributing the social product, the way which alone will keep the system operating, and in turn the distribution creates a structure of social classes, each of which is determined by its position in the system. The method by which a society utilizes natural resources and produces the goods by which it lives is therefore for Marx the mainspring of its existence. Its mode of production at any given time explains its political and indeed its whole cultural condition at that time, and changes in the system of production explain the corresponding changes that occur in its politics and culture. This in bare outline is Marx's theory of economic determinism, which is the concrete social and political meaning that he attached to dialectical materialism.

Considered in relation to the future this theory provided Marx with his programme for a new working-class revolution, which is to abolish social inequality and ultimately to create a socialist and a classless society. Considered in relation to the past the theory provided him with his interpretation of the French Revolution. This was a middle-class revolution by which the new capitalist class of an industrial society destroyed the political privileges of the nobility and the clergy and swept away the remnants of feudal law and government which had hampered the rising system of capitalist production. It had rationalized and sanctified its purposes in the name of the rights of man, which it described as eternal and self-evident natural truths. From the point of view of a working class, however, the civil and political liberties of the democratic government are not the rights of man; they are the rights of the middle class. This does not mean that they are valueless, for the democratic republic is a higher stage of social evolution than the feudal society which it replaced; it is indeed the typical stage of a middle-class society and the highest it can attain, though still far from the highest stage possible. Marx's attitude toward political and civil liberty was thus always ambivalent. In comparison with the undefined liberties which he imputed to a socialist society, he described rights like the suffrage, and political methods like representation, as mere formalities or mere concealments of an underlying class despotism. In general, however, he assumed that socialism would continue and extend political liberty. But this never depended on an analysis of socialism but only on an a *priori* belief that in a developing society nothing valuable can be lost.

Thus Marx arrived at an evolutionary theory of society in which the whole system of natural law fell into place as the ideology appropriate to a specific stage of development. The normal course of social development is feudalism, capitalism, socialism, with a form of political organization fitted to each.

Moreover, his theory of revolution made evident the mechanism by which political change takes place: it is the incompatible interests of social classes and the struggle between them to dominate society in their own interest. The French Revolution relieved the middle class from exploitation by the older classes but left it an exploiting class. The wage-earning proletariat is an inevitable product of capitalism which rises *pari passu* with the bourgeoisie. The success of the bourgeois revolution opens the way for the more thoroughgoing proletarian revolution which in the end will sweep away the new exploiting class. But the final step will complete the process by abolishing classes and exploitation altogether.

Marx made it quite clear that he did not regard himself as having originated the theory of class antagonism. He took over and extended a theory created by French historians to explain the Revolution. In a letter to Engels he referred to Augustin Thierry as "the father of the class struggle in French historical writing."[4] What Marx objected to in the middle-class historians was the presumption that the class struggle had ended with the rise to power of the bourgeoisie, just as he objected to the economists' presumption that the laws of a capitalist economy were external and immutable. In the revolutions of his own day Marx believed that he *saw* a new type of revolutionary uprising which had as its spear point not a middle class intent upon political rights but a working class rising to the consciousness of its own degradation and confusedly determined to alter not the political superstructure but the underlying economic causes of social inequality.

> *What I did that was new was to prove: (1) that the existence of classes is only bound up with particular, historic phases in the development of production; (2) that the class struggle necessarily leads to the dictatorship of the proletariat; (3) that this directorship itself only constitutes the transition to the abolition of all classes and to a classless society.*[5]

The final step in Marx's argument, therefore, is that the structure of classes that exists in a society at any given period is itself an historical product which changes with the forces of economic production that the society is able to utilize. This he regarded as the ultimate cause to which the whole social, legal, and political framework of society can be traced back, while changes in this framework are to correlated with changes in the methods of economic production. Writing in 1859, in one of the few autobiographical passages that occur in his works, Marx explained how a brief editorial experience with economic questions, for which he felt inadequately prepared, drove him back to a reconsideration of his Hegelian studies in philosophy and jurisprudence.

> *I was led by my studies to the conclusion that legal relations as well as forms of state could neither be understood by themselves, nor explained by the so-called general progress of the human mind, but that they are rooted in the material conditions of life, which are summed up by Hegel . . . under the name of "civic society"; the anatomy of that civic society is to be sought in political economy.*[6]

This then was the final significance which Marx attached to materialism in contrast with Hegelian idealism. Hegel's civil society and not his state is the primary factor in social evolution. The legal and institutional relations that make up the state, and all the moral and religious ideas that accompany them, are only a superstructure built upon the underlying economic foundation of civil society.

> *The phantoms formed in the human brain are also, necessarily, sublimates of their material life-process, which is empirically verifiable and bound to material premises. Morality, religion metaphysics, all the rest of ideology and their corresponding forms of consciousness, thus no longer retain the semblance of independence. They have no history no development; but men, developing their material production and their material intercourse, alter, along with their real existence, their thinking and the products of their thinking. Life is not determined by consciousness, but consciousness by life.*[7]

The order of importance and of causal efficacy is reversed: it is the economic order that "produces" while the mind merely "reflects." As Marx said later, in Hegel "dialectic stands on its head"; dialectical materialism "turned it right way up" by removing the "mystifications" of idealism and substituting for them the substantial and tangible realities of the industrial system. Thus the dialectic no longer moves in the realm of logical abstractions but in the realm of real forces.

It is important to note, however, that it was not the dialectic which Marx changed but rather a metaphysical interpretation of it. The dialectic was a method, and it is quite clear that he meant to retain the main outline of Hegelian methodology. The purpose of the method in Hegel has been the essentially metaphysical one of establishing an order of precedence or of "degrees of reality" by which thought can rise from appearances to the Absolute Idea. What Marx "turned right way up" was the order of precedence, while his forces of production remained a kind of material analogue to Hegel's Absolute Spirit. Thus the actual facts and events of social, legal, and political history were still conceived by him as the "phenomenal forms" the appearances or manifestations of this underlying reality, a kind of surface-play of transient and largely accidental circumstance which draws its necessity from the hidden force out of which it arises. On purely empirical grounds the fact that political institutions and moral ideas are "products" of economic conditions would in no way entail the conclusion that they cannot in turn affect these conditions. In short, economic factors in dialectical materialism do not act merely as scientific causes which produce empirical consequences. They are more nearly creative energies that operate like semi-personalized agents, though it is only fair to say that when Marx dealt with an actual problem of historical analysis, he was almost always better than his method. But the important critical question still remains, whether the dialectic was not a pseudo-method. In fact the sociological importance of Marx's materialism depended on the degree in which it ceased to be in any definite sense dialectical and became simply empirical and causal.

In *The Poverty of Philosophy* Marx applied his new point of view to the criticism of economic science, both the classical economics and the economics of contemporary socialism. For the former he had a high admiration, being convinced that as an account of capitalism it was substantially correct. His objections against it were aimed largely at the incredible naivete of the economists in respect to the historical aspects of their subject. As Engels said later, they argue as if Richard the Lion Hearted, had he only known a little economics, might have saved six centuries of bungling by adopting free trade, instead of wasting his time on the crusades. As theologians divide religions into true and false, viz., their own and all others, so the economists treat all economic systems as if they were blundering approximations to capitalism, while they treat capitalism as if its relations and categories were natural and eternal. Against this Marx defended the thesis that economics is an historical science. Its laws are applicable only to the stage of economic production to which they belong; its categories, such as profits, wages, and rent, are "theoretical expressions, the abstractions, of the social relations of production."

> *These ideas, these categories, are as little eternal as the relations they express. They are historical and transitory products.*[8]

Thus economics became for Marx a combination of history and analysis: analysis of the relations prevailing in any given system of production, supplemented by the history of the rise and development of that system.

Toward humanitarian, utopian, and reformist cirticisms of classical economic Marx was less tolerant. Such projects, in his opinion, offer palliatives, sentimentality, and idealist dreams without either history or analysis. In substance they all reduce to some plan for separating the good from the bad in capitalism, usually to some impossible way of uniting capitalist production with socialist distribution. Utopian socialism, he believed, refuses to face the hard fact that, given a system of production, distribution of the social product follows, and the whole class structure and political system with it. In fact, he was much less than just to the utopian socialists, for his own theory of the classless society was as utopian as anything in Proudhon. He merely postponed utopia to an indefinite future. Marx shared with Hegel a contempt for any personal ideal or desire, which he identified with mere caprice. The ideal is all to be attributed to the internal drive of the system itself, and is good merely because it is "inevitable"; that is, the final goal of the system's evolution. The practical effect of this prepossession was that Marx discounted any attempt at reform. He considered legislation to be incapable of changing the industrial system in any important respect, and hence he valued social legislation merely as a step toward revolution. The capitalist system must in the end be "smashed," and Marx never abandoned the essentially utopian idea that smashing one system is a sure way to create a better system.

Ideology and the Class Struggle

It was characteristic of Marx that he was interested less in perfecting dialectical materialism as a philosophy of history than in applying it to concrete situations, especially with the purpose of finding a programme of action for a consciously revolutionary proletariat. Thus in 1848 he and Engels used the class struggle as the key to "all hitherto existing society" in the *Communist Manifesto*, which became one of the great revolutionary tracts of all times. A little later he wrote two pamphlets to explain the failure of the revolutionary struggle which had just occurred in France. They applied the economic interpretation to a problem in contemporary history.[9] These pamphlets illustrate the singular combination of dogmatism with shrewd observation and detailed realistic information characteristic of Marx. They give a very able and incisive analysis of the economic affiliations of the several parties in the revolution and also a clear insight into the inchoate state of the proletarian parties. They are indeed much the kind of analysis of a revolutionary situation which any first-class journalist would now try to make, a clear indication of the extent to which Marxian interpretation has gained general acceptance. At the same time Marx's description is underlain by a largely a *priori* theory of social classes, and the pamphlets certainly do not justify the extravagant claims which Marxists often make for the dialectic as a means of prognosis. Marx's prophecy, that the recurrence of a business depression like that of 1847 would start the revolution anew, was mistaken and, as Engels candidly admitted later, Marx quite failed to appreciate the possibilities for development contained within the capitalist system.

The pamphlets serve also to make clearer Marx's conception of the relation of social classes both to the course of history and also to their own mentality. The class had for Marx a collective unity as the nation had for Hegel. It acts in history as a unit and it produces its characteristic ideas and beliefs as a unit, acting under the compulsion of its place in the economic and social system. The individual counts mainly through his membership in the class, because his ideas—his moral convictions, his esthetic preferences, even the kind of reasoning that seems to him convincing—are in the main a reflection of the ideas generated by the class.

> *Upon the different forms of property, upon the social conditions of existence rises an entire superstructure of distinct and characteristically formed sentiments, illusions, modes of thought and views of life. The entire class creates and forms them out of its material foundations and out of the corresponding social relations. The single individual who derives them through tradition and education may imagine that they form the real motives and the starting-point of his activity.*[10]

This passage suggests the peculiar sense in which Marx used the word ideology. Ideas reflect and more or less misrepresent an underlying economic reality; they are "mystifications" of it, at least in so far as their origin has not been unmasked. As ideal motives or reasons for conduct they are merely appearances or manifestations of something which is in its real nature quite different. And though they seem valid and compelling to their unsophisticated possessor, their compulsive force is really something which is not in his consciousness at all but is concealed in the social position of his class and in its relations to economic production. The theory evidently depends upon Hegel's contrast of appearance and reality. Marx's forces of production, like Hegel's World Spirit, are infinitely cunning in creating all manner of illusions and mystifications to realize their inherent purpose, and Marx's classes give birth to their appropriate ideologies much as Hegel imagined that the spirit of the nation gives birth to a national culture. An expression like "modes of thought and views of life," however, may be very misleading. It can cover a spectrum of beliefs and practices ranging from superstition to science, and the fact that a belief originates in a social class or is characteristic of it does not imply that it is either valid or invalid. Marx no more than anyone else supposed that all beliefs are on the same level of truth or that all practices are equally moral. The notion of ideology was at once one of Marx's most pregnant ideas and also one of the vaguest and most subject to abuse. That people are biased by social position is obvious; it may even be true that bias sometimes helps them to see evidence that other people overlook, but the notion that bias piled on bias adds up to evidence is merely a myth. Ideology as Marx, used it was a powerful controversial weapon but one that can be used with equal force by all contestants until every theory, including Marxism itself, is "unmasked" as a form of special pleading. The Arbiter of every such controversy is power.

The two pamphlets on the revolutionary movement in France laid down also the main outline of Marx's theory of class structure in modern industrial societies. This theory was pretty clearly suggested to him by his observation of French society and his experience with French socialism, though Marx's conception of industrial capitalism and of an industrial proletariat depended in the main on the history of English industry. For no very cogent reason he assumed that this combination provided a type to which all industrial societies would in general approximate. The theory postulated a middle class mainly urban and commercial in its interests and devoted politically to the civil and political liberties of the Revolution, and an industrial proletariat also mainly urban but concerned more with economic security than with political liberty. These classes Marx regarded as the active political forces in a modern society, the forces between which the class struggle mainly takes place, so that the issue is fundamentally the dominance of one or the other. The other classes that the theory recognized, the peasantry and the petty bourgeoisie, he regarded as politically inert though they may, under proper circumstances, be able to affect what the two active classes can do. Marx also considered the ideology of the peasant class and of farmers to be characteristically petty bourgeois.

This theory is obviously tailored to fit the dialectic, which obliged Marx to have two main opponents who generate change by their mutual tensions. For this reason it was largely a *priori* even though it embodied his penetrating perception of the revolutionary consequences of the industrial revolution. Because the dialectic runs in terms of the logical contrariety between two types, details are regarded as merely variations on a theme, and minor differences do not count. Hence the theory records observations of society at large but not detailed observation of any single society. What is left over from the two main classes is merely lumped, with the result that what he calls the petty bourgeoisie is a heterogeneous collection of elements that have little in common except that they resist being classified as capitalists or workingmen. Thus it puts farmers and peasants with independent artisans and small shopkeepers; it has no place for professional people or the increasing number of white-collar workers whose jobs were created by industry. In consequence, though Marxists have always believed the class struggle to be the only reliable guide to political strategy, the vagueness of Marx's concept of a social class was responsible for some of his worst errors in prediction. Throughout the nineteenth century farmers were the despair of Marxian theorists and organizers, and peasants became industrial labourers only under compulsion. No empirical sociology would count independent artisans and office workers as having the same type of work experience. And the expectation that every kind of salaried employee would be absorbed into the class of wage labourers was wide of the mark. It is impossible not to believe that Marx's farsighted predictions of some trends in capitalism were made in spite of the dialectic rather than because of it.

Marx's Summary

The fragmentary manner in which Marx worked out the theory of dialectical materialism justifies the quotation at some length of his only summary statement of it, which was not written, however, until several years after the theory took shape.

> *In the social production which mean carry on they enter into definite relations that are indispensable and independent of their will; these relations of production correspond to a definite stage of development of their material powers of production. The sum total of these relations of production constitutes the economic structure of society—the real foundation, on which rise legal and political superstructures and to which correspond definite forms of social consciousness. The mode of production in material life determines the general character of the social, political, and spiritual processes of life. It is not the consciousness of men that determines their existence, but, on the contrary, their social existence determines their consciousness. At a certain stage of their development, the material forces of production in society come in conflict with the existing relations of production, or—what is but a legal expression for the same thing—with the property relations within which they had been at work before. From forms of development of the forces of production these relations turn into their fetters. Then comes the period of social revolution. With the change of the economic foundation the entire immense superstructure is more or less rapidly transformed. In considering such transformations the distinction*

should always be made between the material transformation of the economic conditions of production which can be determined with the precision of natural science, and the legal, political, religious, aesthetic, or philosophic—in short ideological forms in which men become conscious of this conflict and fight it out. . . . No social order ever disappears before all the productive forces, for which there is room in it, have been developed; and new higher relations of production never appear before the conditions of their existence have matured in the womb of the old society. Therefore, mankind always takes up only such problems as it can solve; since, looking at the matter more closely, we will always find that the problem itself arises only when the material conditions necessary for its solution already exist or are at least in the process of formation.[11]

Marx's theory of cultural development, then, as presented in this passage, included four principal propositions. First, it is a succession of stages each of which is dominated by a typical system of producing and exchanging goods. This system of productive forces generates its own characteristic and appropriate ideology, which include law and politics together with the ideal or so-called spiritual products of the civilization, such as morals, religion, art, and philosophy. As an ideal pattern each stage is complete and systematic, a coordinated whole in which the ideological factors are adjusted to the underlying forces of production and to each other. In actual use, as for example in the descriptive and historical chapters of *Capital,* Marx relaxed the logical rigidity of the theory. At any given time the development of the forces of production has run unequally in different countries and in different industries of a single country; there are remnants of the older economy and beginnings of the newer. Consequently there are correspondingly different ideologies in different strata of population. Second, the whole process is "dialectical"; its motive force is supplied by the internal tensions created by disparities between a newly evolving system of production and the persisting ideology appropriate to an older system. A new method of production finds itself in a hostile ideological environment which must be dissolved before it can grow. The ideology appropriate to the old system becomes more and more restrictive of the new, and the internal stresses and strains build up until they reach a breaking point. A new social class, with an ideology appropriate to its social position in the new system of production, comes into sharper conflict with the older classes having ideologies bred by the obsolescent system. The general pattern of development, therefore, is cyclical, an alternation of periods of evolution, in which a new system of production is gradually formed and new ideologies are gradually created, and periods of revolution in which the whole constellation of forces breaks down and recrystallizes, so to speak, in another pattern. Third, the forces of production—the methods of producing goods and of distributing the products of industry—are always primary as compared with their secondary, ideological consequences. The material or economic forces are "real" or substantial, while the ideological relations are only apparent or phenomenal. Fourth, the dialectical development is an internal process of unfolding or of vitalistic realization. The productive forces inherent in any society develop completely before the dialectical transformation or recrystallization of forces takes place. And since the ideological superstructure merely reflects the internal growth of the underlying metaphysical substance, the problems that appear upon the level of consciousness will always be soluble with the further unfolding and the progressive realization of the substratum behind them.

In this imposing speculative structure, at once so suggestive and so puzzling, it is the third item, the primacy of the "forces of production," which belongs most characteristically to Marx and is also crucial for any empirical use of the theory. For this thesis is what labels the system "materialism," in Marx's sense of that word, and also underlies the claim that the theory provides an especially "scientific" approach to social problems. If the theory is to be used in explaining any historical series of events, it is evidently necessary that the "forces of production" should be clearly distinguishable from the "relations of production," or the foundation from the superstructure. But this distinction is never clearly made by Marx, and seemingly it is impossible in principal that it should be made clear. For a society's forces of production must include at least available raw materials and trade routes, yet they cannot exclude technology, because technology determines whether raw materials are in any effective sense "available." The mere presence of iron or coal does not affect a culture which lacks the technique of smelting. But technology depends, in part at least, on skill and knowledge, or on science, and science must belong to consciousness or to the superstructure. Or to put the difficulty the other way around, the superstructure clearly includes legal institutions that govern the ownership of tools or the accumulation of capital, yet these may determine how raw materials are used or whether they are used at all. Thus when Marx himself used his theory to explain the rise of capitalism in England, he cited the expropriation of the monasteries as a source of capital, and the emancipation of the serfs as a factor in creating a class of free labourers; but these were obviously political or legal changes or, in the case of the monasteries, depended on a change of religious belief. In a tangle of social institutions it is meaningless to insists that some single change is always the "cause" of all other changes. The truth is that Marx's distinction of superstructure and foundation was not empirical. His model was Hegel's metaphysical distinction between appearance and reality, as is evident from his singular conclusion that every social problem must be soluble. The obscurity of Marx's theory became more evident in its elaboration by his collaborator, Friedrich Engels.

Engels on Dialectic

The theory of dialectical materialism was completed by Marx about 1850. From that time forward it was presumed in all that he wrote but even in *Capital* it was nowhere stated; the treatment of socialism in that work turned discussion toward intrinsically less important economic theories such as surplus value. It was not until later in the nineteenth century that the economic explanation of history began to assume the importance it deserved and to extend its influence beyond the circle of professed Marxists. In the meantime the public had been prepared to take an interest in it by the spread of biological evolution, though inherently there was little if any logical relation between the two. Anthropologists like Lewis Morgan, apparently without depending upon Marx, had stressed the importance of technology in primitive cultures. The development of historical scholarship among socialists, especially in Germany, caused the economic interpretation of history to be applied and re-examined. By this time Marx was already in failing health (he died in 1883) and the further exposition of his theory fell to his friend, Friedrich Engels.[12] Unfortunately, Engels, though he was a man of strong common sense and transparent candor, was philosophically not very acute and in no sense original. He elaborated Marx's fragmentary texts but he left the underlying obscurities almost exactly where they were.

In their understanding of the general nature of dialectic and the kind of necessity which it discloses in history, it is clear that both Marx and Engels relied on Hegel. They objected to particular uses of it by Hegel, which Engels said were nearly always arbitrary, and they rejected of course the idealist interpretation of it as a self-development of thought. It is, on the contrary, a self-development of nature itself reflected in thought. But this implied no very serious change of Hegel, since he also believed that the dialectic revealed a development implicit in reality. Hegel's metaphysical logic, therefore, was an assumed major premise in the whole Marxian argument, with this difference only, that Marx and Engels substituted a materialist for an idealist metaphysics. For Engels as for Hegel the value for dialectic lay in the fact that it permitted the discovery of a necessary evolution in history:

> *From this standpoint [of Hegel's philosophy] the history of mankind no longer appeared as a confused whirl of senseless deeds of violence, all equally condemnable before the judgement seat of the now matured philosophical reason . . . but as the process of development of humanity itself.*[13]

In his Feuerbach Engels attributed rationality to nature in exactly the Hegelian sense. The real or rational cannot be equated with existence because much of what exists is irrational and therefore unreal; for example, in 1789 the French monarchy existed but was not real. In other words, for Engels as for Hegel "real" means not existent but significant or valuable. The process of history is inherently selective and self-realizing rather than causal, and in effect the important is regarded as bringing itself into existence simply because it is important, after the manner of an Aristotelian entelechy. The whole conception was fundamentally vitalistic or teleological, just as it was in Hegel. Despite their so-called materialism, the necessity of history for Marx and Engels as for Hegel was really a moral necessity, the "progressive development," as Engels calls it, of civilization by the expansion of its inner forces. The supposed necessity reflected their faith in the inevitable success of the proletarian revolution, as for Hegel it reflected his faith in the mission of Germany.

According to Engels's account of the dialectic in his *Feuerbach* the important difference between Marx and Hegel lay in the fact that Marx adopted a materialist version of dialectic; ideas are not forces, as Hegel supposed, but "pictures of real things," the conscious reflex of the dialectic evolution of the real world." Engels's account of ideas as "pictures" got a posthumous importance when it was reproduced by Lenin in his *Materialism and Empirio-Criticism*. Quite obviously the "picture," used as a collective term for every kind of idea from a scientific theory to an hallucination, was nothing but a meaningless figure of speech. Apparently it was intended to have two connotations. It suggested, first, that ideology is relatively insubstantial as compared with economic forces and that any form of philosophical idealism is a "mystification" whose real purpose is to support reaction. It suggested, second, that ideas do have real counterparts in the world; in this sense it was a figurative way of denying subjectivism. And while subjectivism has never been a serious philosophical position, it was convenient for Engels to regard Kant and Hume in that light. His treatment of modern philosophy was therefore summary in the extreme. He merely assumed that every philosophy must be either idealist or materialist, and thus with hardly more than a sentence he dismissed the whole anti-metaphysical tradition from Hume to Kant. Apparently Engels really believed that their argument could be refuted merely by pointing out that there is such an operation as empirical confirmation! The truth is, of course, that the critical question about dialectic was not metaphysical at all. The question was whether Hume and Kant were right in making the methodological distinctions they did between casual statements and valuations.

Engels made it clear in the *Feuerbach* that what chiefly commended the dialectic to him and to Marx was its power as a solvent of dogmatism. It was this, he said, which made Hegelianism a revolutionary philosophy.

> *Truth, the cognition of which is the business of philosophy, became in the hands of Hegel no longer an aggregate of finished dogmatic statements, which once discovered had merely to be learned by heart. Truth lay now in the process of cognition itself, in the long historical development of science, which mounts from lower to ever higher*

levels of knowledge without ever reaching, by discovering so-called absolute truth, a point at which it can proceed no further and where it would have nothing more to do than to fold its hands and admire the absolute truth to which it had attained.[14]

There are neither self-evident truths in science nor natural and inalienable rights in society; nothing is absolute, final, or sacred. The most that can be said is that a scientific theory or a social practice is "suitable" to its time and conditions, and all theories and practices that prevail are suitable, as is shown simply by the fact that they do prevail. But it is certain that with the passage of time and change of conditions they will pass away and be supplanted by something "higher." He merely assumed, quite uncritically, that civilization as a whole always will progress, or more specifically, that socialism will be an improvement over capitalism.

Both Marx and Engels occasionally played with the idea that dialectic is merely a working hypothesis which implies no substantive conclusion whatever. This was perhaps a mark of deference to Kant that was hard to avoid in Germany in the third quarter of the nineteenth century. It was also a "deviation" that revisionist Marxists were prone to and that Lenin felt it necessary to refute in 1909 when it occurred among Russian Marxists, for if the dialectic were only a working hypothesis, its moral appeal would largely evaporate. Thus Engels in *Anti-Duhring* said that the dialectic proves nothing but is merely a way of advancing to new spheres of research, and that it does away with the need for a metaphysics or a philosophy of history. Marx was even more explicit. In a letter which he wrote in 1877 to a Russian correspondent he said that the account of primitive accumulation in *Capital* did not pretend to do more than trace the path by which capitalism emerged from a feudal economy in Western Europe, and he protested against a critic who, in applying his account to Russia, had metamorphosed an historical sketch into "an historico-philosophic theory of the *marche generale* imposed by fate upon every people."

By studying each of these forms of evolution separately and then comparing them one can easily find the clue to this phenomenon [different historical results from apparently similar conditions], but one will never arrive there by the universal passport of a general

> *historico-philosophical theory, the supreme virtue of which consists in being super-historical.*[15]

If this statement were taken literally, the dialectic would mean about the same as the "comparative method" so popular in anthropology during the last quarter of the nineteenth century. In the same strain Engels in his letters criticized the younger German socialists who, he said, used historical materialism as an excuse for not studying history. Yet it is certain that Marx did not regard the history of capitalism merely as empirical history. Had he done so he would hardly have spoken in the Preface to *Capital* of "tendencies which work out with an iron necessity toward an inevitable goal," or of "the natural phases of evolution," or said that a country more highly industrialized than others, "simply presents those others with a picture of their own future." Either the dialectic is a method that makes historical prediction possible or else the Marxian historian has at his command only the same methods that other historians use. Certainly if the dialectic is only a working hypothesis, it does not warrant the assertion that the proletarian revolution is "inevitable."

Engels on Economic Determinism

Apart from the philosophical principles entering into the dialectic, Engels' elaboration of dialectical materialism dealt mainly with the use of economic interpretation in history. In the letters already referred to, written between 1890 and 1894, he discussed the extent to which such interpretation is possible or useful, his main purpose being to correct what he thought to be the exaggerated claims made for it by younger members of the party. He acknowledged that he and Marx, in putting forward a new idea, had overstated the extent to which economic causes could be found for political and legal institutions. He asserted that it would be pedantic to seek economic causes for all history, instancing the High German consonant-shift as one for which no economic origin cold probably be given. The example was a little strange and one wonders whether he realized that he was taking the history if language, with all its implications for differences of national culture, quite out of the region of economic explanation. He suggested that in the case of religion and mythology economic forces may act negatively rather tan positively. He admitted that, within a general framework of economic forces, political or even dynastic relationships may exert a large historical influence, as in the rise of Prussia from Brandenburg rather than from some other small German state. And he acknowledged that legislation "can close some paths of economic development and open others," though it cannot alter its main course. It had never been Marx's belief, he said, that economic forces are the sole causes of historical change, but only that they are "ultimate" or "fundamental." The economic factor is "the strongest, most elemental, and most decisive." Finally, Engels now argued that it was the special merit of dialectic to take into account the interaction of all the different factors that are present together in a historical situation.

> *According to the materialistic conception of history the factor which is in last instance decisive is the production and re-production of actual life. More than this neither Marx nor I have ever asserted. But when anyone distorts this so as to read that the economic factor is the sole element, he converts the statement into a meaningless, abstract, absurd phrase. The economic condition is the basis, but the various elements of the superstructure—the political forms of the class contests, and their results, the constitutions—the legal forms, and also all the reflexes of these actual contests in the brains of the participants, the political, legal, philosophical, the religious views . . . all these exert an influence on the development of the historical struggles, and in many instances determine their form.*[16]

With all these concessions it is hard to see what there is about the economic explanation of history that the most bourgeois historian would have any concern to deny or that calls for dialectic to explain it. What Engels says amounts in substance to little more than that Marx emphasized a factor in social studies that had been overlooked or undervalued—namely, that in any society prevalent ways of producing or exchanging goods are intricately related to economic, political, and moral institutions and practices. Few if any historians would now question this or deny its importance or refuse to acknowledge Marx's originality. He has been called, perhaps with some exaggeration but certainly with some justification, the "true father of economic history."[17]

At the same time it is obvious that Engels meant to claim a good deal more than this for Marx and for the theory of economic determinism. He insists that the economic factor is the "most elemental," even while he admits that legislation can sometimes control it, and he retains the distinction between foundation and superstructure even while he argues that the superstructure causally influences the foundation. But Marx's philosophy depended on the presumption that the two can always be clearly discriminated, and also that there is a clear sense in which the foundation causes the superstructure but not *vice versa*. Without these presumption there is no sense in calling Marx's philosophy materialism, or in assuming that only a revolution will modify capitalism. On Engels' showing there is no reason why a moral idea—a conscientious revulsion against a fifteen-hour work day for women and children, for example—should not lead to a legal restriction on hours of labour or why the law should not be effective. In effect Engels has undermined any meaning that Marx attached to historical "inevitability."

Engels' letters also expanded somewhat the brief account that Marx had given of ideology and its dependence on the economic system. Even more explicitly than Marx he treated science in a wholly different way from law, morals, philosophy, religion, and art, though all ought logically to count as part of the superstructure. In substance both men treat science simply as true, and because it is true it provides a firm basis for technology. The only senses in which Engels regards science as affected by the economy are, first, that problems invest, gated by scientists may have been set by industry, and second, that scientific discoveries may be socially important because they react on technology. Apparently it never occurred to either Marx or Engels that anyone would try to find an economic derivation for the concept of scientific truth itself, as should be done by a consistent Marxian relativism that treated science in the same way as morals, art, and religion. If this were done the standard of truth accepted in a society ought to depend on its class structure, and proletarian science ought to differ from bourgeois science. Some Marxists, for controversial purposes, have indeed occasionally approached some such conclusion, but this hardly ranks as more than a desperate effort to follow the unworkable distinction between foundation and superstructure. The notion that ideology may in some cases affect what figures in a society as a standard of truth has, however, produced the rather large body of theory now known as sociology of knowledge.[18]

The other parts of the ideological superstructure Engels treated very differently. The validity which men claim for law, morals, politics, art, religion, and philosophy is a "false consciousness" or a deceptive reflection of the interests which the system of production assigns to the various classes engaged in it. Here the thinker is not clearly aware of the motives that actuate him but imagines that his ideas are true merely in and for themselves. To this category Engels attributed especially abstractions like justice, liberty, and supposed esthetic, moral, and religious verities when these are not recognized as belonging in some specific social context. These are what have more recently been named "rationalizations"—specious defenses of wishful thinking or the covert idealization of class interests. At the same time Engels certainly did not regard all ideologies as equally false. The ideology of the proletariat is superior to that of the bourgeoisie presumably for two reasons. In the first place, the philosophy of Marx makes it clear to the proletarian that his ideas of morality, art, and philosophy do depend upon his class and its position in the class struggle. Hence he can adjust his morals to the cause of the revolution. In the second place the proletariat is a "rising" class which present history is bringing to a position of dominance; its ideology is therefore the "wave of the future." In both cases the force of Engels' arguments depended on his faith in progress and in the accuracy of the prediction that the direction of progress is now toward a proletarian revolution and a new proletarian society.

Dialectical Materialism and Politics

The concept of ideology, economic determinism, and the class struggle complete the theoretical parts of Marx's social philosophy. They were to provide the stimulus to a working-class revolution and also a guide to the strategy of revolutionary parties, for the purpose of a philosophy, as Marx said, is not to interpret the world but to change it. They convey the impression of a high degree of intellectual originality and of penetrating observation, but not less of an irritating indefiniteness of meaning. The root of their indefiniteness in every case is the underlying vagueness in Marx's system already mentioned, namely, the impossibility of distinguishing clearly between the economic basis and the superstructure. Because of this indefiniteness the claims that

Marx's socialism is in some special sense "scientific" and that his theories have a unique predictive value are wholly exaggerated. He made several far-sighted predictions about the future of capitalism, but he also was often wrong, as might be true of any man with a great fund of knowledge and keen insight. But this is not the same as science. The great importance of the concepts mentioned merits comment at this point.

The words "ideology" is the only term from Marx's formidable vocabulary that has come into common use, and though Marx did not coin the word, he gave it more of less the meaning that it now has in common usage. The word has long ceased to have any connotation of Marxism. Its meaning hardly admits of precise definition, though it refers to a fact now generally recognized. This is the fact that any social group which acts together as a unit must have a common body of beliefs, values, and convictions that "reflects" its understanding of itself, of its environment, and of other social groups with which it has transactions. Such a body of common beliefs is indeed a condition of its existence as a group. These beliefs range all the way from knowledge to myth, with no very sharp dividing lines between them, because until they are questioned they all seem to those who share them to be merely the "normal" ways for human beings to think or believe. That every society does and must have such a body of shared ideas is now a commonplace of cultural anthropology. In Marx's usage, and to some degree in common usage, the word "ideology" is likely to have a faint—sometimes an explicit—implication of condescension; it assumes the superior sophistication of the user as compared with the simple-minded attitude of those who merely take an idea without question. Sometimes the word has connotations like "rationalization," "wishful thinking," or "prejudice." The distinctive claim of Marx's theory is that ideological beliefs are characteristic of social classes and reflect the position of the class in the class structure of the society, which in turn can be explained by the system of economic production. This is certainly much too limited, for any group may have its typical beliefs and attitudes, and if the word has the usual sense of rationalization; Freud's psychology can provide more examples than economics. In Marx's use the word described especially the theories of natural law in liberal political theory or in classical economics, which he regarded as typical of middle-class people.

The use of "ideology" in politics is almost always controversial. "Unmasking" an opponent is standard Marxian practice: it means showing that his arguments make a pretense of reasonableness but are really covert defenses of class privilege, and seem valid only because of his class prejudices. For controversial purposes it is often very effective, but it is negative and can also be self-defeating; because, since everyone has some sort of ideology, "unmasking" is a game that can be played on everyone and that everyone can play. And when everything, including Marxism itself, has been "unmasked," the positive conclusion has still to be drawn and defended. Any serious reasoning, on politics or any other subject, simply must go on the assumption that good evidence can be distinguished from bad. This capacity is no more characteristic of one social class than of another.

Marx's theory of economic determinism also was an idea of great originality, highly suggestive but also capable of fantastic exaggeration which Engels himself thought it necessary to disclaim and which sometimes brought the idea into unmerited disrepute. As G.D.H. Cole, by no means an unsympathetic critic of Marxism, once said, "There are Marxists who cannot see a flapper use her lipstick without producing pat an explanation of her conduct in terms of the processes of production and the class struggle." The difficulty of seeing the importance of the idea was largely occasioned by Marx himself, by his insistence on the priority of economic to all other explanations and by his description of economic factors as material and therefore more scientific or more open to observation than others. This was in reality a fragment or Marx's metaphysics, his predilection for materialism. But when a social scientist is talking about human behavior—and what people do in economic relations is behavior—drawing a line between mind and matter is neither possible nor useful. Another obstacle that Marx set up against appreciating economic determinism was his tendency to turn it into a philosophy of history. This was a frequent nineteenth-century speculation, quite baseless and often merely a misunderstanding of organic evolution—that there is some standard, straight-line succession of stages that every society runs through. Yet when all the objections are made, economic explanation in political and social history is enormously useful. No historian would now disregard it. Technology, transportation, trade routes, available raw materials, the distribution of wealth in a society have also ways been important for history and politics, and they still are. They are related to the political institutions of a society, its law, its social classes, and its morals and art. All these together form an intricately related complex, and no single factor "explains" them all, but neither can the economy be left out. Economic determinism was one factor—certainly not the only one—in making the study of politics more realistic than was possible with the utilitarian separation of politics from economics, or with an almost wholly legalist approach to the subject. It was a step in the direction of a later tendency to bring it into contact with social and cultural history, or with anthropology and social psychology. The abuses of economic interpretation in history by socialists after Marx came, as Engels said, from those who used it as an excuse for not studying history.

The concepts of ideology and economic determinism underpinned the concept of the class struggle, so that the three together were considered by Marx to provide a strategical guide for the proletariat in accomplishing the social revolution. Marx's theory of social classes was in fact largely a *priori* and designed to fit his theory of social revolution. He certainly never made an empirical study of the class structure of any society. His theory was indeed put together rather incongruously from his experience as a revolutionist in France, supplemented by his valid perception of the social importance of the industrial revolution which, at the time when Marx wrote, was mainly a phenomenon of English society. Thus he assumed a dominant middle class, essentially plutocratic and mainly urban, sharply distinguished from a nobility which was a feudal remnant, and from large body of peasant farmers. None of this applied at all accurately to England, where capitalist agriculture had displaced the peasant proprietor. In England also the wealthy middle class had intermarried extensively with the nobility. Marx's theory, therefore, was in many respects not at all a good guide to political strategy. It never made any significant impression on the English working class, who according to Marx's theory ought to have been its readiest recipients. Marxian party socialism succeeded far better in Germany than in France, yet Marx always looked upon Germany as a backward country in comparison with either France or England.

Marx's account of the behaviour of social classes presented some theoretical peculiarities. A social class is for him a collective entity, as nations were for Hegel, and their members, as he said in the Preface to *Capital*, can be treated as "personifications of economic categories, representations of special class relations and class interests." As a rule, therefore, a social class acts competitively in its own interest, very much like the economic man of classical economics. But he dialectic requires that its ideology should be also at some point self-contradictory and its behaviour suicidal. Though an individual's beliefs and behavior are assumed in the main to be those that the position of his class impresses on him, the class must also occasionally produce unusual individuals who break loose and provide a new ideology for a rising class that will supplant the old ruling class. As Marx said in the *Communist Manifesto*, there is "a portion of the bourgeois ideologists, who have raised themselves to the level of comprehending theoretically the historical movements as a whole." The passage was written at a time when Marx thought of communists not as a political party but as intellectualist revolutionists able to spark and direct discontent from the outside. The passage provided the germ of the role that Lenin assigned to the Marxist intellectual and indirectly therefore of Lenin's theory of the party as the vanguard of the proletariat. The final disappearance of social classes, which Marx expected to happen in the final stage of socialism, seems to be logically no more than a fragment of romantic individualism that Marx never got rid of. It is quite discrepant with the collectivist bent of this social philosophy or the generally realistic temper of his thought. Both he and Engels attributed classes to the division of social labour, and how a society becoming steadily more highly industrialized can simplify its specialization defies explanation.

The struggle for power between social classes provides the driving force for politics, because as Marx understands political organization, some class must at any given time be dominant. It will use its superior power to exploit classes with less power, and the state is merely the apparatus of power which it uses for exploitation, "a committee for managing the common affairs" of the dominant class. The law is a body of rules that upholds what the exploiting class calls its "rights." The key to successful political leadership is the understanding that politics is merely a conventionalized kind of warfare, that a party is the general staff which plans and directs the strategy of whatever class it represents. A conception of politics like this obviously represents the point of view of a revolutionist who regards the existing political system as so unjust that it can only be "smashed." It represents also the point of view of a person so far from power that he never contemplates even in imagination what it would be like to have the responsibility of governing. After the system is smashed, however, the successful revolutionist will have nothing but law and politics to put together a new system, and he will certainly not describe that, even in his own mind, as merely a means of exploitation. Like Stalin he will describe the relations between peasants and industrial workers in Russia as "friendly," which will be as fictitious, or as true, as the same statement made about relations between the classes in any society. For if classes depend on the division of labour, it is as easy to follow Plato in describing their relations as cooperative as to follow Marx in describing them as hostile, the truth being that in some respects they are the one and in some respects the other. Pending the revolution, a party which thinks of social classes as continually at war will give its attention to planning the revolution and will have very hazy plans for doing anything come structive afterward. In general this is what Marx did.

Capitalism as an Institution

The thought of Marx's early writings was heavily influenced by his early Hegelian training. The reasoning by which he constructed its framework was largely deductive, but like Hegel he tended to fit into the framework a great mass of data drawn from his historical studies. It aimed to be a philosophy of history, and following his Hegelian model, Marx assumed that all significant data would in fact fit into a sufficiently spacious framework. As Hegel said, "The real is the rational," and Marx too supposed that dialectical materialism could yield a universal theory of the evolution of civilization. He never abandoned this conception, but after 1850 he devoted his life as a scholar less to this kind of speculation and more to using his ideas in a historical interpretation of contemporary society in Western Europe. In so doing he was developing the most fruitful germ in philosophical Hegelianism—its concept of institutional history—and what in substance Marx was trying to do was to treat capitalism as a social institution. He had no thought, of course, of giving up his original practical purpose of furthering a social revolution or of supplying its intellectual underpinning. Hence without any consciousness of dividing his effort he could at the same time engage in continuous plans to organize socialist parties. His twofold plan involved an intensive study of the economic origins of existing social classes and a thoroughgoing economic analysis of the nature of the antagonism between these classes. These two lines of investigation formed the principal subjects of his work on *Capital*. The first took him into extensive historical research into the origins of the capitalist organization of industry, the rise of the middle class, and the formation of its counterpart, the industrial wage-earning class, which Marx rightly regarded as the major development in modern European society. The second undertook to back history with a precise economic analysis of capitalism, upon lines already set by the classical economists, to show at once the mechanism by which capitalism produces the two chief classes and the grounds for their inevitable and growing antagonism. This part of Marx's work issued in the theory of surplus value, which unfortunately tended to monopolize the discussion of Marxian socialism in its earlier stages.

The historical chapters of *Capital*, especially those which deal with the earlier history of he capitalist organization of industry, prior to the eighteenth century, and with the formation of a class dependent solely upon its wages were the best of all Marx's writings. They have scarcely been superseded even yet, despite the attention given to economic history by later writers, who were in no small degree inspired by the beginning Marx made. He opened up the main avenues of approach to the historical study of capitalism, especially as the new industrial system affected social history: the formation of a proletariat by the divorce of the peasantry from common rights in the land, the destruction of household industry by the growth of capitalist organization, the steady increase in the size and power of the units of such organization, and the acceleration of these processes by the expropriation of the church and the colonial exploitation of America and the Indies. The distinctive feature of Marx's treatment was his stress upon the changes in human and social relations that result from industrial and commercial changes, and particularly upon the cramping, even the distorting, of the workers' lives by the steady advance of the division of labour. Marx's general thesis was that the working class has been subjected by industrial organization to a regimentation at odds with the profession of liberty and equality in the bourgeois democratic philosophy.

> *In manufacture, the enrichment of the collective worker, and therefore of capital, in the matter of social productivity, is dependent upon the impoverishment of the workers in the matter of their individual powers of production.*[19]

Marx believed, mistakenly, that capitalism depended on a progressive reduction of workers' living standards. He was not mistaken in believing that working conditions in mines and factories when he wrote were often scandalous, that hours of labour not only for men but for women and children were outrageously long, or that machine tending involved frustrations and risks that had not existed in a more primitive system of production. The descriptive chapters of *Capital* opened up most of the criticisms of capitalist industry which are current even today and reinforced his criticisms with much statistical and other factual data drawn from public reports. This part of his work was probably assisted by Engels, who had published his book, *The Condition of the Working-Class in England*, in 1844. Marx dealt realistically with such subjects as the periodic recurrence of crises, the existence even in prosperous times of chronic technological unemployment, the destruction of the skilled crafts by new machines, the displacing of skilled by unskilled labour, the sweating of non-industrialized trades, and the growth of an unemployable slum-proletariat. As with his historical studies, the novel and distinctive characteristic of Marx's treatment was his stress upon the social repercussions of industrialization, its tendency to weaken primary social groups like the family, and therefore upon the human problems that it created. The contradictory quality of capitalism seemed to him, as it had to Hegel, to be its paradoxical union of organization and anarchy: the technological organization of production united to an anarchy of exchange, an elaborate social coordination of the units of production united with an almost complete disregard for the adaptation of industrial means to human ends. Though the ideal received only occasional and passing statement, Marx had always in mind the contrast between capitalism and a planed and socialized economy, designed to produce and distribute goods when and where a legitimate need exists for them.

The real force of Marx's book was carried not by theoretical argument but by the stark realism with which it pictured the actual conditions of labour and by so doing pictured unregulated capitalism as a parasite that devours the human substance of society. In fact, though not in intention, *Capital* was the first and probably the most powerful of the ethical attacks on the sheer moral ugliness of an acquisitive society without adequate protection for its industrial labour force. Characteristically, however, Marx never makes his attack on capitalism as an overt moral judgement, nor does his argument that capital exploits labour mean that the workers were better off under some earlier system of production. The dialectic was for him a guarantee, and he often says, that capitalism is an advance over the feudalism that preceded it. Nor do the cruelties of capitalism mean that capitalists personally are cruel; capitalists and workers alike are caught in the system and in general must do what the system requires. From Marx's point of view the system itself is inherently self-contradictory and in the end is therefore self-destructive, but what makes it self-destructive is that it contains the germs of a higher and better system that is struggling to be born. Implicitly, therefore, Marx's criticisms always look toward the future rather than the past: toward what he believes the conditions of the workers will be in a rationally planned and socialized economy. Something of this sort must, he believed, be the logical outcome of an economy from which the contradictions of capitalism have been purged. He tried neither to describe such a future economy nor did he hold it up as an ideal to be striven for. Like Hegel he believed that the course of history is both inevitable and rational: men will indeed strive but in the end their striving will be for what they must desire and must create. Thus in the guise for an arid analysis of economic causes and effects, Marx developed what in fact was an exceedingly powerful moral appeal, backed by a quasi-religious conviction. It was nothing less than an appeal to join the march of civilization and right; and it was this appeal that gathered armies of workingmen to Marxian socialism.

The Collapse of Capitalism

The major purpose of *Capital*, therefore, was to show that capitalism in destroying itself must give rise to socialism, its antithesis. The plan of Marx's argument was to accept the labour theory of value, which Ricardo had made the central principle of classical economics and which Marx regarded as an authentically scientific theory of capitalism, and then to show dialectically that it is logically incoherent. The basic concept of Marx's analysis was "surplus value." The classic defense of capitalism had been the argument that in a system of free exchange everyone would, in the long run, receive back a value equivalent to that which he brought to the market and would thus receive his equitable share of the social product. Against this Marx sought to show that in an industrial system in which capitalists own the means of production, labour will always be forced to produce more than it receives and more than is required to keep the system going. Wages, on the average, will lie close to the subsistence minimum, not as Malthus had argued because of the pressure of population but because of the system of private ownership, and the capitalist's monopolistic position in the system will enable him to sequestrate the surplus in the form of profits and rents. This arguments, with its almost endless ramifications and its excessive technicalities, led to a long controversy which was celebrated in its day but which was outmoded even before it came to an end. For the Ricardian theory of value from which it started became obsolete for non- Marxian economists while the controversy was still in progress. Marx's economics in general and the theory of surplus value in particular, therefore, belong properly to the history of economic theory. It is indeed taken for granted by present-day Marxists, yet an ardent Marxist like Lenin rarely referred to it. For Marx, however, surplus value was the keystone of the argument, since it provided the ground of his conclusion that a capitalist system must ultimately be self-destroying. The theory left in its train two propositions that remain articles of faith for later Marxists: first, that capitalism must inevitably collapse, and second, that its collapse must inevitably give rise to socialism.

Marx's economic analysis, therefore, produced a number of predictions about the course that a capitalist society will run through in its way to ultimate failure. Because of the competition of capitalists among themselves, industry will tend to be concentrated in larger and larger units of production. These will tend to become monopolistic, and wealth will be concentrated in fewer and fewer great fortunes. Competition to keep up profits will make exploitation more severe, and the working class will become more and more impoverished. Because labour is chronically unable to consume all that it produces, a capitalist economy will be subject to periods of overproduction, depression, and unemployment. Small businessmen, farmers, independent artisans—the petty bourgeois remnants of a handicraft economy—will more and more be reduced to the level of wage-earning proletarians, and a capitalist society will tend to be polarized between capitalists, with satellite subclasses, on one side and the proletarian masses on the other. In the end, Marx argued, this must bring about a revolutionary situation in which the expropriators will be expropriated, and the means of production will be socialized.

All these predictions were subjects of prolonged controversy, and judged in the light of what happened after Marx wrote they had widely different values, which suggests that they were not deductions from sound theory but, when correct, were penetrating guesses about the way capitalist industry would work. The tendency of industrial and business units to combine and grow in size and the tendency toward ıecurring cycles of prosperity and depression were verified, though corporate organizations tended to spread ownership and to divest it of the implications of control that Marx attached to it. On the other hand the prediction that the working class would be progressively impoverished was wide of the mark, for industrial societies indubitably raised their standard of living. The prediction that the lower middle class would be absorbed into the wage-earning proletariat also proved to be wrong, for industrialization greatly increased the so-called white-collar class, which in Marx's classification must be called petty bourgeois. Though capitalism assumed international proportions, as Marx expected, the working class of the more highly industrialized countries showed no tendency to unite for an international class struggle, as Lenin in 1914 confidently expected them to do. Nor does it appear that capitalist industrialism sharpened class antagonism. If this kind of broad comparison is to be made, it seems nearer the truth to say that industrial societies are less stratified than handicraft societies, that their class lines are easier to cross, and that they are extraordinarily stable. Social revolutions occurred in Russia and China, not in England or Germany. Marx's certainty about the validity of his method induced a readiness to predict that revolution and the collapse of capitalism were imminent, and these predictions were usually mistaken because the revolutions either did not occur or occurred in the wrong places.

The other half of Marx's prediction—that the collapse of capitalism would be followed by a socialized or collective economy—was a speculation that depended wholly on the dialectic. Behind it there was, to be sure, a perfectly justified mood of revulsion against the brutalities of early capitalism. But the dialectic made it impossible for him to think of this as criticism; it must be prediction, and what is predicted must come about. Development must lead to the opposite of that from which it starts, and the opposite of capitalism is communism. For no substantial reason Marx believed that all the evils of capitalism were concentrated in the private ownership of the means of production, and hence he could believe that the abolition of private ownership would cut off the evil at its root. The "anarchy" of privately owned and competitive production will be succeeded by a planned and harmonized economy, "an association of free individuals who work with jointly owned means of production and wittingly expend their several labour powers as a combined social labour power." The first step to this end is to bring production "under the conscious and prearranged control of society," or in short, public ownership. By reason of this change the whole class structure supported by privately owned industry will be undermined and ultimately destroyed, and a classless society will eventuate in which coercion will no longer be necessary. The state in Engels' famous phrase will "wither away", since it is an organ of repression in a society based on exploitation, and in some inexplicable way specialization and the division of labour will no longer be necessary. Again as Engels said in a famous sentence borrowed from St. Simon, "The government of persons is replaced by the administration of things and the direction of the process of production."[20]

This was Marx's repayment for all the scorn that he had heaped on the utopian socialist, or perhaps it was the apocalyptic vision required to make any theory of social revolution convincing: human relationships that throughout history had been governed by force and exploitation are at some point to be supplanted by relationships that will be wholly idealized and cooperative. The classless society is the myth of the future which compensates for the disillusionments of the present and the disappointments of the revolution itself. Coupled with the idea that history has an inevitable end, however, the myth of the future may be a very dangerous kind of moral philosophy. For the future is the one thing that never arrives, and if the present is the domain of sheer force, force will always be morally justified if it leads toward history's predestined goal, which in practice means, if it succeeds. Marx had in fact, like Hegel, something very like contempt for moral scruples and convictions and ideals, and both temperamentally and by conviction, he believed that reform is impossible. Society as it is must be "smashed" to make a fresh start, and though the revolution must be planned, what is to follow the revolution can be left to the new order. The social morality of the apocalyptic vision is fanaticism, but beyond the vision there is a possibility which Marx's experience never forced him to consider, namely, that the revolution might occur. The social morality of a realized utopia can quite easily be cynicism.

The Strategy of the Social Revolution

Marx always regarded his philosophy as the guide to a successful *proletarian revolution, and his career* was divided between scholarship and socialist leadership. It would be hard to name any form of political radicalism in Western Europe after Marx that was not in some way affected by his thought. But there have been two great political movements both of which claimed to be the authentic version of Marxism, and these are at once so similar and so puzzlingly different that their relation to Marx is an important part of understanding his philosophy. These were, first, party socialism as it existed in Western Continental Europe down to World War I and, second, communism as it has existed since the Russian Revolution of 1917. The latter grew directly from the former, for Lenin was a leader of a Russian Marxian party, yet he was also the destroyer of the Second International or organization of Marxian socialist parties. The enmity between communists and socialists became even more bitter than that between communists and middle-class parties. The strategy of communist parties has been entirely different from that of the socialist parties. For the latter, by 1914, had gained positions of considerable political power in several countries of Western Continental Europe, especially in Germany, and in general their power grew by attracting votes in free elections, after suffrage was extended to the working class. Lenin's party, on the contrary, never was and never aspired to be a popular party gaining its ends by mass support. Yet it is quite true that both party socialism and communism derived their different conceptions of strategy from Marx. A fuller explanation of this seeming paradox must depend on the account of Lenin's version of Marxism in the next chapter; here it is sufficient to point out that Marx himself suggested two different lines of strategy either of which might be taken to be the appropriate implication of his philosophy.

In the first place it seems probable that Marx, perhaps about 1850, did in fact change his mind about the strategy of revolution, though he never said so explicitly. In the *Communist Manifesto* (1848) he denied emphatically that communists form a political party; they are "the most advanced and resolute section of the working class," and this expression is obviously the origin of Lenin's description of his party as the "vanguard" of the proletariat. At this time Marx certainly believed both that a bourgeois revolution was imminent in Germany and also that it would probably be touched off by a socialist revolution in France. Accordingly he could believe that an elite of dedicated revolutionists, with a definite programme and a clear understanding of the historical necessity of social revolution, might successfully operate as a general staff for all radical proletarian movements, such as, for example, left-wing labour unions. Apparently, however, he soon became convinced that these petty bourgeois radical organizations were too strong to be managed in this fashion, and with the failure of the revolutionary attempts of 1848, he concluded that a long period of preparation would be needed, while industrialism created in the workers an effective revolutionary class consciousness. He still believed that the social revolution was inevitable, but he believed also, in line with his theory of social evolution, that a revolution could not be "made" until bourgeois society had developed the full potentialities of the capitalist system. The strategy implied was twofold: a socialist party must indeed press for bourgeois reforms that strengthen the working class but its main consideration must be to preserve its own ideological purity and its freedom of action. It must never involve itself in divided political responsibility by cooperating with middle-class parties. This was conventionalized into standard strategy by the Marxian socialist parties: refusal to accept cabinet posts in governments formed by coalitions with non-socialist parties.

Obviously, however, if this strategy succeeded, it was likely to defeat its original revolutionary purpose. It aims to build its power by attracting voters with reforms that are not intrinsically socialist; even the *Manifesto* had demanded a graduated income tax. But the more a party succeeds in getting reforms through the ballot, the less reason there is for it to remain revolutionary. And this is indeed what tended to happen to successful Marxian socialist parties. In 1895 even Engels boasted that the German Social Democrats were succeeding better by legal than by illegal methods. Socialist intellectuals, being philosophical Marxists, remained revolutionists in theory, and only a few "revisionists," like Eduard Bernstein, became avowed evolutionists, but by the end of the nineteenth century a party like the German Social Democrats was little likely to stage a revolution. In effect a communist society such as Marx imagined had become an ideal to be approximated by liberal political methods through an indefinitely long process. It was assumed that if a revolution ever did happen, it would retain all the democratic political gains that had been made in the meantime. By 1914 some such belief had become the ingrained conviction of Marxists in the socialist parties of Western Europe.

In the second place Marx tended to make a distinction between the strategy appropriate to a socialist party in a country with a "ripening" industrial economy and to one in a country with a relatively backward economy. Only the former could successfully lead a revolution, since the revolution must ultimately be produced by the evolving economy. There was still the question what strategy socialist parties should follow in countries marginal to the main line of development. Marx tended to regard France as the natural leader of a revolution and to consider Germany as relatively backward, as indeed it was in his earlier life, but not by 1914. For obvious reasons Marx's remarks on strategy in a backward country had special significance for Russian Marxists. Thus it happened that two documents which Marx himself never published but which Engels printed after Marx died assumed an importance for Trotsky and Lenin such as they never had for German socialists.[21]

In 1850, believing that a middle-class revolution was about to break out and succeed in Germany, Marx wrote an Address for the Central Committee of the Communist League (for which the *Manifesto* had been written), advising the socialist minority about its strategy relative to this revolution. A socialist party, he says, must cooperate with middle-class revolutionists until the revolution succeeds. It must then turn against its allies; it must keep its own center of power intact; and though it cannot hope to make a successful socialist revolution, it must use every means of subversion and obstruction to prevent either business or government from becoming settled. It must set poor peasants against rich peasants; it must aim to nationalize the land; and it must force the revolutionary government as far as possible toward an attack on private property. In short, the battle cry of the proletarians must be: "The Revolution in Permanence." Thus in 1850 Marx supplied the concept of permanent revolution which Trotsky adopted and developed in 1906, and which laid down substantially the policy that Lenin followed in 1917 relative to the middle-class revolution in Russia.

Of much greater importance were Marx's comments on the programme produced by the Gotha Congress, which in 1875 brought about a combination of radical organizations in Germany that made the beginning of what proved to be an effective socialist party. Marx's comments were fragmentary and bitterly vituperative and were suppressed at the time in the interest of harmony, but they were directed to a state of affairs in Germany which, more than anything else that Marx wrote, was directly relevant to the state of affairs in Russia forty years later. As Marx said bluntly, "The 'toiling people' in Germany consist of peasants and not of proletarians." What the peasants consciously "want" is quite different from what they ought to want and hence what they "really" (or dialectically) do want. In a society becoming more highly industrialized they are politically impotent for any constructive purpose, but by sheer weight of numbers they are a critical factor in the situation. Though they are incapable of leadership they can be steered and guided, and their discontent can be channeled into support of the proletarian minority, which alone can be the leader toward a genuine socialist revolution. The objectives set by the Program that Marx was criticizing he condemned as not socialist at all but merely those of any middle-class revolution: suffrage and other popular political rights. These have a value in a pre-socialist society, but in relation to socialism they are merely "pretty little gewgaws." Marx's hints for the control of a prevailingly peasant society by a proletarian "vanguard" pretty clearly suggested Lenin's plan in 1905 for a "Democratic-revolutionary Dictatorship of the Proletariat and the Peasantry." Marx's marginal notes on the Gotha Program contained also his most extended reference to the transition from a capitalist to a socialist society, though characteristically this is a reference rather than a description. The transition will take place in two stages. The public ownership of the means of production will of itself abolish the appropriation of surplus value and will achieve the bourgeois profession of giving to workers the full value of what they produce. This, however will still fall short of genuine communism, which must abolish the division of labour and increase the social product to permit the realization of the communist ideal: "From each according to his ability, to each according to his needs." In the transition period between capitalism and communism "the state can be nothing but the revolutionary dictatorship of the proletariat." Quite obviously Marx's notes on the Gotha Program, together with remarks made elsewhere, contain the germ of much that Lenin in 1917 put into his pamphlet, *The State and Revolution*.

Marx's social philosophy, therefore, supported two conceptions of political strategy which proved in practice to be divergent. The one line, developed by Marxian party socialism, looked to the evolution of industrialism to produce a class-conscious proletariat which would grow in strength until it could take over a society already politically democratic. Down to 1914 this seemed clearly the main line of Marxian strategy already in a fair way to succeed through the political organization of the working class in great popular parties such as the German Social Democrats. For this strategy political liberalism was the necessary antecedent, and the revolution would be the consummation of a long course of political and economic development and of popular education. The other line, which after 1914 marked out the strategy of Leninism, harked back to the earlier stages of Marx's thought, which took communism to be the ideal of an intellectual elite or of a proletarian minority submerged in a society prevailingly peasant and without liberal political rights. For this line revolution was a present reality and the antecedent of political and economic transformation. It leaned heavily on Marx's somewhat incidental remarks on the strategy appropriate to communist parties in backward societies. As far as their intentions were concerned, Russian Marxists had no thought of abandoning or changing the central principal of Marx's social philosophy, namely, economic determinism, yet inevitably to the Western Marxist they seemed to be discarding it.

NOTES

1. *Deutsch-franzosische Jahrbucher*, 1844; *Die heilige Familie*, 1845; selections from these are translated by H.J. Stenning under the title, *Selected Essay by Karl Marx*, New York, 1926. *Die deutsche Ideologie*, 1846 (first published in full in the Gesamtausgabe); The German Ideology, Eng. trans. of Parts I and III by R. Pascal, New York, 1939. *La misere de la philosophie*, 1847; Eng. trans. *The Poverty of Philosophy*, ed. by C.P. Dutt, New York, 1936. *The Communist Manifesto*, 1848. The standard edition of he works of Marx and Engels (which is not complete) is *Karl Marx, Friedrich Engels, historischkritische Gesamtausgabe, Werke, Schriften, Briefe*. Im Auftrage des Marx-Engels-Instituts, Moskau, hrsg. v. D. Rjazanov. Frankfurt a. M., 1927—.
2. Letter to Lasalle, January 16, 1861; *Marx-Engels Correspondence, 1846-1895* (1934), p. 125. *Cf. Capital*, Vol. I, Eng. trans. by E. and C. Paul, p. 392, n.2.
3. *The German Ideology*, Eng. trans. by R. Pascal, p. 22.
4. July 27, 1854; *Marx-Engels Correspondence, 1846-1895*, p. 71.
5. Letter to Weydemeyer, March 5, 1852; ibid., p. 57. The italics are Marx's.
6. *Critique of Political Economy*, Preface; Eng. trans. by N. I. Stone (1904), p. 11.
7. *The German Ideology*, Eng. trans. by R. Pascal, p. 14 f.
8. *The Poverty of Philosophy*, Eng. trans. ed. by C.P. Dutt, p. 93.

9 *Die Klassenkample in Frankreich, 1848-1850*, articles in the *Neue Rheinische Zeitung*, 1850, published by Engels, 1895; Eng. trans. ed. by C.P. Dutt, *The Class Struggles in France* (1848-50), New York, 1934. *Der achtzehnte Brumaire des Louis Bonaparte*, 1852; Eng. trans. ed. by C.P. Dutt, *The Eighteenth Brumaire of Louis Bonaparte*, New York, 1935.

10 *The Eighteenth Brumaire*, Eng. trans., pp. 40 f.

11 *Critique of Political Economy*, Preface; Eng. trans. by N. I. Stone, pp. 11 ff.

12 *Herrn Eugen Duhrings Umwalzung der Wissenschaft*, 1878 (usually referredt to as "Anti-Duhring"; Marx cooperated in writing this work); Eng. trans. by E. Burns. *Herr Eugen Duhring's Revolution in Science*, New York, 1935. *Ludwig Feuerback und der Ausgang der deutsfchen Philosophie* (1884); Eng. trans. *Ludwig Feuerback and the Outcome of Classical German Philosophy*, New York, 1934. Letters to Conrad Schmidt, August 5 and October 27, 1890, July 1 and November 1, 1891, *Marx-Engels Correspondence*, 1846-1895, pp. 472, 477, 487, 494; to J. Bloch, September 21, 1890, *ibid.*, p. 475; to Franz Mehring, July 14, 1893, *ibid.*, p. 510.

13 *Anti-Duhring*, Eng. trans. by E. Burns, p. 30.

14 *Ludwig Feuerbach*, Eng. trans., p. 11.

15 *Marx-Engels Correspondence*, 1846-1895, pp. 354 f.

16 Quoted by E.R.A. Seligman, *The Economic Interpretation of History* (1902), pp. 142 f. From a letter published in *Der sozialistische Akademiker*, October 15, 1895.

17 Isaiah Berlin, *Karl Marx* (1948), p. 144.

18 See for example Karl Mannheim's *Ideology and Utopia: An Introduction to the Sociology of Knowledge*, Eng. trans. by Louis Wirth and Edward Shils, 1936, which contains an extensive bibliography. There is a more recent treatment in W. Stark's *The Sociology of Knowledge: An Essay in Aid of a Deeper Understanding of the History of Ideas*, 1958.

19 *Capital*, Vol. I, Eng. trans. by E. and C. Pual, pp. 382 f.

20 *Anti-Duhring*, Eng. trans. by E. Burns, p. 315. Cf. Engels' letter to Bebel, March 18-28, 1875; *Marx-Engels Correspondence*, 1846-1895, pp. 332 ff.

21 *Address of the Central Committee of the Communist League, March, 1850*, published by Engels in 1885. *Marx and Engels: Selected Works* (Moscow, 1955), Vol. I, pp. 106-117. *Marginal Notes to the Programme of the German Workers Party, 1875* (Critique of the Gotha Program), published by Engels in 1891, *Ibid.*, Vol. II, pp. 18-37.

REFERENCES

The Social and Political Thought of Karl Marx. By Shlomo Avineri. Cambridge, 1968.

Karl Marx, His Life and Environment. By Isaiah Berlin. 3rd Edition. New York, 1963.

Karl Marx's Interpretation of History. By Mandell M. Bober. 2d ed., rev. Cambridge, Mass., 1948.

Marxism, Past and Present. By R.N. Carew Hunt. London, 1954.

The Theory and Practice of Communism. By R.N. Carew Hunt. 2d ed. London, 1957. Part I.

The Meaning of Marxism. By G.D.H. Cole. London, 1948.

The Philosophical Foundations of Marxism. By Louis Dupre. New York, 1966.

The Materialist Conception of History: A Critical Analysis. By Karl Federn. London, 1939.

Marx's Concept of Man. By Erich Fromm. New York, 1961.

Towards the Understanding of Karl Marx: A Revolutionary Interpretation. By Sidney Hook, New York, 1933.

From Hegel to Marx: Studies in the Intellectual Development of Karl Marx. By Sidney Hook, New York, 1936.

Reason, Social Myths, and Democracy. By Sidney Hook, New York, 1940.

Chs. 9-12.

Marx, Proudhon, and European Socialism. By John H. Jackson. London, 1957.

The Ethical Foundations of Marxism. By Eugene Kamenka. New York, 1962.

Karl Marx: An Essay. By Harold J. Laski. London, 1922.

Karl Marx's Capital: An Introductory Essay. By A.D. Lindsay. London, 1925.

Democracy and Marxism. By H.B. Mayo. New York, 1955.

Karl Marx: The Story of His Life. By Franz Mehring. Eng. trans. by Edward Fitzgerald. New York, 1935.

Marxism: The Unity of Theory and Practice. By Alfred G. Meyer. Cambridge, Mass., 1954.

Alienation: Marx's Conception of Man in Capitalist Society. By Bertell Ollman. Cambridge, 1971.

German Marxism and Russian Communism. BY John Plamenatz. London,

1954. Part I.

The Open Society and Its Enemies. By K.R. Popper. Rev. ed. Princeton, N.J., 1950. Chs. 13-21.

Marx in the Mid-Twentieth Century. By Gajo Petrovic. Garden City, 1962.

An Essay on Marxian Economics. By Joan Robinson. London, 1942.

Democracy and Socialism: A Contribution to the Political History of the Past 150 Years. By Arthur Rosenberg. Eng. trans. by George Rosen. New York, 1939.

Karl Marx, His Life and Work. By Otto Ruhle. Eng. trans. by E. and C. Paul. New York, 1949.

Philosophy and Myth in Karl Marx. By Robert C. Tucker. Cambridge, 1961.

Human Nature: The Marxian View. By Vernon Venable. New York, 1945.

Marxism: A Re-examination. By Irving M. Zeitlin. Princeton, 1967.

9

World Communism To-day

Communism as we know it today had its origin in Russia in 1917 with the overthrow of the Tsarist regime by the Bolsheviks. Although it is only a little over thirty years old, it has spread its tentacles practically to every part of the world. Such rapid expansion is nothing short of a miracle.

Soon after the Bolsheviks came into power, there was considerable opposition to them both from within and without. From without active military support came from some of the Western democracies in the form of support for the White Russians. This support of their enemies, just at a time when they were struggling to stand on their feet, Russian Communists have not yet forgotten; and that partly accounts for their suspicion of Western democracies to the present day.

Whatever may have been the reaction of the West to Soviet Communism in the years immediately after World War I, many in the Orient believed that it contained within it the germs of a new world order. They looked upon it as a Godsend. What was of special appeal to them was its passion for economic and social justice and its determination to wage a relentless warfare against imperialism and racial discrimination practised in various degree by Western democracies. The Orient was particularly impressed by its various five year plans for the agricultural and industrial improvement of Russia, the virtual liquidation of illiteracy within the borders of Russia, the granting of cultural autonomy to the various racial and linguistic groups within the Soviet Union, the punishment of racial discrimination as at reason against the state, and the renunciation of extra-territorial rights in China which the Western democracies were loath to renounce. The Orient also believed that Soviet Russia was pledged to conducting a vigorous campaign for world peace and disarmament.

All of these favourable elements which the Orient saw or thought it saw in Russian communism were in striking contrast to the economic exploitations and political domination practised by several of the Western democracies in many Eastern lands. The Orient, for instance, could not easily forget the strenuous opposition put up by these democracies to the plea of racial equality made by Japan around the peace table at Versailles in 1918-19. Nor could it forget the White Australia policy of the Dominion of Australia, the gross racial discrimination of the Union of South Africa against Asiatics, the social distance maintained by the British between themselves and the dependent people in their far-flung empire or the colour-consciousness amounting to obsession on the part of some Americans.

In the relations between Great Britain and India, complete self-government for the latter country had been promised when Britain was in the throes of World War I. But once the war was over, Britain used every possible excuse including the rivalry between the Hindus and Muslims and the comparative helplessness of Hindu out-castes to postpone the implementation of her promise. In return for the many voluntary and involuntary services which India had rendered to Britain during World War I, Britain visited her with the Amritsar massacre and Rowlatt Act of 1919, the wholesale imprisonment of her national leaders, and the suppression of their legitimate national aspirations.

As against this picture presented by Western democracies, Soviet Russia appeared to be a paragon of virtue. But the Orient soon began to detect the clay feet of Achilles. The wholesale liquidation of the *'kulaks'* and others in opposition, the hounding of Trotsky until he was finally assassinated on foreign soil, the entrenchment of one party government, the suppression of freedom of speech, freedom of discussion, and freedom of writing, the exile of political opponents to Siberia, the practice of forced labour on a mass scale by the state, the wholesale disappearance of military leaders suspected to be lacking in complete loyalty to the powers that be, the suppression of religion by the fist of the state, the active promotion of Godlessness, and the disruption of family life—all of this made the orient wonder whether after all

Russia was the exemplar and saviour that she had expected her to be. Question was raised whether Russia was justified in thinking that the whole world was to become communist in order that her own communism might succeed. It is true that this fear was set at rest for some time by Stalin's belief held for a while that world communism was not necessary for the success of Russian communism and by the suspension of the Comintern. But in recent years the Russian authorities seem to have reversed their position and have revived the idea of world communism in the form of the Cominform.

As Russian communism began to develop in the twenties and thirties it became clear that it was becoming more and more authoritarian, nationalistic, and militaristic, not without its own form of imperialist ambitions. In pursuit of her avowed goal of world-wide communism, Russia set up or helped to create secret Communist cells in different parts of the world. In the early twenties, the U.S.A. which has a reputation for witch-hunting, indulged in this pastime in relation to her local Communists. The Meerut trials took place in India resulting in harsh prison sentences being imposed upon certain English and Indian Communists working under cover in India. Subject India was not much interested in these trials, regarding them as an imperialist device to divert the attention of the people from their own sufferings under the imperialist yoke to an outside enemy.

This was also the time when their was considerable academic interest in the doctrinal teachings of Communism. For a while Pandit Jawaharlal Nehru, the idol of Indian youth at this time, seemed to be in sympathy with several of the Communist doctrines and aspirations. Increasing numbers of college and university students became openly sympathetic towards Communism. Communist literature was avidly devoured. It is true that quite a few who were only Socialists called themselves Communists, not taking the trouble to distinguish between the two. To many of them any kind of stick was good enough with which to beat British imperialism. But to one and all Communism represented a commendable eagerness to improve the lot of the masses.

Communism since the outbreak of World War II

With the outbreak of World War II, the feelings of the Orient towards Soviet Russia began to undergo a rapid change. The non-aggression pact—concluded with Hitler in 1939—came as a blow to all liberty-loving peoples. Even the man with the meanest intelligence was able to see that it was dictated solely by considerations of expediency, and not by any high principles. Yet many looked upon it as the natural reaction of a proud people to the way in which Great Britain and France had kept Soviet Russia out of their counsels on the eve of the Munich Pact of 1938. Lord Halifax showed a singular lack of imagination in dealing with Russia. His mistake was later corrected partially by Sir Stafford Cripps when he became the British ambassador to Soviet Russia.

The events which came in quick succession after the outbreak of World War II filled the friends of Soviet Russia with dismay. Portions of Poland were overrun with the help of Germany and brought under Russian domination. The non-Slavic states of Latvia, Estonia, and Lithuania were annexed without hesitation under some pretext or other. War was provoked against the people of Finland, and although they put up an unexpectedly stiff resistance, they had finally to surrender some of their territory to Russia. Such unscrupulous expansion was justified by Soviet sympathisers on the ground that Russia required these strategic areas in the interest of her self-defence. But that was to justify what may be a good end by questionable means.

Even if it is possible to accept this explanation, there is no justification for the way in which Russia spread her tentacles into Hungary, Bulgaria, Roumania, Albania, Yugoslavia (until Tito's deflection), Czechoslovakia, and Eastern Germany. While all of these countries maintain their nominal independence, they have all adopted the one-party idea of the state, practised by Mussolini and Hitler until their downfall and defeat and by Stalin ever since he came into power. It is significant that in all of these countries, Russia achieved her goal without firing a single shot, although military pressure was always present. Her method has been to inspire and organize local Communists and use infiltration tactics and deceit in winning people to the Communist ideology and Communist regime.*

*Mr. Justice Jackson writes that Communism has crept over Eastern Europe 'by deception, coercion coup d'etat, terrorism, and assassination'.

The local Communist parties are so well entrenched that it seems impossible to uproot them without a world revolution of some sort.

Similar inroads have been made into northern Korea and China. Soviet Russia waited until the last moment before she was willing to fight Japan, but when she agreed to do it, it was at a big price to be paid by the people of Korea and of China, more especially of the people of Manchuria. This price has been paid since the termination of the war.

The Communist party in China was organized in Shanghai in 1922 under the leadership of men like Mao Tse-tung. It was a revolutionary party from the beginning with a strong agrarian programme. In the last two years of his life Sun Yat-sen, the father of modern China, was favourably disposed towards Communism and organized his own Kuo-mintang one the model of the Communist party. But after his death, his party supporters gradually forgot his revolutionary teachings and became militaristic and reactionary both in the economic and political fields. Chiang Kai-shek became the undisputed leader of the Kuo-mintang and, after defeating the war lords with the aid of the Communists, he broke away from the latter in 1927 and rejected 'a super-government under Borodin' who had been in China as a political adviser from the Soviet Union. The fight between Chaing Kai-shek and Chinese Communists went on for decade, and Chiang ruthlessly suppressed many Communists. But with the Japanese aggression which commenced in 1937, the two rivals came together and fought shoulder to shoulder all through the war, although there were mutual suspicions on both sides. The Communists had all along regarded this truce as only a 'temporary compromise'. So when the war was over, the rift appeared again and neither side was willing to yield. General Marshall was sent out by President Truman to see whether he could not pour oil on troubled waters. But it was too late already. Chiang Kai-shek's government and the people's Party (the Kuo-mintang) were fast discrediting themselves by their inefficiency and corruption and by their failure to attend to the pressing economic needs of the masses and the poor working conditions of the soldiers. All of this resulted in a swing of Chinese sympathy towards the Communists. Many of Chiang's soldiers went over to the other side; and weapons of warfare furnished to the nationalists by the U.S.A. were unscrupulously sold to the communists. It is reported that the U.S. spent more that three billion dollars in bolstering up Chiang Kai-shek against the Communists. Yet within a space of five years since the close of the war, the whole of China has fallen like a ripe fruit into the laps of the Communists and there are very few left to fight for Chiang and his party, now marooned in Formosa.

Contrary to popular opinion Chinese Communism is not merely a party of agrarian reformers. The party is composed of Marxists of varying degrees. Mao Tse-tung, the leader, born in 1893 of a well-to-do peasant family and a self-educated man, has added both to the theory and practice of Communism on the agrarian side, and Chinese Communism is still in the process of evolution. Li Li-san, a principal aide and former rival of Mao, is a Russian trained man and, when opportunity presents itself, is likely to lead Chinese Communism into the orthodox channels of Russian Communism.

So far Mao Tse-tung has been popular with his people. His soldiers have behaved admirably in their dealings with them. There has been a marked reduction in the huge rents paid by peasants for the use of land and in taxes. Educational facilities are being provided for the masses. But the more well-to-do are not having an easy time of it. Individual rights are still respected, but how long that will continue it is difficult to say. Both religion and irreligion are allowed to have free play. While the Y.M.C.A. and Protestant Christian bodies in general are left unmolested, Roman Catholics whose official position is one of unmitigated opposition to Communism and Taoists whose religion is full of superstitions are not receiving any favours. Indoctrination of every group of people including housewives in the doctrines of Communism is going on rapidly. There is not much appreciation for India which has recognized Mao Tse-tung's regime and occupies a middle position in the controversy between the two major power groups led by the U.S.A. and the U.S.S.R. respectively. India is regarded as another imperialist power. After a period of several weeks of negotiations, Mao Tse-tung has been able to extract terms from Stalin which appear to be favourable to China on the whole. But which of the two giants will out-manoeuvre the other in the end, it is difficult to forecast. It is possible that Mao may turn out to be the Tito of the East, holding on to a vigorous nationalism and Communism at one and the same time. It is equally possible that China may become a satellite of a dominant Russia. What may prevent the latter alternative are the sturdy independence of the Chinese people, their pragmatic outlook which refuses to make too much of ideological differences, the vastness of the country, and poor transportation facilities, as well as the Chinese tradition of turning against any of her rulers who forfeits his 'mandate from heaven'. Chinese Communism can still prove itself to be the saviour of Asia if it will carry out its reforms with moderation, clean the Augean stable of its corruption, and give itself whole heartedly to the service of the people, instead of losing itself in the fantastic and suicidal ideas of world revolution and imperialist domination.

Communism is spreading its influence to other parts of Asia, too, through vigorous propaganda, the setting up of local Communist cells, and the fomenting of trouble. The Communist party in North Korea is so well organized that the U.S.A. is afraid to relax her indirect control of South Korea. The Huks in the Phillipines who fought the Japanese by means of guerilla warfare are Communist led, but not definitely Communists. The same is true of a good many in Malaya too, where the Chinese influence is strong. Of late the British overlords have been high-handed in the treatment of Communists. But that only makes martyrs of them in the eyes of many of their countrymen.

In Indo-China with the active support of the U.S.A. and Great Britain, the French are seeking to re-impose their imperial rule. Bao Dai, a puppet, has been set up as the leader; and the national leader, Ho Chih Minh, an ardent Nationalist and Communist is discredited. The republic of Viet Nam, which he founded, is on the black list. The Viet Nam of the French is made up of three 'independent' states—Annam, Cambodia, and Iaos The American government is giving military and economic aid in putting down the Communists; and the extent to which this aid weakens the Nationalist forces and strengthens French imperialism, the U.S.A. is unpopular with Asian leaders. The Communists in their turn may be receiving help from their Chinese allies massed on the borders of the country and from Russians; but there is no proof in support of it.

Communism is knocking not only at the doors of Indo-China and Malaya, but also at the doors of the whole of southern and south-eastern Asia, many of whose national leaders are leftist in their economic views, Indonesia, which is the last of the countries in this region to secure her political freedom, is not yet a complete master in her own household. There are still internal frictions to overcome. In this state of affairs, if Indo-China falls to the Communists, Indonesia may follow suit. But the probability is that Indonesia will pull herself together and move in the direction of a mixed economy.

Siam has a mild from of military rule with a democratic paraphernalia. But there is no genuine democratic rule yet, although the people by nature seem to be peaceable and non-revolutionary. The present government has yielded to the economic and military pressure of the U.S.A. which is assuming an increasingly influential role in Asian affairs. If Siam can withstand Communism at all, it can only be with the aid of outside powers.

Since her political independence in January 1948, Burma has been an unhappy country and has known no peace. The energies of the government have been sapped by the civil war with the Karens as well as by unsettled economic conditions throughout the country. The present prime minister, Thakin Nu, is not the equal of his predecessor, Aung San. Recently he has announced that he is becoming a hermit premier, interested more in a life of personal devotion than in the day to day administration of his country. What this may mean is the further deterioration of political conditions in Burma.

Tibet is becoming nervous of her autonomous existence. If Communists China becomes stronger than she is at present, she may swallow her up without any compunction. To avoid this possibility Tibet needs to free herself from her mediaevalism and outmoded theocracy. Free political institutions and radical economic improvement contain the key to survival.

The Communists party in India which was organized in 1922 is a force with which the government of that country has to reckon. Though small in numbers, it is vigorous. It has won over the All-India Trade Union Congress to its side, with a present membership of 300,000. It has its strong support in some of the big cities as well as among peasants and workers in several parts of India. Madras and West Bengal have banned the Communist party but no similar action has been taken by the Central government.

The policy pursued by Indian Communists has been frankly and openly opportunist. It is one of fishing in troubled waters. When the war was on and when the Indian National Congress was striving to wring freedom from the unwilling hands of Britain, Indian Communists threw their weight on the side of Britain. At a time when national leaders were striving hard to prevent the dismemberment of the country, the Communists advanced specious reasons for partition. Once partition was brought about, they turned turtle and agitated for unification. During the days when the Razakars were carrying on a reign of terror in Hyderabad, the Communists joined hands with them and set up parallel governments in several villages which have not yet been liquidated. Since the close of the war there have been Communist-inspired strikes and several acts of sabotage, including the wrecking of trains. All of this has put a severe strain on a government which is fast losing its popular support.

The Muslim countries as a whole are not yet seriously threatened by Communism. Martin Ebon writes: "Marx cannot compete with Allah, nor Stalin with Mohammed'. But what happens in Burma and Assam, where Communist influence is strong, is bound to influence Eastern Pakistan. Likewise, what happened in Calcutta, Delhi and Bombay will have its repercussions in Lahore and Karachi. Recently the Prime Minister of Pakistan was in the United State asking for military aid in order to safeguard the territorial integrity of his country. He took care, however, not to mention against whom that integrity was to be protected.

Organized Communism is practically non-existent in Afghanistan. But this fortunate circumstance may not always last on account of its proximity to both Communist Russia and Communist China. Any inroads into their independence are likely to be seriously resisted by Afghans who are 'fiercely nationalist, tough, and fanatically religious'. (Ebon). Communism has reared it ugly head in Egypt from time to time. But it is not yet a formidable force. In the Arab countries as a whole Communism is kept at bay by feudalism and foreign investments, but they alone cannot stop the sweep of an idea and philosophy which is a curious mixture of human idealism and complete unscrupulousness in the realization of it. Communism in Turkey is illegal and no Communist party functions there. Up till now Turkey has been able to resist Communism with American dollars and military equipment. Russia has been agitating for the joint control of Dardanelles. Although she is not pressing the claim just now because of considerations of expediency, she may come back to the claim with renewed determination when circumstances are more auspicious.

Communism is spreading in several parts of the continent of Africa too. The Communist party has strong supporters among young Africans in the Union of South Africa. It is possible that Communism in this area may prove to be a blessing in disguise in removing racialism of the worst kind to be practised since the downfall of the Nazis. 'The Communist party of South Africa', says Martin Ebon, 'has the support of a group of Europeans who disagree with the race policy of the leading parties, as well as of an increasing number of Indians'.

Communism has taken over several countries in Europe. In France and Italy, too, it has been strong and may have won some of the recent elections had it not been for strong outside influences working in the opposite direction.

How is the challenge of Communism to be met?

Communism is undoubtedly totalitarianism, dictatorial, and tyrannical. It attaches little or no importance to democratic methods or parliamentary procedure, although the Soviet is called the people's Republic. In an article in the New York Times of May 21, 1950, Justice Robert H. Jackson of the U.S. Supreme Court sums up the undemocratic methods of the American Communist party in the following terms: (1) 'The goal of the Communists party is to seize powers of government by and for a minority rather than to acquire power through the vote of a free electorate'. (2) 'The Communist party alone among American parties past or present is dominated and controlled by a foreign government'. The Communist ideology is to place loyality to the party and to world Communism above loyalty to one's own country or even to one's conscience. (3) 'Violent and undemocratic means are the calculated and indispensable methods to attain the Communist

Party's goal'. It is significant, as Mr. Jackson points out, that in none of the states in Eastern Europe where Communism is dominant was it elected by a free or contestable election. In none can it be evicted by any election. (4) 'The Communist party has sought to gain this leverage and hold on the American population by acquiring control of the labour movement'. (5) 'Every member of the Communist party is an agent to execute the Communist programme'. Ample evidence of it has been seen in the number of spy trials in the U.S. since 1947.

In spite of all these charges, every one of which is true, modern Communism is not sheer naked force devoid of all human idealism, as was the case with Fascism and Nazism. It is rooted in despair and may well be described as 'organized desperation'. World War I gave it its first innings and World War II gave it a unique opportunity to spread over a great part of the world. World War III, if and when it comes, will create conditions of universal misery where Communism may attain its goal of world domination without much effort or sacrifice on its part. The warmongers of our day who are agitating for immediate war with Russia will, instead of defeating Communism, help it to ride to success on their backs.

Communism cannot be stopped by exaggerating its evils or by painting it in lurid colours. Communism cannot be argued down, nor can it be shouted down. It can and should be lived down. The best way of doing it is to take immediate steps for the removal of every form of social, economic, and political in justice. Pandit Nehru is a true prophet of our day when he says 'Political subjection, racial inequality, economic inequality, and misery—these are the evils we have to remove if we would insure peace'. Equally right is Mr. Henry Wallace, a former Vice-President of the U.S., when he writes, 'No powerful idea—and Communism is a powerful idea—can be countered by guns and money'.

The Roman Catholic call to arms against Communism because of its totalitarianism is much like fighting with one's own shadow. It is not as though Communism was all materialistic and Godless, and the systems opposed to it, spiritual and Godfearing. Present day capitalism has certain things to its credit, such as, large scale production, provision of opportunity for individual initiative, and leadership, and philanthropy up to a point. But nobody will pretend that Capitalism is altogether Godly and righteous. If much of Communism is flagrantly antigod, Capitalism professes to be religious, but does not often demonstrate it in practice. Unlimited private profit is its bedrock and foundation. At times it becomes supremely indifferent to human values, especially when its operations become impersonal, as through the control of stocks and shares and foreign investments. If power corrupts man, money does it even more.

If the world is to be saved from the menance of Communism, it is necessary rapidly to replace private profit motive by social welfare motive. Every country in the world requires more of co-operatives and more of social security services. The time is not far off when progressive opinion everywhere should demand a civic minimum below which nobody should be allowed to fall and possibly a civic maximum above which nobody should be allowed to rise, except in the case of those who use their wealth in the production of greater directly beneficial to a wide range of people. If abject poverty is a sin against God and man, so are great riches. The time is ripe for the realization of the Roman motto: 'Private property small, common property large'.

Capitalism suffers further from the fact that it is wasteful and extravagant and creates artificial needs merely for the sake of keeping the industrial machinery moving. It does not have a rational, national or world planning. What planning there is, is planning with the consent of the capitalist and banker; and that is a one-need planning. The new order of our day calls for 'planned production for community consumption'. If such planning is not to become impersonal, tyrannical, and soul-crushing, it is necessary to begin at the primary levels of production and consumption and move up to higher levels. National and world planning should arise out of a series of plans at the local community levels.

The Orient in particular wants neither unadulterated Capitalism nor the present Soviet form of Communism. The future in Asia belongs to some form or another of socialism. Thoughtful people everywhere should realize that there is no one economic system suited to all times and all places. Each country should evolve its own system adopting features of value from other systems and fitting them into the national tradition and genius.

Vast and economically backward countries such as India will do well to follow the middle economy of such countries as Sweden, Switzerland, and New Zealand, making what local variations and adaptations are found necessary. The non-aggressive and non-imperialist Scandinavian countries have more to contribute to the economic life and thinking of the world than either Capitalism or Communism.

Nehru's idea of a mixed economy for India is conceived along sound lines. At the top level—the level of heavy industries and services of a monopolistic character, such as, the railways, postal and telegraph system, and communications—there should be national ownership and national control. In the case of industries which are well established in the country and are rendering tolerably good service such as the textile industries, the need is for private ownership with state control. Where private enterprise is not able to meet all the needs of the country, as in the case of the steel industry of India, it is right and proper that the state should supplement private enterprise by organizing industries of its own or entering into partnership with private interests. As regards the ownership of land, there can be no two opinions on the need for the liquidation of landlordiness. While there is scope for large scale collective farming, in certain areas, the prevailing type should be that of peasant proprietorship. In no circumstance is there justification for absentee landlordism.

One other feature of the mixed economy suited to India is the retention, improvement, and dovetailing of cottage industries. When it is remembered that there are some six million artisans in India who have held their own in the face of adverse conditions brought about by industrialism, it is wrong to let any of them languish for lack of work or patronage. India should not go the way of Western countries, sacrificing handicrafts to mammoth machine production.

Even the capitalist countries do not have simon-pure capitalism any longer. The U.S.A. in recent years has placed severe restrictions on monopolies and has adopted a system of taxation and social security services so as to equalize wealth and opportunity up to a point at least.

Although co-operatives are not wide-spread, they are bound to make headway as time goes on.

Great Britain has made great strides in the direction of nationalization—railways, coal mines, banking, etc. But as yet she does not have wholesale socialism. Private property and private profit motive have not been eliminated, but are regulated.

The U.S.S.R. likewise has no complete Communism. It is more accurate to describe Soviet economy as state capitalism rather than as state socialism. Private property within limits prevails. So do differential rewards for different types of work and different quantities produced.

Thus it looks as though the world as a whole is moving in the direction of a middle or mixed economy. If the differences between the various systems are not grossly exaggerated, as they are at times for propaganda purposes, it is possible for both qualified capitalism and qualified communism to live together in peace and stimulate each other to greater production and better distribution and consumption.

Communism challenges the present-day world not only in the economic and industrial fields, but also in the social. Western democracies so called have been guilty of racialism and arrogant imperialism. Among these democracies, the Union of South Africa has the poorest record. She not only insults her Negro majority, the legitimate owners of the country, but also the Indian minority whom she originally brought into the country in order to develop its resources in her own interest. Her administration is marked by naked and unashamed racialism; and communism offers her a fitting challenge. The imperialist exploitation of Africa by Great Britain, France, Portugal, and Belgium, in spite of the trusteeship system, offers a fertile soil for Communism. The Belgian treatment of the Congo, the South African treatment of South West Africa, the French treatment of Indo-China, and the British treatment of Malaya in particular, give Communism the opportunity it needs for spreading its propaganda. Communism is shrewd enough not to provoke a war if it can help it, but fully avails itself of the opportunities provided by the racial arrogance and exploitation of democracies for its own expansion. This does not mean that the record of Soviet Russia as regards imperialism is anything to be proud of. She started her career as the friend of the oppressed all over the world. Later she became intensely nationalistic. At present she is nationalistic and aggressively imperialistic.

A further challenge of Communism is in the political and international fields. It is a common mistake of democracies to assume that they are the true and sole exponents of fundamental rights and of popular sovereignty. The facts are that compared with Communism they concede many rights to the citizens which are denied by the Communists. But there are at the same time many aberrations. True, the press is not gagged as in a Communist country. But indirect pressure is put upon it through vested interests of one kind or another. While different news papers may cancel out each other's brand of propaganda, the press as a whole is not free, but highly selective. Furthermore, even if the hand of the government is not always in evidence in worming into the private lives of citizens, the local community in a time of hysteria, an ill-informed and skilfully directed public opinion, and employing agencies which play for safety can virtually become tyrants. One has known of persons in public employment who had voted for Henry Wallace in the 1948 presidential election, living in perpetual dread lest they should be found out.

Democracy, furthermore, in some of the advanced countries is extravagant and wasteful. The number of primaries and elections one witnesses in the U.S. are sure to break the back of a poor country like India. In spite of the mounting cost involved, democracy does not often succeed in getting honest, public-spirited and godfearing men at the helm of affairs. The intricate and often corrupt party organizations and the immense cost of campaigns mean that unscrupulous machine politicians frequently get the upper hand. When the electorate is sufficiently round, it can defeat machine politics; but that does not often happen. The remedy is not to overthrow democracy, but to make democratic processes simple and, as far as possible, remove private gain from the reach of politicians. It is equally necessary to restrict the vast powers given to chairmen and members of legislative committees in the U.S.A. and the opportunity, derived from responsibility, they have for witch-hunting and character assassination. If these charges are not promptly brought about, there is not much to distinguish a democracy from totalitarianism.

In the international field the neutral powers in current world politics can see how the policy of the Western world has been to isolate Russia as far as possible. Even during the war when Russia poured her blood like water and suffered incalculable material damages, her leaders were not taken into the full confidence of American and British leaders. Soviet Russia, in her turn, was pursuing her own interests, sometimes surreptitiously. During and since the war, with her superior material resources, the U.S.A. has acquired naval and aerial forces all over the world at practically every strategic point, thus giving Russia the impression that she is being encircled and that the scene is being laid for World War III. One of the main provisions of the Atlantic Charter—its provision which guarantees to all countries including enemy countries, equal access to the raw materials and trade of the world has been consigned to the limbo of oblivion. Soviet Russia is jockeyed out of position when it comes to her access to oil in the Near and Middle East. Access to warm seaports such as the Dardanelles also is denied to her.

It is possible to argue that every one of these grievances can be set right by negotiations, but that Russia does not want it. In her present mood it is likely that Russia will regard negotiations with a view to removing certain injustices as appeasement. But those who stand for justice, fair play, and equality ought not to get frightened at the very mention of the word 'appeasement'. They should take courage in both hands and open the doors wide for negotiation and agreement which is a more commonsense and less expensive thing to do than to precipitate World War III.

A country such as China has been noted in the past for her capacity to absorb various dynasties and various systems of thought. Even in their religious life the Chinese have reached such a high degree of tolerance and mutual accommodation that it is possible for them to be part-time Confucianists, part-time Taoists, and part-time Buddhists. Such cosmopolitanism makes one wonder whether if they are not pushed around too much by outsiders, they may not become part-time Communists and part-time Capitalists. It may be that Mao Tse-tung will succeed in shooting a Chinese object with a Marxist arrow. Dividing the world with a sharp sword into two antagonistic groups can only result in the crystallizing of present differences and denying to them the opportunity for natural growth, development, and change.

In the inflammatory situation which obtains in the world today, Jawaharlal Nehru is right in refusing to join one or the other of the two power blocs,* neither of which has the entire truth on its side. Both the U.S. and U.S.S.R. seem to be blundering giants. It may be that in the end Nehru will have to throw the moral weight of his country on the side of democracies in spite of their imperfections. But before doing that it is necessary to make them surrender imperialism in every form or shape in different parts of the world and abandon imperialism. As matters stand at present, it seems that the powerful nations of the world are anxious to forget their battles on other people's lands with other people's lives, though with their arms and other material resources. National leaders, therefore, should exercise utmost care to prevent their countries from becoming cockpits for other people's benefit. They should further insist that the elaborate machinery provided by the UN should be fully utilized before any country is led into a war by its nose. In recent months and years many important decisions affecting the peace of the world have been taken outside the ambit of the United Nations, although for the sake of politeness, care is always taken to render lip service to the UN.

Constructive ways of dealing with Communism

During the presidential election of 1948, President Truman went on record as saying: ' Communism succeeds only when there is weakness or misery or despair. It cannot succeed in a strong and healthy society'. Mr. John Foster Dulles, a Republican with a high reputation in the U.S., says that to oppose Communism simply because it is dynamic and seeks change is 'both wrong and stupid'. It is wrong because existing institutions are never perfect and stupid because the state never prevails against forces seeking change. Dulles further says: ' Communism, in its present challenge, seeks to manoeuvre the free socialists into the position of being the defenders of the *Status quo*, leaving Communism as the proponent of change. We must not allow ourselves to be drawn into that death trap'.

The best way to stop Communism is to stop poverty. The Oriental world in particular requires a prosperous middle class. Standards of living should be substantially raised. The working

*Nehru said that Indian foreign policy is 'the pursuit of peace, not through alignment with any major power or group, but through an independent approval to each controversial or disputed issues'.

classes and peasants should be given a living wage. Social gaps should be bridged through revised taxation measures. Trade unions should be strengthened. The under-privileged of the world should be educated and emancipated from economic and social slavery.* Social security laws should be extended so as to include insurance against unemployment, intermittent employment, old age, accident, sickness, and death. If qualified capitalism is to be the prevailing economy, it should discover means for the prevention of periodic 'booms and busts'. Trade barriers should be lowered so that in times to come, the whole world might become a single free trade area. Both business and labour should be trained to rise above group selfishness and regard themselves as partners with each other and trustee for the vast consuming public. Severe checks should be placed on the irresponsibility and one-sidedness of the press and the predatory instincts of commercial and military groups. Those in government employ should be selected and trained for service and uprightness of character. The corruption and selfishness of public servants are a canker which can destroy the mightiest of structures. Where the salaries and allowances of public servants are way beyond the average income of the people, there should be no hesitation to apply the pruning knife. Both economics and politics should be decentralized so as to vitalize and re-vivify local communities. Peasant movements should be strengthened and directed along constructive lines. Brotherhood should be substituted for vulgar caste and clan distinctions and more vulgar racial discrimination. Religion and worship should be related to life in all its phases and to the social needs of mankind. Disarmament should be pressed vigorously. Experience shows clearly that preparation for war is invitation to war.

These changes may appear to be too slow of realization. But there is no short-cut to success. War with Soviet Russia seems to be the short and easy way out. But experience shows that short-cuts are at times the most tedious and round-about way of reaching the goal. Martin Ebon, to whom we are indebted for some of the

---

* The Huks in the Philippines are disaffected because the government controlled mainly by large landowners, has taken no steps to improve the lot of the peasants. The income tax paid by the rich is negligible, this means that the burden of government falls largely on the shoulders of the poor.

suggestions set forth above, is right when he says: 'The tractor is, in the end a weapon superior to the tank. The fire in the hearth sheds more warmth than a flame thrower.'

NOTES

1. Mr. Justice Jackson writes that Communism has crept over Eastern Europe 'by deception, coercion coup d'etat, terrorism, and assassination'.
2. Recently Nehru said that Indian foreign policy is 'the pursuit of peace, not through alignment with any major power or group of powers, but through an independent approval to each controversial or disputed issue.'
3. The Huks in the Philippines are disaffected because the government controlled mainly by large landowners, has taken no steps to improve the lot of the peasants. The income tax paid by the rich is negligible, this means that the burden of government falls largely on the shoulders of the poor.

REFERENCES

Bazilevich, K.G., *A History of the U.S.S.R.*
Berdyaev, N., *The Russian Idea.*
Beuer, G., *New Czechoslovakia.*
Bothereau, R., *Histoire du Syndicalisme France, ais.*
Burns, E., *What is Marxism.*
Cole, G.D.H., *What Marx Really Meant.*
Crankshaw, E., *Russia and the Russians.*
Dallin, D. J., *The Rise of Russia in Asia.*
Dobb Maurice, *Studies in the Development of Capitalism.*
Gorer, G. & J. Rickman, *The People of Great Russia.*
Hunt, R.N.C., *The Theory & Practice of Communism.*
Koestler, A., *The Yogi & the Commissar.*
Plamenatz, J., *What is Communism.*
Marx, Karl, *Selections from his Writings.*
Stalin, J., *Leninism.*
Schlesinger, R., *The Spirit of Post-war Russia.*
Stratchey, J., *The Theory & Practice of Socialism.*
Timasheef, N.S., *Religion in Soviet Russia.*
Towster, J., *Political Power in the U.S.S.R.*
Trotsky, L., *Stalin.*
Webb, S. and Webb, B., *Soviet Communism.*

APPENDIX I

G.W.F. HEGEL

Freedom in Nature and Society*

At the present time, the idea that freedom of thought, and of mind generally, evinces itself only in divergence from indeed in hostility to, what is publicly recognized, might seem to be most firmly rooted in connection with the state, and it is chiefly for this reason that a philosophy of the state might seem essentially to have the task of discovering and promulgating still another theory, and a special and original one at that. In examining this idea and the activity in conformity with it, we might suppose that no state or constitution had ever existed in the world at all or was even in being at the present time, but that nowadays—and this "nowadays" lasts for ever-we had to start all over again from the beginning, and that the ethical world had just been waiting for such present-day projects, proofs, and investigation. So far as nature is concerned, people grant that it is nature as it is which philosophy has to bring within its ken, that the philosopher's stone lies concealed somewhere, somewhere within nature itself, that nature is inherently rational and that what knowledge has to investigate and grasp in concepts is this actual reason in it; not the formations and accidents evident to the superficial observer, but nature's eternal harmony, its harmony however, in the sense of the law and essence immanent within it. The ethical world, on the other hand, the state (i.e. reason as it actualizes itself in the element of self-consciousness), is not allowed to enjoy the good fortune which springs from the fact that it is reason which has achieved power and mastery within that element and which maintains itself and has its home there. The universe of mind is supposed rather to be left to the mercy of chance and caprice, to be God-forsaken, and the result is that if the ethical world is Godless, truth lies outside it, and at the same time, since even so

*From G.W.F. Hegel, Philosophy of Law (1821); translated by T.M. Knox as Philosophy of Right, Oxford University Press, 1942). By permission.

reason is supposed to be in it as well, truth becomes nothing but a problem. But it is this also that is to authorize, nay to oblige, every thinker to take his own road, though not in search of the philosopher's stone, for he is saved this search by the philosophizing of our contemporaries, and everyone nowadays is assured that he has this stone in his grasp as his birthright. Now admittedly it is the case that those who live their lives in the state as it actually exists here and now and find satisfaction there for their knowledge and volition (and of these there are many, more in fact than think or know it, because ultimately this is the position of everybody), or those at any rate who consciously find their satisfaction in the state, laugh at these operations and affirmations and regard them as an empty game, sometimes rather funny, sometimes rather serious, now amusing, now dangerous. Thus this restless activity of empty reflection, together with its popularity and the welcome it has received, would be a thing on its own, developing in privacy in its own way, were it not that it is philosophy itself which has earned all kinds of scorn and discredit by its indulgence in this occupation. The worst of these kinds of scorn is this, that, as I said just now, everyone is convinced that his mere birthright puts him in a position to pass judgement on philosophy in general and to condemn it. No other art or science is subjected to this last degree of scorn, to the sup position that we are masters of it without ado.

At the present time, the pettifoggery of caprice has usurped the name of philosophy and succeeded in giving a wide public the opinion that such trifling are philosophy. The result of this is that it has now become almost a disgrace to go on speaking in philosophical terms about the nature of the state, and law-abiding men cannot be blamed if they become impatient so soon as they hear mention of a philosophical science of the state. Still less is it a matter of surprise that governments have at last directed their attention to this kind of philosophy, since, apart from anything else, philosophy with us is not, as it was with the Greeks for instance, pursued in private like an art but has an existence in the open, in contact with the public, and especially, or even only, in the service of the state. Governments have proved their trust in their scholars who have made philosophy their chosen field by leaving entirely to them the construction and contents of philosophy-though here and there, if you like, it may not have been so much confidence that has been shown as indifference to learning itself, and professorial chairs of philosophy have been retained only as a tradition (in France, for instance, to the best of my knowledge, chairs of metaphysics at least have been allowed to lapse). Their confidence, however, has very often been ill repaid, or alternatively, if you preferred to see indifference, you would have to regard the result, the decay of thorough knowledge, as the penalty of this indifference. Prima facie, superficiality seems to be extremely accommodating, one might say, at least in relation to public peace and order, because it fails to touch or even to guess at the substance of the things; no action, or at least no police action, would thus have been taken against it in the first instance, had it not been that there still existed in the state a need for a deeper education and insight, a need which the state required philosophical science to satisfy. On the other hand, superficial thinking about the ethical order, about right and duty in general, starts automatically from the maxims which constitute superficiality in this sphere, i.e. from the principles of the Sophists which are so clearly outlined for our information in Plato. What is right these principles locate in subjective aims and opinions, in subjective feeling and particular conviction, and from them there follows the ruin of the inner ethical life and a good conscience, of love and right dealing between private persons, no less than the ruin of public order and the law of the land. The significance which such phenomena must acquire for government is not likely to suffer any diminution as a result of the pretentiousness which has used that very grant of confidence and the authority of a professorial chair to support the demand that the state should uphold and give scope to what corrupts the ultimate source of achievement, namely universal principles, and so even to the defiance of the state as if such defiance were what it deserved. "If God gives a man an office, he also gives him brains" is an old joke which in these days surely no one will take wholly in earnest.

What is rational is actual and what is actual is rational

On this conviction the plain man like the philosopher takes his stand, and from it philosophy starts in its study of the universe of mind as well as the universe of nature. If reflection, feeling, or whatever form subjective consciousness may take, looks upon the present as something vacuous and looks beyond it with the eyes of superior wisdom, it finds itself in a vacuum, and because it is actual only in the present, it is itself mere vacuity. If on the other hand the Idea passes for "only an idea," for something represented in an opinion, philosophy rejects such a view and shows that nothing is actual except the Idea. Once that is granted, the great thing is to apprehend in the show of the temporal and transient the substance which is immanent and the eternal which is present. For since rationality (which is synonymous with the idea) enters upon external existence simultaneously with its actualization, it emerges with an infinite wealth of forms, shapes and appearances. Around its heart it throws a motley covering with which consciousness is at home to begin with, a covering which the concept has first to penetrate before it can find the inward pulse and feel it still beating in the outward appearances. But the infinite variety of circumstance which is developed in this externality by the light of the essence glinting in it-this endless material and its organization-this is not the subject matter of philosophy.

It is a fact that the ethical order is the system of these specific determination of the Idea which constitutes its rationality. Hence the ethical order is freedom or the absolute will as what is objective, a circle of necessity whose moments are the ethical powers which regulate the life of individuals. To these powers individuals are related as accidents to substance, and it is in individuals that these powers are represented, have the shape of appearance, and become actualized.

The bond of duty can appear as a restriction only on indeterminate subjectivity or abstract freedom, and on the impulses either of the natural will or of the moral will which determines its indeterminate good arbitrarily. The truth is, however, that in duty the individual finds his liberation; first, liberation from dependence on mere natural impulse and from the depression which as a particular subject he cannot escape in his moral reflections on what ought to be and what might be; secondly, liberation from the indeterminate subjectivity which, never reaching reality or the objective determinacy of action, remains self-enclosed and devoid of actuality. In duty the individual acquires his substantive freedom.

Virtue is the ethical order reflected in the individual character so far as that character is determined by its natural endowment. When virtue displays itself solely as the individual's simple conformity with the duties of the station to which he belongs, it is rectitude.

But when individuals are simply identified with the actual order, ethical life (*das Sittliche*) appears as their general mode of conduct, i.e. as custom (*Sitte*), while the habitual practice of ethical living appears as a second nature which, put in the place of the initial, purely natural will, is the soul of custom permeating it through and through, the significance and the actuality of its existence. It is mind living and present as a world, and the substance of mind thus exists now for the first time as mind.

In this way, the ethical substantial order has attained its right, and its right its validity. That is to say, the self-will of the individual has vanished together with his private conscience which had claimed independence and opposed itself to the ethical substance. For, when his character is ethical, he recognizes as the end which moves him to act the universal which is itself unmoved but is disclosed in its specific determinations as rationality actualized. He knows that his own dignity and the whole stability of his particular ends are grounded in this same universal, and it is therein that he actually attains these. Subjectivity is itself the absolute form and existent actuality of the substantial order and the distinction between subject on the one hand and substance on the other, as the object, end, and controlling power of the subject, is the same as, and has vanished directly along with, the distinction between them in form.

The state is the actuality of concrete freedom. But concrete freedom consists in this, that personal individuality and its particular interests not only achieve their complete development and gain explicit recognition for their right (as they do in the sphere of the family and civil society) but, for one thing, they also pass over of their own accord into the interest of the universal, and, for another thing, they know and will the universal; they even recognize it as their own substantive mind; they take it as their end and aim and are active in its pursuit. The result is that the universal does not prevail or achieve completion except along with particular interests and through the co-operation of particular knowing and willing; and individuals likewise do not live as private persons for their own ends alone, but in the very act of willing these they will the universal in the light of the universal and their activity is consciously aimed at none but the universal end. The principle of modern states has prodigious strength and depth because it allows the principle of subjectivity to progress to its culmination in the extreme of self-subsistent personal particularity, and yet at the same time brings it back to the substantive unity and so maintains this unity in the principle of subjectivity itself.

In contrast with the spheres of private rights and private welfare (the family and civil society), the state is from one point of view an external necessity and their higher authority; its nature is such that their laws and interests are subordinate to it and dependent on it. On the other hand, however, it is the end immanent within them, and its strength lies in the unity of its own universal end and aim with the particular interest of individuals, in the fact that individuals have duties to the state in proportion as they have rights against it.

To hold that every single person should share in deliberating and deciding on political matters of general concern on the ground that all individuals are members of the state, that its concerns are their concerns, and that it is their right that what is done should be done with their knowledge and volition, is tantamount to a proposal to put the democratic element without any rational form into the organism of the state, although it is only in virtue of the possession of such a form that the state is an organism at all. This idea comes readily to mind because it does not go beyond the abstraction of "being a member of the state," and it is superficial thinking which clings to abstractions. The rational consideration of a topic, the consciousness of the Idea, is concrete and to that extent coincides with a genuine practical sense. Such a sense is itself nothing but the sense of rationality on the idea, though it is not to be confused with mere business routine or the horizon of a restricted sphere. The concrete state is the whole, articulated into its particular groups. The member of a state is a member of such a group, i.e. of a social class, and it is only as characterized in this objective way that he comes under consideration when we are dealing with the state. His mere character as universal implies that he is at one and the same time both a private person and also a thinking consciousness, a will which wills the universal. This consciousness and will, however, lose their emptiness and acquire a content and a living actuality only when they are filled with particularity, and particularity means determinacy as particular and a particular class-status; or, to put the matter otherwise, abstract individuality is a generic essence, but has its immanent universal actuality as the generic essence next higher in the scale. Hence the single person attains his actual and living destiny for universality only when he becomes a member of a Corporation, a society, &c., and thereby it becomes open to him on the strength of his skill, to enter any class for which he is qualified, the class of civil servants included.

Another presupposition of the idea that all should participate in the business of the state is that everyone is at home in this business-a ridiculous notion, however commonly we may hear it sponsored. Still, in public opinion a field is open to everyone where he can express his purely personal political opinions and make them count.

Since the laws and institutions of the ethical order make up the concept of freedom, they are the substance or universal essence of individuals, who are thus related to them as accidents only. Whether the individual exists or not is all one to the objective ethical order. It alone is permanent and is the power regulating the life of individuals. Thus the ethical order has been represented by mankind as eternal justice, as Gods absolutely existent, in contrast with which the empty business of individuals is only a game of see-saw.

Duty is a restriction only on the self-will of subjectivity. It stands in the way only of that abstract good to which subjectivity adheres. When we say: "We want to be free," the primary meaning of the words is simple: "We want abstract freedom," and every institution and every organ of the state passes as a restriction on freedom of that kind. Thus duty is not a restriction on freedom, but only on freedom in the abstract, i.e. on unfreedom. Duty is the attainment of our essence, the winning of positive freedom.

The intrinsic worth of courage as a disposition of mind is to be found in the genuine, absolute, final end, the sovereignty of the state. The work of courage is to actualize this final end, and the means to this end is the sacrifice of personal actuality. This form of experience thus contains the harshness of extreme contradictions; a self-sacrifice which yet is the real existence of one's freedom; the maximum self- subsistence of individuality, yet only a cog playing its part in the mechanism of an external organization; absolute obedience, renunciation of personal opinions and reasonings, in fact complete *absence* of mind, coupled with the most intense and comprehensive *presence* of mind and decision in the moment of acting; the most hostile and so most personal action against individuals, coupled with an attitude of complete indifference or even liking towards them as individuals.

The State Divine*

Subjective volition—Passion—is that which sets men in activity, that which effects "practical" realization. The Idea is the inner spring of action; the State is the actually existing, realized moral life. For it is the Unity of the universal, essential Will, with that of the individual; and this is "Morality." The Individual living in this unity has a moral life; possesses a value that consists in this substantiality alone. Sophocles in his Antigone, say, "The divine commands are not of yesterday, nor of to-day; no, they have an infinite existence, and no one could say whence they came." The laws of morality are not accidental, but are the essentially Rational. It is the very object of the State that what is essential in the practical activity of men, and in their dispositions, should be duly recognized; that it should have a manifest existence, and maintain its position. It is the absolute interest of Reason that this moral Whole should exist; and herein lies the justification and merit of heroes who have founded states,—however rude these may have been. In the history of the World, only those peoples can come under our notice which form a state. For it must be understood that this latter is the realization of Freedom, i.e. of the absolute final aim, and that it exists for its own sake. It must further be understood that all the worth which the human being possesses—all spiritual reality, he possesses only through the State. For his spiritual reality consists in this, that his own essence—Reason—is objectively present to him, that is possess objective immediate existence for him. Thus only is he

* From G.W.F. Hegel, *Philosophy of History* (1837; translated by J. Sibree, Willey Book Co., 1900).

fully conscious; thus only is he a partaker of morality—of a just and moral social and political life. For Truth is the Unity of the universal and subjective Will; and the Universal is to be found in the State, in its laws, its universal and rational arrangements. The State is the Divine Idea as it exists on Earth. We have in it, therefore, the object of History in a more definite shape than before; tat in which Freedom obtains objectivity, and lives in the enjoyment of this objectivity. For Law is the objectivity of Spirit; volition in its true form. Only that will which obeys law, is free; for it obeys itself—it is independent and so free. When the State or our country constitutes a community of existence; when the subjective will of man submits to laws,—the contradiction between Liberty and Necessity vanishes. The Rational has necessary existence, as being the reality and substance of things, and we are free in recognizing it as law, and following it as the substance of our own being. The objective and the subjective will are then reconciled, and present one identical homogeneous whole. For the morality (*Sittlichkeit*) of the State is not of that ethical (*moralische*) reflective kind, in which one's own conviction bears sway; this latter is rather the peculiarity of the modern time, while the true antique morality is based on the principle of abiding by one's duty (to the state at large). An Athenian citizen did what was required of him, as it were from instinct: but if I reflect on the object of my activity, I must have the consciousness that my will has been called into exercise. But morality is Duty—substantial Right—a "*second nature*" as it has been justly called; for the *first* nature of man is his primary merely animal existence.

The development *in extenso* of the Idea of the State belongs to the Philosophy of Jurisprudence; but it must be observed that in the theories of our time various errors are current respecting it, which pass for established truths, and have become fixed prejudices. We will mention only a few of them, giving prominence to such as have a reference to the object of our history.

The error which first meets us is the direct contradictory of our principle that the state presents the realization of Freedom; the opinion, viz., that man is free by *nature*, but that in *society*, in the State—to which nevertheless he is irresistibly impelled—he must limit this natural freedom. That man is free by Nature is quite correct in one sense; viz., that he is so according to the Idea of Humanity; but we imply thereby that he is such only in virtue of his destiny—that he has an undeveloped power to become such; for the "Nature" of an object is exactly synonymous with its "Idea". But the view in question imports more than this. When man is spoken of as "free by Nature," the mode of his existence as well as his destiny is implied. His merely natural and primary condition is intended. In this sense a "state of Nature" is assumed in which mankind at large are in the possession of their natural rights with the unconstrained exercise and enjoyment of their freedom. This assumption is not indeed raised to the dignity of the historical fact; it would indeed be difficult, were the attempt seriously made, to point out any such condition as actually existing, or as having ever occurred. Examples of a savage state of life can be pointed out, but they are marked by brutal passions and deeds of violence; while, however rude and simple their conditions, they involve social arrangements which (to use the common phrase) *restrain* freedom. That assumption is one of those nebulous images which theory produces; an idea which it cannot avoid originating, but which it fathers upon real existence, without sufficient historical justification.

What we find such a state of nature to be in actual experience, answers exactly to the idea of a *merely* natural condition. Freedom as the *ideal* of that which is original and natural, does not exist as *original and natural*. Rather must it be first sought out and won; and that by an incalculable medial discipline of the intellectual and moral powers. The state of Nature is, therefore, predominantly that of injustice and violence, of untamed natural impulses, of inhuman deeds and feelings. Limitation is certainly produced by Society and the State, but it is a limitation of the mere brute emotions and rude instincts; as also, in a more advanced stage of culture, of the premeditated self-will of caprice and passion. This kind of constraint is part of the instrumentality by which only, the consciousness of Freedom and the desire for its attainment, in its true—that is Rational and Ideal form—can be obtained. To the Ideal of Freedom, Law and Morality are indispensably requisite; and they are in and for themselves, universal existences, objects and aims; which are discovered only by the activity of thought, separating itself from the merely sensuous, and developing itself, in opposition thereto; and which must, on the other hand, be introduced into and incorporated with the originally sensuous will, and that contrarily to its natural inclination. The perpetually recurring misapprehension of Freedom consists in regarding that term only in its *formal*, subjective sense, abstracted from its essential objects and aims; thus a constraint put upon impulse, desire, passion—pertaining to the particular individual as such—a limitation of caprice and self-will is regarded as a fettering of Freedom. We should on the contrary look upon such limitation as the indispensable proviso of emancipation. Society and the State are the very conditions in which Freedom is realized.

If the principle of regard for the individual will is recognized as the only basis of political liberty, viz., that nothing should be done by or for the State to which all the members of the body politic have not given their sanction, we have, properly speaking, no *Constitution*. The only arrangement that would be necessary, would be, first, a centre having no *will* of its own, but which should take into consideration what appeared to be the necessities of the State; and, secondly, a contrivance for calling the members of the State together, for taking the votes, and for performing the arithmetical operations of reckoning and comparing the number of votes for the different propositions, and thereby deciding upon them. The State is an *abstraction*, having even its generic existence in its citizens; but it is an actuality, and its simple generic existence must embody itself in individual will and activity. The want of government and political administration in general is felt; this necessitates the selection and separation from the rest of those who have to take the helm in political affairs, to decide concerning them, and to give orders to other citizens, with a view to the execution of their plans. If e.g. even the people in a Democracy resolve on a war, a general must head the army. It is only by a Constitution that the *abstraction*—the State—attains life and reality; but this involves the distinction between those who command and those who obey.—Yet obedience seems inconsistent with liberty, and those who command appear to do the very opposite of that which the fundamental idea of the State, viz. that of Freedom, requires. It is, however, urged that,—though the distinction between commanding and obeying is absolutely necessary, because affairs could not go on without it—and indeed this seems only a compulsory limitation, external to and even contravening freedom in the abstract—the constitution should be at least so framed, that the citizens may obey as little as possible, and the smallest modicum of free volition be left to the commands of the superiors;—that the substance of that for which subordination is necessary even in its most important bearings, should be decided and resolved on by the People—by the will of many or of all the citizens; though it is supposed to be thereby provided that the State should be possessed of vigour and strength as a reality—an individual unity.—The primary consideration is, then, the distinction between the governing and the governed, and political constitutions in the abstract have been rightly divided into Monarchy, Aristocracy, and Democracy; which gives occasion, however, to the remark that Monarchy itself must be further divided into Despotism and Monarchy proper; that in all the divisions to which the leading Idea gives rise, only the generic character is to be made prominent,—it being not intended thereby that the particular category under review should be exhausted as a Form, Order, or Kind in its *concrete* development. But especially it must be observed, that the above-mentioned divisions admit of a multitude of particular modifications,—not only such as lie within the limits of those classes themselves,—but also such as are mixtures of several of these essentially distinct classes, and which are consequently misshapen, unstable, and inconsistent forms. In such a collision, the concerning question is, what is the *best constitution*; that is, by what arrangement, organization, or mechanism of the power of the State its object can be most surely attained. This object may indeed be variously understood; for instance, as the calm enjoyment of life on the part of the citizens, or as Universal Happiness. Such aims have suggested the so-called Ideals of Constitutions, and,—as a particular branch of the subject,—Ideals of the Education of Princes (Fenelon), or of the governing body—the aristocracy at large (Plato); for the chief point they treat of is the condition of those subjects who stand at the head of affairs; and in these Ideals the concrete details of political organization are not at all considered. The inquiry into the best constitution is frequently treated as if not only the theory were an affair of subjective independent conviction, but as if the introduction of a constitution recognized as the best,—or as superior to others,—could be the result of a resolve adopted in this theoretical manner; as if the form of a constitution were a matter of free choice, determined by nothing else but reflection.

Of this artless fashion was that deliberation,—not indeed of the Persian *people*, but of the Persian *grandees*, who had conspired to overthrow the pseudo-Smerdis and the Magi, after their undertaking had succeeded, and when there was no scion of the royal family living,—as to what constitution they should introduce into Persia; and Herodotus gives an equally naive account of this deliberation.

In the present day, the Constitution of a country and people is not represented as so entirely dependent on free and deliberate choice. The fundamental but abstractly (and therefore imperfectly) entertained conception of Freedom, has resulted in the Republic being very generally regarded—in *theory*—as the only just and true political constitution. Many even, who occupy elevated official positions under monarchical constitutions—so far from being opposed to this idea—are actually its supporters; only they see that such a constitution, though the best, cannot be realized under all circumstances; and that—while men are what they are—we must be satisfied with less freedom; the monarchical constitution—under the given circumstances, and the present moral condition of the people-being even regarded as the most advantageous. In this view also, the necessity of a particular constitution is made to depend on the condition of the people in such a way as if the latter were non-essential and accidental. This representation is founded on the distinction which the reflective understanding makes between an idea and the corresponding reality; holding to an abstract and consequently untrue idea; not grasping it in its completeness, or—which is virtually, though not in point of form, the same,—not taking a concrete view of a people and a state. We shall have to show further on, that the constitution adopted by a people makes one substance—one spirit—with its religion, its art and philosophy, or, at least, with its conceptions and thoughts—its culture generally; not to expatiate upon the additional influences, *ab extra*, of climate, of neighbours, of its place in the World. A State is an individual totality, of which you cannot select any particular side, although a supremely important one, such as its political constitution; and deliberate and decide respecting it in that isolated form. Not only is that constitution most intimately connected with and dependent on those other spiritual forces; but the form of the entire moral and intellectual individuality—comprising all the forces it embodies—is only a step in the development of the grand Whole,—with its place pre-appointed in the process; a fact which gives the highest sanction to the constitution in question, and establishes its absolute necessity.—The origin of a state involves imperious lordship on the one hand, instinctive submission on the other. But even obedience—lordly power, and the fear inspired by a ruler—in itself implies some degree of voluntary connection. Even in barbarous states this is the case; it is not the isolated will of individuals that prevails; individual pretensions are relinquished, and the general will is the essential bond of political union. This unity of the genera and the particular is the Idea itself, manifesting itself as a *state*, and which subsequently undergoes further development within itself. The abstract yet necessitated process in the development of truly independent states is as follows:—They being with regal power, whether of patriarchal or military origin. In the next phase, particularity and individuality assert themselves in the form of Aristocracy and Democracy. Lastly, we have the subjection of these separate interests to a single power; but which can be absolutely none other than one outside of which those spheres have an independent position, viz. the Monarchical. Two phases of royalty, therefore, must be distinguished,—a primary and a secondary one. This process is necessitated, so that the form of government assigned to a particular stage of development *must* present itself: it is therefore no matter of choice, but is that form which is adapted to the spirit of the people.

In a Constitution the main feature of interest is the self development of the *rational*, that is, the *political* condition of a people; the setting free of the successive elements of the Idea: so that the several powers in the State manifest themselves as separate,—attain their appropriate and special perfection,—and yet in this independent condition, work together for one object, and are held together by it—i.e. form an organic whole. The State is thus the embodiment of rational freedom, realizing and recognizing itself in an objective form. For its objectivity consists in this,—that its successive stages are not merely ideal, but are present in an appropriate reality; and that in their separate and several workings, they are absolutely merged in that agency by which the totality—the soul—the individuate unity—is produced, and of which it is the result.

The State is the Idea of Spirit in the external manifestation of human Will and its Freedom. It is to the State, therefore, that change in the aspect of History indissolubly attaches itself; and the successive phases of the Idea manifest themselves in it as distinct political *principles*. The Constitutions under which World-Historical peoples have reached their culmination, are peculiar to them; and therefore do not present a generally applicable political basis. Were it otherwise, the differences of similar constitutions would consist only in a peculiar method of expanding and developing that generic basis; whereas they really originate in diversity of principle. From the comparison therefore of the political institutions of the ancient World-Historical peoples, it so happens, that for the most recent principle of a Constitution—for the principle of our own times—nothing (so to speak) can be learned. In science and art it is quite otherwise; e.g., the ancient philosophy is so decidedly the basis of the modern, that it is inevitably contained in the latter, and constitutes its basis. In this case the relation is that of a continuous development of the same structure, whose foundations—stone, walls, and roof have remained what they were. In Art, the Greek itself, in its original form, furnishes us the best models. But in regard to political constitution, it is quite otherwise: here the Ancient and the Modern have not their essential principle in common. Abstract definitions and dogmas respecting just government—importing that intelligence and virtue ought to bear sway—are, indeed, common to both. But nothing is so absurd as to look to Greeks, Romans, or Orientals, for models for the political arrangements of our time. From the East may be derived beautiful pictures of a patriarchal condition, of paternal government, and of devotion to it on the part of peoples; from Greeks and Romans, descriptions of popular liberty. Among the latter we find the idea of a Free Constitution admitting all the citizens to a share in deliberations and resolves respecting the affairs and laws of the Commonwealth. In our times, too, this is its general acceptation; only with this modification, that—since our states are so large, and there are so many of "the Many," the latter,—direct action being impossible,—should by the indirect method of elective substitution express their concurrence with resolves affecting the common weal; that is, that for legislative purposes generally, the people should be represented by deputies. The so-called Representative Constitution is that form of government with which we connect the idea of a free constitution; and this notion has become a rooted prejudice. On this theory People and Government are separated. But there is a perversity in this antithesis; an ill-intentioned *ruse* designed to insinuate that the People are the totality of the State. Besides, the basis of this view is the principle of isolated individuality—the absolute validity of the subjective will—a dogma which we have already investigated. The great point is, that Freedom in its Ideal conception has not subjective will and caprice for its principle, but the recognition of the universal will; and that the process by which Freedom is realized is the free development of its successive stages. The subjective will is a merely formal determination—a *carte blanche*—not including what it is that is willed. Only the *rational* will is that universal principle which independently determines and unfolds its own being, and develops its successive elemental phases as organic members. Of this Gothic-cathedral architecture the ancients knew nothing.

Sovereignty : Monarchical or Popular?*

The state is the actuality of the ethical Idea. It is ethical mind *qua* the substantial will manifest and revealed to itself, knowing and thinking itself, accomplishing what it knows and in so far as it knows it. The state exists immediately in custom, mediately in individual self-consciousness, knowledge, and activity, while self-consciousness in virtue of its sentiment towards the state finds in the state, as its essence and the end and product of its activity, its substantive freedom.

The *Penates* are inward gods, gods of the underworld; the mind of a nation (Athens for instance) is the divine, knowing and willing itself. Family piety is feeling, ethical behaviour directed by feeling; political virtue is the willing of the absolute end in terms of thought.

The state is absolutely rational inasmuch as it is the actuality of the substantial will which it possess in the particular self-consciousness once that consciousness has been raised to consciousness of its universality. This substantial unity is an absolute unmoved end in itself, in which freedom comes into its

* From G.W.F. Hegel, *Philosophy of Law* (1821; translated by T.M. Knox as *Philosophy of Right*, Oxford University Press, 1942). By permission.

supreme right. On the other hand this final end has supreme right against, the individual, whose supreme duty is to be a member of the state.

If the state is confused with civil society, and if its specific end is laid down as the security and protection of property and personal freedom, then the interest of the individuals as such becomes the ultimate end of their association, and it follows that membership of the state is something optional. But the state's relation to the individual is quite different from this. Since the state is mind objectified, it is only as one of its members that the individual himself has objectivity, genuine individuality, and an ethical life. Unification pure and simple is the true content and aim of the individual, and the individual's destiny is the living of a universal life. His further particular satisfaction, activity, and mode of conduct have this substantive and universally valid life as their starting point and their result.

Rationality, taken generally and in the abstract, consists in the thorough-going unity of the universal and the single. Rationality, concrete in the state, consists (a) so far as its content is concerned, in the unity of subjective freedom (i.e. freedom of the universal or substantial will) and subjective freedom (i.e. freedom of everyone in his knowing and in his volition of particular ends); and consequently, (b) so far as its form is concerned, in self-determining action on laws and principles which are thoughts and so universal. This Idea is the absolutely eternal and necessary being of mind.

Another question readily presents itself here: "Who is to frame the constitution?" This question seems clear, but closer inspection shows at once that it is meaningless, for it presupposes that there is no constitution there, but only an agglomeration of atomic individuals. How an agglomeration of individuals could acquire a constitution, whether automatically or by someone's aid, whether as a present or by force or by thought, it would have to be allowed to settle for itself, since with an agglomeration the concept has nothing to do. But if the question presupposes an already existent constitution, then it is not about framing but only about altering the constitution, and the very presupposition of a constitution directly implies that its alteration may come about only by constitutional means. In any case, however, it is absolutely essential that the constitution should not be regarded as something made, even though it has come into being in time. It must be treated rather as something simply existent in and by itself, as divine therefore, and constant, and so as exalted above the sphere of things that are made.

The conception of the monarch is therefore of all conceptions the hardest for ratiocination, i.e. for the method of reflection employed by the Understanding. This method refuses to move beyond isolated categories and hence here again knows only *raisonnement*, finite points of view, and deductive argumentation. Consequently it exhibits the dignity of the monarch as something deduced, not only in its form, but in its essence. The truth is, however, that to be something not deduced but purely self-originating is precisely the conception of monarchy. Akin, then, to this reasoning is the idea of treating the monarch's right as grounded in the authority of God, since it is in its divinity that its unconditional character is contained. We are familiar, however, with the misunderstandings connected with this idea, and it is precisely this "divine" element which it is the task of a philosophic treatment to comprehend.

We may speak of the "sovereignty of the people" in the sense that any people whatever is self-subsistent vis-à-vis other peoples, and constitutes a state of its own, like the British people for instance. But the peoples of England, Scotland, or Ireland, or the peoples of Venice, Genoa, Ceylon, &c., are not sovereign peoples at all now that they have ceased to have rulers or supreme governments of their own.

We may also speak of the sovereignty in home affairs residing in the people, provided that we are speaking generally about the whole state and meaning only what was shown above, namely, that it is to the state that sovereignty belongs.

The usual sense, however, in which men have recently begun to speak of the "sovereignty of the people" is that it is something opposed to the sovereignty existent in the monarch. So opposed to the sovereignty of the monarch, the sovereignty of the people is one of the confused notions based on the wild idea of the "people". Taken without its monarch and the articulation of the whole which is the indispensable and direct concomitant of monarchy, the people is a formless mass and no longer a state.

It lacks every one of those determinate characteristics—sovereignty, government, judges, magistrates, class-divisions, &c., —which are to be found only in a whole which is inwardly organized. By the very emergence into a people's life of moments of this kind which have a bearing on an organization, on political life, a people ceases to be that indeterminate abstraction which, when represented in a quite general way, is called the "people"

At the stage of which constitutions are divided, as above mentioned, into democracy, aristocracy, and monarchy, the point of view taken is that of a still substantial unity, abiding in itself, without having yet embarked on its infinite differentiation and the plumbing of its own depths. At that stage, the moment of the final, self-determining, decision of the will does not come on the scene explicitly in its own proper actuality as an organic moment immanent in the state. Nonetheless, even in those comparatively immature constitutional forms, there must always be individuals at the head. Leaders must either be available already, as they are in monarchies of that type, or, as happens in aristocracies, but more particularly in democracies, they may rise to the top, as statesmen or generals, by chance and in accordance with the particular needs of the hour. This must happen, since everything done and everything actual is inaugurated and brought to completion by the single decisive act of a leader.

To define freedom of the press as freedom to say and write whatever we please is parallel to the assertion that freedom as such means freedom to do as we please. Talk of this kind is due to wholly uneducated, crude, and superficial ideas. Moreover, it is in the very nature of the thing that abstract thinking should nowhere be so stubborn, so unintelligent, as in this matter of free speech, because what it is considering is the most fleeting, the most contingent, and the most personal side of opinion in its infinite diversity of content and tergiversation. Beyond the direct incitation to theft, murder, rebellion, &c., there lies its artfully constructed expression—an expression which seems in itself quite general and vague, while all the time it conceals a meaning anything but vague or else is compatible with inferences which are not actually expressed, and it is impossible to determine whether they rightly follow from it, or whether they were meant to be inferred from it. This vagueness of matter and form precludes laws on these topics from attaining the requisite determinacy of law, and since the trespass, wrong, and injury here are so extremely personal and subjective in form, judgement on them is reduced equally to a wholly subjective verdict. Such an injury is directed against the thoughts, opinions, and wills of others, but apart from that, these form the element in which alone it is actually anything. But this element is the sphere of the freedom of others, and it therefore depends on them whether the injurious expression of opinion is or is not actually an effective act.

Laws then may be criticized by exhibiting their indeterminacy as well as by arguing that they leave it open to the speaker or writer to devise turns of phrase or tricks of expression, and so evade the laws or claim that judicial decisions are mere subjective verdicts. Further, however, against the view that the expression of opinion is an act with injurious effects, it may be maintained that it is not an act at all, but only opining and thinking, or only talking. And so we have before us a claim that mere opining and talking is to go unpunished because it is of a purely subjective character both in form and content, because it does not mean anything and is of no importance. And yet in the same breath we have the claim that this same opining and talking should be held in high esteem and respect—the opining because it is personal property and in fact preeminently the property of mind; the talking because it is only this same property being expressed and used.

But the substance of the matter is and remains that traducing the honour of anyone, slander, abuse, the contemptuous caricature of government, its ministers, officials, and in particular the person of the monarch, defiance of the laws, incitement to rebellion, &c., are all crimes or misdemeanours in one or other of their numerous gradations. The rather high degree of indeterminability which such actions acquire on account of the element in which they are expressed does not annul this fundamental character of theirs. Its only effect is that the subjective field in which they are committed also determines the nature and form of the reaction to the offence. It is the field in which the offence was committed which itself necessitates subjectivity of view, contingency, &c., in the reaction to the offence, whether the reaction takes the form of punishment proper or of police action to prevent crimes. Here, as always, abstract thinking sets itself to explain away the fundamental and concrete nature of the thing by concentrating on isolated aspects of its external appearance and on abstractions drawn therefrom.

The sciences, however, are not to be found anywhere in the field of opinion and subjective views, provided of course that they be sciences in other respects. Their exposition is not a matter of clever turns of phrases, allusiveness, half-utterances, and semi-reticences, but consists in the unambiguous, determinate, and open expression of their meaning and purport. It follows that they do not fall under the category of public opinion. Apart from this, however, as I said just now, the element in which views and their expression become actions in the full sense and exist effectively, consists of the intelligence, principles, and opinions of others. Hence this aspect of these actions, i.e. their effectiveness proper and their danger to individuals, society, and the state, depends on the character of the ground on which they fall, just as a spark falling on a heap of gunpowder is more dangerous than if it falls on hard ground where it vanishes without trace. Thus, just as the right of science to express itself depends on and is safeguarded by its subject-matter and content, so an illegitimate expression may also acquire a measure of security, or at least sufferance, in the scorn which it has brought upon itself. An offence of this sort is punishable on its own account too, but part of it may be accounted that kind of nemesis which inner impotence, feeling itself oppressed by the preponderating abilities and virtues of others, is impelled to vent in order to come to itself again in face of such superiority, and to restore some self-consciousness to its own nullity. It was a nemesis of a more harmless type which Roman soldiers vented against their generals when they sang scurrilous songs about them in triumphal processions in order to get even with them for all the hard service and discipline they had undergone, and especially for the omission of their names from the triumphal honours. The former type of nemesis, the bad and hateful type, is deprived of its effect by being treated with scorn, and hence, like the public, which perhaps forms a circle of spectators of scurrility, it is restricted to futile malice and to the self-condemnation which it implicitly contains.

APPENDIX II

THOMAS JEFFERSON

Rebellion and Liberty*

The British ministry have so long hired their gazetteers to repeat and model into every form lies about our being in anarchy, that the world has at length believed them, the English nation has believed them, the ministers themselves have come to believe them, and what is more wonderful, we have believed them ourselves. Yet where does this anarchy exist? Where did it ever exist, except in the single instance of Massachusetts? And can history produce an instance of rebellion so honourably conducted? I say nothing of its motives. They were founded in ignorance, not wickedness. God forbid we should ever be twenty years without such a rebellion. The people cannot be all, and always, well informed. The part which is wrong will be discontented in proportion to the importance of the facts they misconceive. If they remain quiet under such misconceptions it is a lethargy, the forerunner of death to the public liberty. We have had thirteen states independent for eleven years. There has been one rebellion. That comes to one rebellion in a century and a half, for each state. What country before ever existed a century and a half without a rebellion? And what country can preserve its liberties if their rulers are not warned from time to time that their people preserve the spirit of resistance? Let them take arms. The remedy is to set them right as to facts, pardon and pacify them. What signify a few lives lost in a century or two? The tree of liberty must be refreshed from time to time with the blood of patriots and tyrants. It is its natural manure.

---

*From a letter to Colonel William Stephens Smith (November 13, 1787)

HORALD J. LASKI

Challenge to Authority*

There is, outside the purely formal realm, no obligation to obey the actual state. Our obedience, is, and can only be, a function of our judgement upon its performance. That judgement, moreover, is never one which each citizen can make upon the same postulates, intellectual or emotional. What he decides will be the product of the place he occupies in the state, and the relation of that place to his view of what he ought to attain. He may be wrong in the view he takes; but he has never any rational alternative to action in the light of his own certainties. Upon this attitude there hinges a view of law the implications of which are important. It regards the validity of law as unrelated to the source from which it comes. Law becomes law as it goes into application; it is made law by being accepted. That is not to say that accepted law is right law; for law may be accepted by the might which is behind it. We have, in fact, to distinguish between three different senses in which the idea of law can be used. There is the formal juristic sense, which is no more than an announcement, ultimately dependent upon the sovereign authority, of the will to enforce certain decisions. There is the political sense, in which the formal announcement is validated by the acceptance of it by those to whom it applies. There is, finally, the ethical sense in which the decision announced ought to be obeyed, because it is morally right that what it proposes should be done.

Now it is clear that in the first two of these three senses the citizen has no inherent duty to obey. Few people would seriously claim that the juristic sense is always to be equated with the ethical; certainly, to take an obvious example, no Quaker could admit that a state whose government ordered its citizens to make

---

* From Harold J. Lasi, *The State in Theory and Practice*. By permission of The Viking Press, New York.

war had, for this purpose, a title to their obedience. Nor can it, I think, be seriously claimed, either, that the political and ethical senses are identical; the commands of the Hitlerite state on June 30,1934, were law in the sense that they went into effective operation, and were accepted by the population over whom it ruled; but most people in a position to make an independent judgement would, I suggest, regard them as ethically outrageous. Might, however profound, does not make right; effective operation of law still leaves undecided the question of ethical adequacy.

Neither formal competence, then, nor political power can confer a just title to obedience. With what are we left? Only, I think, with the insistence that law to be ethically valid must confirm with the requirements of the system of rights the purposes of which the state exists to maintain. And since law is a command seeking to control my behaviour in some particular way, I must judge that conformity for myself as the test of its ethical adequacy. The roots of valid law, that is, are, and can only be, within the individual conscience. I make law legal, so to say, by giving to its operation the consent of my conscience.

If it is said that such a view, by justifying refusal to obey, opens the door to anarchy, the answer is that the accusation is true. But it is not a serious accusation. In the life of states the door to anarchy is always open because men are never willing to admit the unconditional conference of power. If, further, it be said that the individual conscience is at least as likely to be wrong as the consciences of those who rule the state, the answer, again, is that while this may be true, the citizen who yields his conviction on the ground that he may be mistaken will soon cease, in any meaning sense, to be a citizen at all. There is no way of making a state active in the fulfillment of its function except the knowledge that men will refuse to obey its commands where they regard them as a violation of that function. That was the truth that Pericles saw when he told the citizens of Athens that the secret of liberty was courage. Unless men are prepared to act by the insights they have, even when these insights are erroneous, they are bound to become no more than the passive recipients of orders to whose moral quality they are indifferent. When they do that, they poison the foundations of the state. For they then cease to be moral beings in any sense of the word that has meaning. They associate truth and justice and right automatically with the possession of physical power. No people prepared in that fashion to abdicate its humanity is likely to be long capable of creative achievement. For so to abdicate the duty of moral judgement is to sell oneself into slavery.

It is said that the individual is powerless, and that he wastes his energy by acting upon his judgement. But there are at least two answers to this view. A moral obligation is not less compelling because it may end in failure. To adopt that canon of effort is to accept the view that justice is the will of the stronger-a doctrine against which, as I have pointed out, the whole history of humanity is a protest. And to argue, secondly, that the individual is powerless is, on the record, quite untrue. He is powerless only when his perceptions are so completely unshared that he fails to arouse any note of response among his fellow-citizens; and he has always to remember that the shift of events may cause them to be shared at a later stage. The early Christians must have appeared singularly futile to their own generation when they challenged the majesty of Rome; but their steadfastness conquered the Western world. Luther's recalcitrance must have appeared akin to madness to a church which remembered its successful emergence from the stresses of the Conciliar revolt; but he changed the history of the world by his courage. Even so liberal a mind as Emerson could write of the American abolitionists that they were "narrow, self-pleasing, conceited men, and affect us as the insane do";[1] but it was hardly a generation afterwards that so respectable an observer as Oliver Wendell Holmes, not given to extreme views, could say of his friend's judgement that "it would have taken a long time to get rid of slavery if some of Emerson's teachings had been accepted as the whole gospel of liberty."[2]

History, indeed, abounds with such instances. The individual who protests against the law he deems unjust is far less alone than he is likely to imagine. He is acting in a mental climate in which the experience borne in upon him is likely to be shared by others; and the gesture he makes may awaken others to the understanding of their obligations. No one who looks back upon their history can doubt that the suffragettes who, for eight years, defied the law awakened the British government to a sense that their claims were serious in a way that altered the whole perspective of those claims. No one can doubt either that the unbreakable will of Lenin was central to the success of the Bolshevik Revolution in 1917. That we must fight for our philosophy if we believe in it, seems to me the inescapable implication of the record.

Against this view two considerations are urged, in both of which there is, unquestionably, considerable force. It is said that to challenge the government is to weaken the authority of all law, and that to do so is to open the flood-gates to chaos. It was the sense of this danger which made T.H. Green who admitted, in the last resort, the right to revolution, insist that we must approach the state in fear and trembling. But it is surely not less important to realise that respect for law must always mean respect for what the law does; and if the individual, whether alone or in concert with others, judges what the law does to be ethically intolerable, he must act upon the basis of his judgement. To decide otherwise is to argue that the highest duty of the individual is to maintain order, without regard to the quality of the order that is maintained. I do not find this argument compatible with the notion of the individual as a moral being.

It is said, secondly, that this view admits the right of any doctrine to support itself by force, if it can. Men have only to announce that they are moved by some profound conviction to be justified in using violence to attain their ends. Such an attitude, it is argued, is utterly destructive of the foundations of social well-being.

But the answer is surely that no doctrine, however evil, moves to the use of force unless it is rooted in profound grievance which it sees no other way to remedy. We may believe the Bolshevik Revolution to have been wholly evil; but it is clear that the previous conditions of the Russian state alone account for its origin and methods. We may argue, with the Communists, that Hitler has been no more than the agent of finance-capitalism in Germany;[3] but is also clear that his victory was built upon the profound grievances of millions of Germans who saw no adequate redress for them in the habits of the Weimar republic. The truth is that men in general are so accustomed to obey that their departure from the normal canons of political behaviour is always an index to grave disease in the state. They have, as Burke said, "no interest in disorder; where thev do wrong it is their error and not their crime." We need not argue that a doctrine which arms itself is wise or right to do so. But, on the facts, we have to argue that no doctrine ever does successfully arm itself unless the government it attacks has failed to deal with the grievances it expresses in a reasonable way.

That is, I think, apparent in the history of most revolutions. Certainly the student of the English civil wars, of the revolutions of France and of Russia, will note as not the least remarkable of their features, the patient efforts of the common people to await reform before they turned to violence. And in any society violence is unlikely if the conviction is widespread that the state is seriously attempting to fulfil its obligations. Violence comes when the facts persuade men to believe that the bona-fides of their rulers is no longer to be trusted.

NOTES

1. Quoted in V.F. Calverton, *The Liberalism of Ameriacn Literature* (1932), p. 330.
2. Ibid., p. 331.
3. Cf. E. Henry, *Hitler Over Europe* (1933).

Bibliography

A Character of the Trimmer: Being a Short Life of the First Marquis of Halifax. By H.C. Foxcroft. 2 vols. Cambridge, 1946.

A History of Cynicism from Diogenes to the 6th Century A.D. By Donald R. Dudley. London, 1937.

A History of the U.S.S.R. By Bazilevich, K.G.

Alienation: Marx's Conception of Man in Capitalist Society. By Bertell Ollman. Cambridge, 1971.

An Essay on Marxian Economics. By Joan Robinson. London, 1942.

Baron d' Holbach: A Prelude to the French Revolution. By W.H.. Wickwar. London, 1935.

Condorcet and the rise of Liberalism. By J. Salwyn Schapiro. New York, 1934.

Condorcet on the Progress of :he Human Mind. By Sir James George Frazer. Oxford, 1933.

Democracy and Marxism. By H.B. Mayo. New York, 1955.

Democracy and Socialism: A Contribution to the Political History of the Past 150 Years. By Arthur Rosenberg. Eng. trans. by George Rosen. New York, 1939.

Diogenes of Sinope: A Study of Greek Cynicism. By Farrand Sayre. Baltimore, 1938.

Epicurus and His Gods. By A. M. J. Festugiere. Eng. Trans. By C.W. Chilton. Oxford, 1955.

French liberal Thought in the Eighteenth Century: A Study of Political Ideas from Bayle of Condorcet. By kingsley Martin. 2d ed. Rev. London 1954.

From Hegel to Marx: Studies in the Intellectual Development of Karl Marx. By Sidney Hook, New York, 1936.

German Marxism and Russian Communism. BY John Plamenatz. London, 1954. Part I.

Gorer, G. & J. Rickman, *The People of Great Russia*.

Hellenistic Civilization. By W.W. Tarn. 3d ed. Rev. by the author and G.T.

Griffith. London, 1952. Ch. 10.

Histoire du Syndicalisme France, ais. By Bothereau, R.,

Human Nature: The Marxian View. By Vernon Venable. New York, 1945.

Jean-Jacques Rousseau, Moralist. By Charles W. Hendel. 2 vols. London, 1934.

Jean-Jacques Rousseau: A Critical Study of His Life and Writings. By F.C. Green. Cambridge, 1955. Ch. 7.

Jean-Jacques Rousseau: Discours sur les sciences et les arts. Ed. by George R. Havens. New York, 1946. Introduction.

John Locke and the Doctrine of Majority-rule. By Willmoore Kendall. Urbana, III., 1941.

John Locke, A Biography. By M.W. Cranston. London, 1957.

John Locke, A Critical Introduction. By John D.O'Connor. Baltimore, 1952.

John Locke: Essays on the Law of Nature. Ed. By W. von Leyden. Oxford, 1954.

John Locke's Political Philosophy. By J. W. Gough. Oxford, 1950.

Karl Marx, His Life and Environment. By Isaiah Berlin. 3rd Edition. New York, 1963.

Karl Marx, His Life and Work. By Otto Ruhle. Eng. trans. by E. and C. Paul. New York, 1949.

Karl Marx: An Essay. By Harold J. Laski. London, 1922.

Karl Marx: The Story of His Life. By Franz Mehring. Eng. trans. by Edward Fitzgerald. New York, 1935.

Karl Marx's Capital: An Introductory Essay. By A.D. Lindsay. London, 1925.

Karl Marx's Interpretation of History. By Mandell M. Bober. 2d ed., rev. Cambridge, Mass., 1948.

Koelln, Fritz C. A., and James P. Pettegrove, *The Philosophy of the Enlightment.* Ernst Cassirer. Eng. Trans. By . Princeton, N. J., 1951.

La pensee de Jean-Jacques Rousseau: essai d' interpretation nouvelle. By Albert Schinz. Paris, 1929.

Life and Letters of Sir George Savile, Bart., First Marquis of Halifax. By H.C. Foxcroft. 2 vols. London, 1898.

Locke on Peace and War. By Richard Cox. New York, 1960.

Locke's Theory of the State. Pollock, Sir Frederick, In: *Essay in the Law.* London, 1922. Ch. 3.

Marx in the Mid-Twentieth Century. By Gajo Petrovic. Garden City, 1962.

Marx, Proudhon, and European Socialism. By John H. Jackson. London, 1957.

Marx's Concept of Man. By Erich Fromm. New York, 1961.

Marxism, Past and Present. By R.N. Carew Hunt. London, 1954.

Marxism: A Re-examination. By Irving M. Zeitlin. Princeton, 1967.

Marxism: The Unity of Theory and Practice. By Alfred G. Meyer. Cambridge, Mass., 1954.

Montesquieu and Burke. By Courtney, C.P., Oxford, 1963.

Montesquieu and English Politics (1750-1800). By F.T.H. Fletcher, London, 1939.

Montesquieu in America, 1760-1801. By Paul M. Spurlin. University, Louisiana, 1940.

Montesquieu: A Critical Biography. By Robert Shacleton. New York, 1961.

Natural Rights: *A Criticism of Some Political and Ethical Coriceptions*. By David G. Ritchie. London, 1895.

New Czechoslovakia. By Beuer, G.

Philosophy and Myth in Karl Marx. By Robert C. Tucker. Cambridge, 1961.

Plamenatz, J., *What is Communism*.

Political Thought in England from Locke to Bentham. By Harold J. Laski. London, 1920.

Progress in the Age of Reason. By R.V. Sampson, Canbridge, Mass., 1956.

Property in the Eighteen Century, with Special Reference to England and Locke. By Paschal Larkin. London, 1930.

Reason, Social Myths, and Democracy. By Sidney Hook, New York, 1940.

Religious Toleration in England." By H.M. Gwatkin. In the *Cambridge Modern History*, Voll. V. (1908), ch.1.

Representative Government in Greek and Roman History. By J.A.O. Larsen. Berkeley, Calif., 1955.

Rousseau and Burke: A Study of the Idea of Liberty in Eighteenth-century Political Thought. By Annie M. Osborn. New York, 1940.

Rousseau and Romanticism. By Irving Babbitt. Boston, 1919.

Rousseau and the French Revolution. By Joan McDonald. London, 1965.

Rousseau and the Idea of Progress. By Frederick C. Green. Oxford, 1950.

Rousseau and the Modern State. By Alfred Cobban. London, 1934.

Rousseau: A Study of His Thought. By J.H. Broome. London, 1963.

Rousseau's Political Religion, *Review of Politics* (October, 1965). By Fred H. Willhoite, Jr.

Rousseau-Totalitarian or Liberal? By John W. Chapman. New York, 1956.

Russia and the Russians. By Crankshaw, E.

Schlesinger, R., *The Spirit of Post-war Russia.*

Selections from his Writings. By Marx, Karl.

Smith, Arthur Lionel, English Political Philosophy in the Seventeenth and Eighteenth Centuries." In: *The Cambridge Modern History*, Vo,l. VI (1909), ch.23.

Stalin, J., *Leninism.*

Stoic and Epicurean. By R.D. Hicks. London, 1911. Ch. 5.

Stratchey, J., *The Theory & Practice of Socialism.*

Studies in the Development of Capitalism. By Dobb Maurice.

The Age of Reason." Diderot." by Harold J. Laski. In *Studies in Law and Politics*. London, 1932.

The Early Rousseau. By Mario Einaudi. Ithaca, 1967.

The English Revolution and Locke's Two Treatises of Government. By Peter Laslett. *In the Cambridge Historical Journal*, Vol. XII (1956), pp. 40-55

The Ethical Foundations of Marxism. By Eugene Kamenka. New York, 1962.

The Faith of Reason: The Idea of Progress in the French Enlightenment. By Charles Frankel. New York, 1948.

The Greek Atomists and Epocurus. By Cyril Bailey. Oxford, 1928. Ch. 10.

The Greek City from Alexander to Justinian. By A.H.M. Jones. Oxford, 1940.

The Greek Cynics. By Farrand Sayre. Baltimore, 1948.

The Idea of Nationalism: A Study in Its Origins and Background. By Hans Kohn. New York, 1944. Ch. 5.

The Library of John Locke. By John Harrison and Peter Laslett. Oxford 1965.

The Materialist Conception of History: A Critical Analysis. By Karl Federn. London, 1939.

The Meaning of Marxism. By G.D.H. Cole. London, 1948.

The Meaning of Rousseau. By Ernest H. Wright. London, 1929. Ch. 3.

The Moral and Political Philosophy of John Locke. By Sterling P. Lamprecht. New York, 1918.

The Open Society and Its Enemies. By K.R. Popper. Rev. ed. Princeton, N.J., 1950. Chs. 13-21.

The Philosophical Foundations of Marxism. By Louis Dupre. New York, 1966.

The *Pioneers of the French Revolution*. By Marius Roustan. Eng. trans. by Frederic Whyte. Boston, 1926.s

The Political Doctrine of Montesquieu's Esprit des lois. By Lawrence M. Levin. New York, 1936.

The Political Philosophy of Rousseau. By Roger D. Masters. Princeton, 1968.

The Political Tradition of the West: A Study in the Development of Modern Liberalism. By Frederick M. Watkins. Cambridge, Mass., 1948.

The Political Writings of Jean-Jacques Rousseau. Ed. by C.E. Vaughan. 2 vols. Cambridge, 1915. Introduction.

The Question of Jean-Jacques Rousseau. By Ernst Cassirer. Eng. trans. and ed. by Peter Gay. New York, 1954.

The Rise of European Liberalism: An Essay in interpretation. By Harold J. Laski. London, 1936. Ch. 3.

The Rise of Russia in Asia. By Dallin, D. J.

The Rise of Totalitarian Democracy. By J.L. Talmon. Boston, 1952.

The Russian Idea. By Berdyaev, N.

The Social and Economic History of the Hellenistic World. By M. Rostovtzeff. Oxford, 1941

The Social and Political Ideas of Some English Thinkers of the Augustan Age, A.D. 1650-1750. Ed. By F.J. C. Hearnshaw, London, 1928. Chs. 3, 4.

The Social and Political Ideas of Some Great French Thinkers of the Age of Reason. Ed. by F.J.C. Hearnshaw. London, 1930. Ch. 7.

The Social and Political Ideas of Some Great French Thinkers of the Age of Reason. Ed. by F.J. C. Hearnshaw. London, 1930. Chs. 5, 6, 8.

The Social and Political Thought of Karl Marx. By Shlomo Avineri. Cambridge, 1968.

The Social Contract. By J.W. Gough. 2d ed. Oxford, 1957. Ch. 9.

The Theory & Practice of Communism. By Hunt, R.N.C.

The Theory and Practice of Communism. By R.N. Carew Hunt. 2d ed. London, 1957. Part I.

The Yogi & the Commissar. By Koestler, A.

Timasheef, N.S., *Religion in Soviet Russia*.

Titi Lucreti Cari De rerum natura Ed. With Prolegomena, Critical

Apparatus, Translation and Commentary by Cyril Bailey. 3 vols. Oxford, 1947. Prolegomen, Section IV.

Towards the Understanding of Karl Marx: A Revolutionary Interpretation. By Sidney Hook, New York, 1933.

Towster, J., *Political Power in the U.S.S.R.*

Trotsky, L., *Stalin*.

Turgot. By C.J. Gignoux. Paris, 1945

Vaughan. C.E., *Studies in the History of Political Philosophy before and after Rousseau*. By. 2 vols. Manchester, 1925. Vol. 1, Ch. 4

Voltaire and the State. By Constance Rowe. New York, 1955.

Voltaire: *Man of Justice*. By Adolph Meyer. London, 1952.

Voltaire's Politics: The Poet as Realist. By Peter Gay. Princeton, N.J., 1959.

Webb, S. and Webb, B., *Soviet Communism*.

What is Marxism. By Burns, E.

What Marx Really Meant. By Cole, G.D.H.,

Yolton, John W., "Locke on the Law of Nature." In: *The Philosophical Review*, Vol. LXVII (1959), pp. 477-498.

Index

C

D

E

Z